Daniela Böhm

AGRI-ENVIRONMENTAL DECISION-MAKING OF CHINESE FARMERS

Economic, social and cognitive determinants of farmers' nitrogen overuse in Shandong Province

ibidem-Verlag
Stuttgart

Bibliografische Information der Deutschen Nationalbibliothek
Die Deutsche Nationalbibliothek verzeichnet diese Publikation in der Deutschen Nationalbibliografie; detaillierte bibliografische Daten sind im Internet über http://dnb.d-nb.de abrufbar.

Bibliographic information published by the Deutsche Nationalbibliothek
Die Deutsche Nationalbibliothek lists this publication in the Deutsche Nationalbibliografie; detailed bibliographic data are available in the Internet at http://dnb.d-nb.de.

Cover picture:	Chinese farmer working on his field in Shouguang, Shandong Province. © Daniela Böhm.
D7	Dissertation Faculty of Agricultural Sciences, Georg-August-University Göttingen, Germany Supervisor: Prof. Dr. Rainer Marggraf Co-supervisor: Prof. Dr. Achim Spiller

∞

Gedruckt auf alterungsbeständigem, säurefreien Papier
Printed on acid-free paper

ISBN-13: 978-3-8382-0383-6

© *ibidem*-Verlag
Stuttgart 2012

Alle Rechte vorbehalten

Printed in Germany

"Economics is all about how people make choices.
Sociology is all about why they don't have any choices to make."

James Duesenberry 1960, p. 233

SUMMARY

Over the past 30 years, China has successfully increased food production, which has led to significant negative external impacts at subsequent escalating environmental costs (Ash and Edmonds 1998). In particular, in the intensive agricultural production areas of the fertile North China Plain, farmers' nitrogen overuse for winter wheat/ summer maize crop rotations contributes greatly to nitrates leaching into soil and aquifers, causing significant environmental problems (Ju *et al.* 2004). The majority of these farmers are smallholders, usually of advanced age and with very little technical knowledge; instead of advancing the agricultural sector, younger rural family members increasingly migrate to urban areas for better-paid off-farm labour (Hoering 2010; Xu and Wang 2009). Recently, these issues have garnerd widespread attention, and the Chinese government attaches great importance to achieving more sustainable agricultural production (UNDP 2006).

However, currently, farmers are caught in the crossfire of various contextual influences, such as structural reforms accompanied by ongoing socio-economic and cultural development (Zheng and Fewsmith 2008). They face uncertainty regarding new agricultural technologies and the rising market structure of agro-chemicals without having access to independent professional vocational training (Huang *et al.* 1999). The environmental damage that results from this lack of knowledge is not afforded a high priority, especially regarding the background of farmers who must secure their agricultural income for family subsistence. Thus, the challenge to be overcome is to enhance well-grounded approaches that accomplish effective agricultural training, encouraging farmers to adopt optimised practices, even though the environmental awareness of the general public is rising only very slowly (Harris 2004).

In this regard, the theoretical framework is about the decision-making theories of individual behaviour. Since – in addition to economic concerns – successful local policy implementation is closely related to an individual's social and cognitive preferences, the approach was to link the socio-psychological theory of human behaviour proposed by Fulton *et al.* (1996) to the leading principles of the economic model of individual decision-making (*cf.* Kirchgässner 2000). Therefore, a comprehensive theoretical model of individual decision-making was developed as a basis for the empirical research. In particular, fundamentals of cognitive processes seek to extend the traditional concept of the *homo oeconomicus*. The cognitive hierarchy model of Fulton *et al.* (1996) was used as a basis; then, Schwartz' (1994) theory of fundamental value types was applied. These defined universal goals represent the core of human cognition and have been proven to be universal for all cultures. Tailored to the Chinese context, the concept of *guānxi* relationships as well as agri-environmental attitudes were included in the next level of the hierarchy. These cognitions are attached to former experiences in certain situations; hence, they show how the mental decision-making process is related to the cultural, institutional and historical context (Wertsch 1998).

In order to address the various research objectives, in 2009 a quantitative survey of 1,342 farm households was conducted in rural Shandong Province, which is a major agricultural production area in China. Since the survey was part of a broader research project, the questioning was accomplished in close cooperation with counterparts from the Chinese Centre for Agricultural Policy (CCAP). The aim was to investigate the agro-economic and agri-environmental situation of Chinese agriculture. Out of the original subjects, 394 farmers were interviewed more intensively, surveying in particular social and cognitive determinants of farmers' decision-making. Moreover, the statistical data were underpinned by qualitative personal interviews and findings from group discussions with the intention of acquiring additional information regarding policy recommendations.

Univariate descriptives were used for statistical data analysis in order to provide an overview of the sample, local agricultural practices and the environmental situation. Moreover, calculations, such as the apparent Nitrogen Use Efficiency of farmers' fertilisation practices and the Standard Gross Margins, were used to evaluate the farms' production efficiency and the profitability of the cultivated crops, as well as to estimate the dimension of particular cost factors. Bivariate or multivariate methods were used to analyse cognitive and social determinants. The relationships between several conclusions concerning the relevance of respective variables for the research approach were explained by means of a structural equation model.

The descriptive agro-economic results of farms' status quo, especially of their wheat/ maize crop production systems, confirmed the information gained from literature concerning the study area. Besides excessive nitrogen overuse (about 540 kg N/ ha) and low production efficiencies due to poorly adapted management practices, decreasing profitability gave evidence of the poor environmental and economic situation of small-scale farmers. As a result, since it appears clear that small-scale farming has no future perspective, farm households are increasingly diversifying their income strategies. In particular, assuming opportunity costs for family labour, farms are no longer profitable. A major problem detected is the lack of technical knowledge and the ineffective, non-credible extension system, followed by increased urban migration of the farm labour, in particular among the younger generation. As a consequence, Chinese agriculture lacks well-educated trainees.

So as to encourage young farmers to continue farming, well-adapted incentives have to be established that comply with farmers' preferences. In this regard, initial advances were accomplished by studying the impact of the contextual framework on farmers' inherent cognitions and preferences. The study results revealed in particular that China is undergoing dramatic economic and structural changes, and that even the society in rural areas is in transition. Thus, the findings on farmers' fundamental values have shown that farmers still rely on traditional Confucian values, such as conformity and harmony, and that family security prevails over farmers' own interests. However, there is also a tendency towards secular-rational values, hence towards more self-enhancing and achievement values, diminishing farmers' will to strive towards intrinsic universal goals. Moreover, underlying values demonstrate a tendency towards a stronger instrumental bias with regard to farmers' *guānxi* relationships. Nevertheless, reliance on *guānxi* is still indispensable, as it provides farmers' with a strategy for coping with the insecure conditions in the agricultural sector. Thus, agricultural information is transferred by long-established trustworthy social networks, on which farmers rely more than on the remote extension system. However, most of them farm using traditional methods or based on their own experience. Furthermore, an evaluation of farmers' agri-environmental attitudes showed a consequential ranking of economic above environmental issues. Referring to farmers' nitrogen overuse, they make risk-averse decisions since they have only experienced positive effects from agro-chemicals and since environmental damage could not be easily traced back to their fertilisation behaviour.

In order to implement well-grounded approaches for the enhancement of farmers' agricultural knowledge and behaviour, in addition to their contextual framework, their agri-environmental decision-making was analysed on the basis of the theoretical model. The results affirmed that, besides economic reasons, fundamental values and *guānxi* relationships indeed influence farmers' agri-environmental attitudes as well as their disposition towards environmental services and their fertilisation behaviour. Depending on their cognitive position, either farmers do not question the use of agro-chemicals at all, or they think carefully about their use, but ultimately make their decision based on their desire not to lose income. Both of these farmer types are older and of lower income and driven by self-enhancing and traditional value positions. The difference between them is their disposition towards their social relationships. Those farmers who rely on *guānxi* relationships might indeed care more about environmental issues, but tend to make their decisions based on economic factors; as a result, they fertilise more. Farmers who think more in individual categories do not feel responsible for environmental concerns, yet fertilise less. The latter are not negatively influenced by information acquired through their social network; instead, they seem to farm more independently, making farming decisions based on their own experience. In contrast, open and self-determined farmers with universal values and collectively orientated *guānxi* relationships are more concerned about environmental issues, although they still do not have the knowledge to act accordingly.

Finally, based on the theoretical background and survey findings, policy recommendations are drawn in the fields of education, political incentives and institutional reforms. In the field of education, the development of the extension system and reliance on social networks as informative multiplicators is crucial. Monetary incentives and subsidies for planned behaviour change in situations of financial scarcity are political measures for averting economic risk considerations. Lastly, institutional reforms were found to be indispensable with regard to the absorption of negative effects for the sake of a sustainable agricultural transition covering social, economic and environmental aspects. In the end, in order to improve Chinese agriculture and the environmental situation, a new agricultural paradigm is needed that adresses in particular the preferences of young, open-minded farmers and encourages them to continue farming under improved and secure conditions.

ACKNOWLEDGEMENTS

Many people from various institutions have accompanied me during the process of working on this dissertation and in the related projects. I am deeply indebted to everyone who has supported my work.

First of all, I want to express my gratitude to my supervisors from the Department of Agricultural Economics and Rural Development. Sincere thanks go to my first supervisor, Prof. Dr. Rainer Marggraf of the Section for Environmental and Resource Economics, for making this research possible and accepting such an interdisciplinary topic for a doctoral study. I am glad to have had his professional advice and honest support during this time. I am also very grateful to my co-supervisor, Prof. Dr. Achim Spiller of the Section for Marketing of Food and Agricultural Products, who promptly agreed to evaluate the thesis from the perspective of his research focus on analysing decision making. I would also like to thank Jun. Prof. Dr. Ulf Liebe of the Section for Rural Sociology, with whom I had constructive discussions and who immediately agreed to be a part of my board of examiners. My thanks go also to Dr. Holger Bergmann. He constantly pushed me to trust myself and offered me the freedom to follow my own ideas. Since he accompanied the project objectives closely, we had fruitful discussions while he provided advice, particularly on agronomic questions. His commitment to my work enabled me to learn a great deal; I appreciate it very much. Furthermore, I gratefully acknowledge the financial support of the BMBF. For his help in the course of the project, I would like to offer special thanks to the coordinator, Dr. Marco Roelcke from the Technical University of Braunschweig, Institute of Geoecology, for his valuable support in coping with administrative matters. He kindly intermediated regarding culturally sensitive issues and provided agronomic information from his comprehensive treasure trove of experience with Chinese agriculture.

Regarding the organisation of the surveys and participatory group discussions in rural China, I would like to mention a word of gratitude for our Chinese partners from the Chinese Centre for Agricultural Policy, Prof. HUANG Jikun, Prof. HU Ruifa, Dr. JIA Xiangping and Ms. XIANG Cheng. I am indebted to them for their support during my stays in the rural areas as well as the preparatory and follow-up discussions; I am grateful not only for the insights they provided me into their research approach and Chinese culture, but also for their openness towards my own cultural background.

There are also a number of partners in Germany who supported me with information in fruitful discussions, in various workshops and informal get-togethers. Sincere thanks go to our project partners from the TU-BS-coordinated Research Group: Prof. Dr. Rolf Nieder, Dr. Marco Roelcke and Mr. Maximilian Hofmeier from the TU Braunschweig (Geoecology), Prof. Dr. Torsten Müller, Prof. Dr. Volker Römheld and Mr. Tobias Hartmann from the University of Hohenheim (Crop Science); and PD Dr. habil. Kurt Christian Kersebaum and Ms. Anna Michalczyk from the Leibniz-Centre for Agricultural Landscape Research (ZALF) in Müncheberg (Landscape Systems Analysis). I greatly enjoyed the fruitful teamwork with you.

There are still more people who accompanied me during the process of writing my dissertation. In particular, I would like to thank my colleagues for creating a fantastic working atmosphere. Whenever needed, they gave me advice and moral support.

Moreover, I want to express my gratitude to all my friends who supported me throughout the last three years. Special thanks go to my parents for their unconditional encouragement. Finally, my husband, Justus Böhm, deserves my unending gratitude. I cannot imagine that any person could be more loving and supporting. His constant reassurance and reliable advice was indispensable.

TABLE OF CONTENTS

LIST OF FIGURES

LIST OF TABLES

LIST OF ABBREVIATIONS

AD   *Anno Domini* [latin]; after Christ

aNUE   apparent Nitrogen Use Efficiency

AVE   Average Variance Extracted, measure of discriminant validity

BC   Before Christ

BMBF   German Federal Ministry of Education and Research

CAU   China Agricultural University in Beijing

CCAP   Chinese Centre for Agricultural Policy

cf.   *confer* [Latin]; compare

CFA   Confirmatory Factor Analysis

CNY   Chinese *yuán*; Currency of the PRC

DAP   Diammon phosphate $(NH_4)_2HPO_4$; commercial phosphorus fertiliser; defined ratio 18 % N : 46 % P_2O_5

DE   *Dungeinheit*; key converter to determine the maximal stocking rate for different types of animals per hectare (1.4 DE/ ha)

e.g.   *exempli gratia* [latin]; for example

ESS   European Social Survey

etc.   *et cetera* [latin]; and so on

EUR   Euros; European currency

EFA   Exploratory Factor Analysis

f^2 Effect size is a measure of the strength of the relationship

FA   Factor Analysis

GDP   Gross Domestic Product

GONGO   Government-organised non-governmental organisation

h²	communalities
ha	hectare
HRS	Household Responsibility System
i.e.	*id est* [latin]; this is
incl.	including
jīn	Chinese weight unit (1 *jīn* = 1 pound or 500 grammes)
Kg	kilogramme
km	kilometre
KMO	Kaiser-Meyer-Olkin measure of sampling adaquacy
LV	latent variable
m	metre
MDS	Multiple Dimensional Scaling
MOA	Chinese Ministry of Agriculture
MOST	Chinese Ministry of Science and Technology
mŭ	Chinese area unit (15 *mŭ* = 1 ha)
N	Nitrogen
NCP	North China Plain; geographical region in Northeast China
NGO	Non-governmental organisation
n.p.	not paginated
nPID	next PID; personal identificaton number of the respondent of part II of the questionnaire
NPK	Commercial fertiliser containing nitrogen (N), phosphorus (P) and potassium (K); defined ratio 15 % N : 15 % P_2O : 15 % K_2O
p.	page [singular]
PASW	Predictive Analytics SoftWare
PCA	Principal Component Analysis
pp.	pages [plural]
PID	Personal Identification
PLS	Partial least squares
PRC	People's Republic of China
pPID	previous PID; personal identification number of the respondent of part I of the questionnaire
PVQ 21	Portrait Values Questionnaire; an alternative developed order to the SVS measure of the ten basic values, including short verbal portraits of 21 people

r^2	Coefficient of determination, gives information about the goodness of fit of a model
RMB	Renminbi; Currency of the PRC; sign: ¥; code: CNY
SEM	Structural equation modelling
SGM	Standard Gross Margins
SPSS	Statistical Package for the Social Sciences [software programme]
SSA	Similarity Structure Analysis, alternatively Smallest Space Analysis
Std. D.	Standard Deviation
SVS	Schwartz Value Survey, first instrument to measure values as desirable end-states in noun form, lateron in active form
t	tons
TVE	Township and Village Enterprises
UN	United Nations
USD	United States Dollar; Currency of the United States of America
USSR	Union of Soviet Socialist Republics
WTP	Willingness to Pay
α	Cronbach's Alpha; coefficient of reliability
β	Beta weights
σ	Sigma; Statistical significance
€	Euro, European currency
¥	*Yuán*, Chinese currency (1¥ ≈ 0.1€)

1 INTRODUCTION

1.1 Agricultural and environmental background

China's demographic and economic growth over the past decades has had a critical impact on the country's environment and natural resources. In addition to the growing industrial sector and the low environmental awareness of the general public, intensive agriculture contributes considerably to environmental problems (Ash and Edmonds 1998).

1.1.1 Agricultural development – Striving for self-sufficiency

The population of the Peoples' Republic of China (PRC) is about 1.3 billion people. It must feed 21 percent of the world's total population with food production on only 8.5 percent of the world's total arable land and 6.5 percent of the world's water resources (De Schutter 2010). Due to economic reforms, China achieved a grain self-sufficiency rate of at least 95 percent in 2010, with a remarkable production of 546 million tonnes (De Schutter 2010). During the late 1970s, the agricultural sector was restructured by Deng Xiaoping as one of "The Four Modernisations". Important economic reforms towards market-based mechanisms followed, as did the introduction of the household responsibility system (HRS)[1] in agriculture, the development of township and village enterprises (TVEs)[2] in rural areas and export-led growth, stimulated by the opening up of the economy to global trade and investment (De Schutter 2010). Furthermore, agricultural inputs, in particular synthetic fertilisers were heavily subsidised (Lin 1992; Gale et al. 2005). Thus, the nation's agricultural production increased 5 percent on average annually (Hoering 2010). Nevertheless, most of the agricultural activity is carried out by more than 200 million small-scale farmers who have only user rights for very small plots of 0.65 hectares on average (De Schutter 2010), and the PRC hopes to further increase agricultural efficiency. However, since 1998, the average grain yields per plot have begun to stagnate, levelling out at about 4.9 t/ ha in 2010 (Schüller 2004), and the improper use of agro-chemicals and exiguous agricultural training often lead to low use efficiencies (Ju et al. 2006; Huang 1999).

1.1.2 Nitrogen fertilisation – A fundamental problem

In particular, nitrogen fertilisation causes massive environmental problems. China's nitrogen fertiliser consumption is the highest in the world (Cui et al. 2010). In the intensive agricultural east and southeast of China, current agricultural fertilisation practices use a range of 550 to 600 kg N/ ha annually (Ju et al. 2008). With political and structural change, fertilisers were heavily subsidised and hence cheap to purchase. Farmers experienced almost doubled grain yields. However, without training with regard to adapted application and which amount of fertiliser to apply for the best use efficiency of the plants, farmers had little knowledge and were uncertain as to the best fertiliser practice. In addition, Ju et al. (2004) point out a certain recalcitrance regarding an advised reduction of fertilisers, as farmers had

---

[1] The HRS allowed households to contract land, machinery and other facilities from collective organisations. Farmers could make operating decisions independently and surplus production could be sold in free markets. This incentive caused one of the largest increases in agricultural production in such a short time.

[2] TVEs refer to rural companies sponsored by townships and villages, to private stock companies formed by peasants and to individual enterprises. Since they were established after the breakup of the agricultural collectives, many of them are "collectively"-owned and run by the local government.

experienced higher yields in the past. For instance, Zhen *et al.* (2005) identified that only about 6 percent of surveyed households apply the recommendations for balanced input use. Further, Ju *et al.* (2004) stated that the nitrogen application in wheat cultivation in the North China Plain (NCP) shows broad variation.

In general, nitrogen fertiliser application increased from 1977 to 2005 by 271 percent, resulting in severe environmental degradation since the 1990s (Ju *et al.* 2008). In China, especially in the NCP, overfertilisation and the resulting low nitrogen use efficiency is typical of the agricultural production (Ju *et al.* 2007). It leads to total loss rates of nitrogen between 45 percent and 50 percent followed by nitrate and heavy metal leaching into aquatic systems, causing groundwater pollution and the enrichment of reactive nitrogen in the soil system (Ju *et al.* 2004; Ju *et al.* 2008; Cui *et al.* 2010). In addition to the unnecessary economic costs to farmers, the amount of mineral fertilisers applied does not significantly increase crop yields. Current application rates could be reduced by 30 to 60 percent (Ju *et al.* 2008). Especially for the calcareous soils and intense summer rainfall where the wheat/ maize double-cropping systems occur in the NCP, these surpluses (19 percent for wheat and 24 percent for maize) should be reduced for the sake of the environment (Ju *et al.* 2008).

1.1.3 Agri-environmental situation – A matter of urgency

The national government has become aware of the environmental damage resulting from intensified agricultural production. Especially in fertile, but also drought-ridden areas like the North China Plain, the increasing influence of irrigation systems causes declining groundwater levels. In addition, the inappropriate and excessive use of agro-chemicals like synthetic fertilisers contaminates water resources. Soils acidify in the long-run and fallow periods have shortened, with concomitant land degradation (UNDP 2006). According to calculations by the Chinese Academy of Sciences, the cost of exploitation of natural resources, ecological degradation and environmental pollution in 2005 was 13.9 percent of GDP, while growth was just 11.3 percent (De Schutter 2010). Although these problems have already become a popular issue in China and the government attaches great importance to the formulation of laws and regulations on environmental protection, there are still no working legislative controls (Ju *et al.* 2008; Qing and Vermeer 1999), and China faces challenges in implementing sustainable modes of agricultural productivity.

1.1.4 General environmental awareness – A question of education

In China, there is low environmental awareness among the general public. Most Chinese seem to have very limited concern for the natural environment beyond its utility, particularly poorly educated people in rural areas (Qing and Vermeer 1999).

Since the opening of the Chinese economy by Deng Xiaoping in the 1970s, the government has emphasised individualism, entrepreneurship and materialism (Harris 2004). Young people in particular have been influenced by hedonistic values (Kwong 1994). Consequently, consumerism has permeated society at all levels (Kwong 1994). Hence, environmental values are not altruistic, given that they are generally associated with personal well-being rather than protection of nature per se (Harris 2004). The Chinese government is aware of the problems, but environmental policies often compete with overriding commitment to economic growth (Qing and Vermeer 1999).

Nevertheless, environmental concern is slowly rising (Harris 2004). There are only a few registered environmental protection organisations, however, they are organised by the government (GONGO[3]), and their environmental knowledge is not very professional. They receive little media attention, and most are driven by love of nature and duty. In addition, there are some NGOs or student organisations with only a low impact (Qing and Vermeer 1999). Thus, environmental awareness is not established among the general public and does not reach rural areas.

1.1.5 "The Three Rural Issues" – A future challenge

In terms of economic relevance, the agricultural share in China's GDP has declined to less than 10 percent, but the sector's social and political importance persists. Due

---

[3] GONGOs (Government-organised non-governmental organisations) are officially run by the government. They have much more power and influence than ordinary NGOs, but their environmental interest primarily stems from emotional affection and a sense of responsibility (Qing and Vermeer 1999).

the restrictive system of land tenure, the low education level of rural people and their low-income opportunities in agriculture, financial burdens accompany increasing labour emigration (Hoering 2010; Xu and Wang 2009). Those who remain in rural areas are primarily the elderly, woman and children, who are hardly in the position to shoulder the further development of this sector (Xu and Wang 2009). The PRC recognised that the heavy emphasis on grain self-sufficiency contributed to this situation and that the younger generation's motivation to invest in new agricultural technologies instead of working off-farm has to be strengthened (Wen 2006). To this end, the Chinese government has again highlighted "The Three Rural Issues"[4], namely agriculture, rural areas and farmers. During the course of this effort, President Hu Jintao revitalised the promotion of a harmonious society in 2005 during the National People's Congress. He promoted the old Confucian doctrine as a socio-economic vision to solve the worsening social tensions in China (Zheng and Fewsmith 2008). In particular, to appeal to the rural population, banners and slogans were visible throughout the country. This policy could be regarded as a backlash against Deng Xiaoping's focus on materialist economic values.

1.1.6 Farmers' decision-making in the crossfire of influences

In addition to political and societal developments, farmers have to make their own decisions regarding agricultural production and their daily lives, which affect the welfare of their families. The basic features of their peasant economy include choice of crops, methods of cultivation and the role of non-farming activities. However, their decision-making is furthermore restricted by geographical and political constraints like the form of land tenure and restricted access to water for irrigation. For example, farmland in China is contracted from the village committee to each

---

[4] "The Tree Rural Issues" is a concept that stands for solving the main rural problems in a sustainable way at economic, social and institutional level. It is assumed that social problems are a result of economic and regional disintegration, and can be solved only by overcoming the opposition between rural and urban structures. For the 11th Five-year program (2006-2010), the Communist Party set off new guidelines designed to promote social equity by reducing the wealth gap (Hoering 2010).

Hùkǒu[5]-registered inhabitant according to an officially defined size. Hence, it cannot be sold easily and also serves as a retirement arrangement (Chan and Zhang 1999). Moreover, irrigation systems with access to big rivers (*e.g.*, the Yellow River) depend on centrally controlled water gates; thus, irrigation times are out of farmers' control (Farmer in Huimin County, March 2011, personal communication).

Accordingly, the peasant economy is defined by various determinants. Farmers are caught in the crossfire of influences of which they have no overview. In addition, farmers' agricultural decision preferences as well as their attitudes, values and beliefs are influenced at least to some extent by their socio-political and cultural environment. They must continuously adapt to political and structural reforms (agricultural tax, subsidies, guarantied market prices, land use rights, *etc.*). Moreover, they face uncertainties regarding new agricultural technologies and the rising market structure of agricultural chemical inputs without having access to independent professional vocational training. Environmental damage as a result of this lack of knowledge is not taken into account. Due to rural households' low income, farmers' interest is primarily focussed on economic benefit. Some are not even aware of the harmful consequences of their agricultural behaviour.

In short, the development policies of the last 20 years have increased food production through advertising good output and an intensive use of external inputs. Due to failed knowledge transfer, however, this has caused significant negative external impacts and environmental costs, especially in the fertile North China Plain, which is the food-grain production base of the country (Zhen and Zoebisch 2006). The challenge at present and in future is to enhance a sustainable agricultural production in terms of both quantity and quality to feed the growing population without degradation of the production resources and the environment (Brklacich *et al.* 1991). Therefore, new, integrated approaches are necessary to improve the environmental and economic situation of Chinese agriculture.

---

[5] The *Hùkǒu* system is the official system of residence in China, which rules public administration. Registered status is used to control the movement of people between rural and urban areas, because it binds people to their place of origin. People who live and work outside their *Hùkǒu* registration (regional boundary) do not qualify for fixed social services, education, health care, employer-provided housing, *etc.* (Fan 2008).

1.2 Research framework

Project setting

The cooperative Sino-German project, within the scope of which this research takes place, seeks to meet that challenge. The goal of the Nitrogen Project is to improve agricultural production and environmental protection in intensive agriculture on the North China Plain. It aims to implement innovative nitrogen management practices and extension work in different representative cropping systems and for different farm sizes.[6] With regard to the implementation of scientific findings, this study focuses not only on economic and environmental issues but also on social aspects related to sustainability in the agriculture of the region. It is assumed that improvements in China's agriculture and environmental situation could be achieved by a reduction in excessive nitrogen fertilisation, which in turn will dramatically optimise farmers' low income in terms of productivity and cost efficiency, as well as resilience and self-sufficiency. Furthermore, inherent determinants of decision-making are taken into consideration since they are crucial, in particular, for the successful implementation of environmentally sensitive production techniques.

Scientific relevance

Projects optimising sustainability in various cultural contexts often run the risk of failing during the implementation period or with regard to adoption by the local popula. Sometimes, applied research focuses on a very specialised topic, such as agricultural production, without looking more closely at the social system, the contextual conditions or the personal background of the decision-makers. However, the different and often very sensitive decision-making determinants are highly responsible for the adaption process of optimised ideas. This problem indicates the

---

[6] The project "Innovative nitrogen management technologies to improve agricultural production and environmental protection in intensive agriculture" is funded by the German Federal Ministry of Education and Research (BMBF), project number 0330800A-F, and the Chinese Ministry of Science and Technology (MOST), grant number 2007DFA30850. For further information related to the project see http://www.nitrogen-management.org/.

increasing need for further research in the analysis of farmers' decision behaviour to guide culturally adapted development projects in agricultural systems.

Theoretical background

In environmental economics, the standard neoclassical economic model of rational behaviour is a common approach, especially for local policy implications (van der Bergh 2000). However, the maximisation hypothesis and its methodological foundation have been criticised on many grounds (cf. van der Bergh et al. 2000; Kirchgässner 2000). A range of innovative economic studies has shown that decisions are not only linked to rational and monetary incentives, but also to a wide range of other inherent determinants (Simon 1959; Becker 1976; Gasson 1973; Deci and Ryan 1985). In particular, farmers are not always only motivated by profit (Anosike and Coughenour 1990; Gartrell and Gartrell 1985; Herath et al. 1982). More than in any other business, there are external pressures (Errington 1991; Napier and Foster 1982; Potter 1995); extrinsic motivations also make them behave apart from the rational profit-maximisation axiom. Despite considerable effort to understand the decision-making of farmers, there has been little attempt to integrate social and psychological variables in particular within a comprehensive research framework (Willock et al. 1999). Furthermore, little literature is available about specific inherent decision-making determinants of Chinese farmers and their impact on a definite behaviour.

Theoretical approach

The research approach results from the described gap in the knowledge about farmers' inherent behaviour motivations and the assumption that production decisions depend not only on economic factors, but on social, cognitive and contextual factors as well. Therefore, this thesis attempts to link the economist's approach to modelling farm households according to their financial situation with the social psychologist's close analysis of individual behaviour. In this way, it hopes to analyse farmers' relevant behaviour determinants and define their impact in order to support well-adapted agricultural training approaches and successful implementation of policy recommendations.

For the theoretical aspect, the neoclassic model of individual decision-making with its various concepts of the *homo oeconomicus* is extended by incorporating social and cognitive aspects in particular into a comprehensive model.

The cognitive hierarchy model of Fulton *et al.* (1996) is especially relevant. This socio-psychological concept is based on values that refer to fundamental cognitions as the foundation for beliefs, attitudes, subjected norms and behaviour intentions, which are, according to Ajzen and Fishbein (1980), the best predictors of definite behaviour.

Since economic action is strongly embedded in social structure, another focus is on the meaning and influence of social relationships (Granovetter 1985). Since social and personal relationships are necessary for everyone, individuals do not make decisions only according to their intrinsic self-interest outside a social context (Granovetter 1985). Chinese society is dominated by *guānxi* relationships. *Guānxi* relationships are defined as personalised networks of influence. They seek to accumulate social capital, but in spite of that, the concept differs in its traits.

Based on theory, general assumptions are formulated in a comprehensive hypothetical economic model of individual behaviour that seeks to evaluate agri-environmental decision-making from a different perspective.

Empirical approach

Out of the empirical analyses, a detailed description of the study area and the agricultural and economic situation of farm households arises. It provides an overview of farming in intensive agricultural areas of China (Shandong Province) in order to evaluate the efficiency and profitability of Chinese farms and its future perspectives and to characterise the surveyed farmers. In addition to socio-demographic information, the farmers' fundamental value positions and social embeddedness as well as their agri-environmental attitudes give evidence regarding their personal constitutions and psychological motivations. The questions to be answered are these: Why do farmers not apply less fertiliser, and why do they not relate the environmental damage to their behaviour? This study will seek to clarify whether this behaviour stems solely from a lack of knowledge or if farmers have other (intrinsic/ extrinsic) reasons for their decisions. The information gained determines utilisable capacities and, hence, taps the full potential of individuals for future agricultural development in China. Based on this, preliminary policy recommendations are suggested in order to improve the agricultural and environmental situation in China with special regard to problems covering farmers' fertilisation behaviour.

Furthermore, selected paths of the hypothetical model are proved in a structural equation model (SEM) that give in particular evidence if and how agri-environmental decision-making is influenced by such cognitive values and *guānxi* relationships. Thus, the thesis delivers insights into theoretical decision-making processes and enables distinctions between different farmer types. For example, do farmers with particular value orientations or differing emphases on social relationships behave differently, and can they be distinguished according to their inherent cognitions? Supplemented by additional contextual information, the research produces arguments in addition to the neoclassic utility maximisation axiom as to why, for example, some farmers apply too much fertiliser without regard for environmental issues while others care more about their agri-environmental behaviour. Thus, the assumption is proved that farmers do not consistently decide solely as rational economic utility maximisers, but that they are equally affected by inherent fundamental values and their social embeddedness through their *guānxi* relationships. Finally, the research opens up perspectives on how to change farmers' behaviour through structural changes or well-placed incentives.

Data acquisition

For data acquisition, a broader quantitative survey of farmers was conducted in Shandong Province in 2009. In total 1,342 farmers were questioned in two steps. The first questioning dealt primarily with agro-economic variables, and the second focussed mainly on the social and cognitive questions. The second questioning also had a smaller sample size of 394. Personal identification numbers link the two questionnaires. The data provide a basis for agro-economic analyses and act as indicators for the empirical verification of the hypothetical model.

Furthermore, additional information was gathered in personal interviews and from two group discussions with farmers and scientists in March 2010. The personal interviews and discussions aimed to underpin the data gathered with the questionnaire through detailed information from the farmers themselves. Confronting them with specific problems related to fertilisation made their agri-environmental knowledge gaps observable in detail. Inherent doubts on recommended practices were expressed, fears appeared and opportunities to change were discussed from their perspective. Thus, the information was quite helpful in understanding the context of their decision behaviour and the agri-environmental attitudes of some farmers, enabling better explanations to be obtained.

Results at a glance

The results reveal the problematic agronomic and socio-economic situation of farm households in Shandong Province. An overview is presented of farmers' agricultural practices and, in particular, their nitrogen overuse. Findings concerning the profitability of the cropping system show that fertilisation accounts for a large share of the production costs, while, at the same time, fertilisers are very ineffectively applied. Thus, better Standard Gross Margins could be reached simply by increasing the apparent Nitrogen Use Efficiency.

Although the problem seems obvious and the solution clear, according to economic theory, farmers do not decide purely rationally; thus, the results reveal that besides farmers' lack of technical and agri-environmental knowledge, socio-psychological determinants also play a remarkable role in their decision-making.

Since farmers do not have sufficient agricultural knowledge, they rely instead on technical information from their social networks rather than trust the advice of agricultural extension agents. On the one hand, this behaviour is explained by contextual factors, including the remote agricultural extension system, as well as ongoing structural, political and economic developments in rural areas for the last few decades. On the other hand, their behaviour is also influenced by Chinese cultural traditions and their value system, which relies heavily on experience and habit, as well as particular on information from personal ties rather than from non-credible extension agents.

Referring to training approaches for a better implementation of optimised agricultural practices, farmers' agri-environmental attitudes show different underlying value positions and dispositions towards their *guānxi* relationships. Since the comprehensive individual model has been verified, these various attitudes, values, and *guānxi* traits are decisive determinants regarding farmers' nitrogen fertilisation. Finally, these cognitive and social determinants of decision-making act as relevant parameters for the development of policy implications and indicate preliminary recommendations.

Prior to presenting the theoretical framework, a short outline provides an overview of the main structure of the thesis.

1.3 Outline of the thesis

The thesis is divided into five parts. An abbreviated picture of the main parts is presented in Figure 1. This chart visualises the "road map" and covers the main points in keywords summarising the headings of the main sections.

Beginning with the introduction, the first part gives a brief overview of the agricultural and environmental background of Chinese agriculture and related environmental problems. The main areas of interest are sketched and followed by a rough overview of the research framework.

The second part of the thesis provides the theoretical framework by reviewing the literature about the economic theory of individual behaviour and introducing the socio-psychological theory of human behaviour. The underlying economic model presented is based on the individualistic approach of Kirchgässner (2000), but also discusses structural functionalist perspectives. Thus, various modified approaches, including cognitive and social motivations, are highlighted, as is Granovetter's (1985) social embeddedness concept. The socio-psychological theory is adapted from the cognitive hierarchy model of Fulton *et al.* (1996), in particular. Based on the theoretical behaviour models presented, selected decision-making determinants are emphasised. To this end, Schwartz' (1996) theory of fundamental values is presented, as is a sketch of Chinese value positions drawn from other research approaches; then, the Chinese concept of *guānxi* relationships and different classifications is introduced, followed by an overview of Chinese attitudes towards the environment. Finally, the second part concludes with a hypothetical model outlining a comprehensive approach to modelling individual decision-making.

Chapter 3 describes the empirical research. In the first section, the study area is addressed and an overview of the regional agricultural conditions given. The socio-economic and environmental conditions are presented, and structural aspects outlined. Next, issues concerning the questionnaire design are explored. These include techniques for formulating questions and response scaling, adapting the questionnaire to the local situation and a critical reflection on the research ethics involved. The following section explains how the sample was selected. This is followed by a description of how the survey data was collected – including interviewer training and survey methodology. The final section of Chapter 3 details how errors and item nonresponse were dealt with, also data entry and screening.

The fourth chapter presents the data analysis results. First, the statistical methods used are described. Then, an overview of household and farm characteristics is given, followed by a review of the agronomic and economic results achieved. These focus on farmers' wheat and maize management practices – in particular, their fertiliser use – as well as the current profitability of the cropping system. In this context, critical environmental and economic parameters are revealed. The next section reviews the analysis results of the farm decision-maker. Here, the main characteristics of the respondents, the households and the farms are again described, since the results refer to another sample size. The results reveal farmers' agri-environmental knowledge and general attitudes towards environmental issues as well as their perception and evaluation of water pollution and its quality. Additionally, evidence is provided about farmers' fundamental value positions and current evaluation of their *guānxi* relationships as well as the correlation of farmers' values with these *guānxi* relationships and with agri-environmental attitudes. The final section analyses the impact of cognitive and social factors on farmers' decision-making by using a structural equation model. After evaluating the model, the influence of several factors on agri-environmental attitudes is revealed and the focus narrows to farmers' fertilisation behaviour and willingness to pay for environmental goods. Finally, the relevance of cognitive and social decision-making determinants for better adapted agricultural training is argued.

The fifth and final chapter presents the conclusions. The results of Chapter 4 are summarised and applied at a higher, more general level. Subsequently, the strengths and limitations of the research are outlined and, finally, the decision-making determinants are assessed in the context of policy implications for the sustainable development of Chinese agriculture.

Figure 1   Outline of the thesis

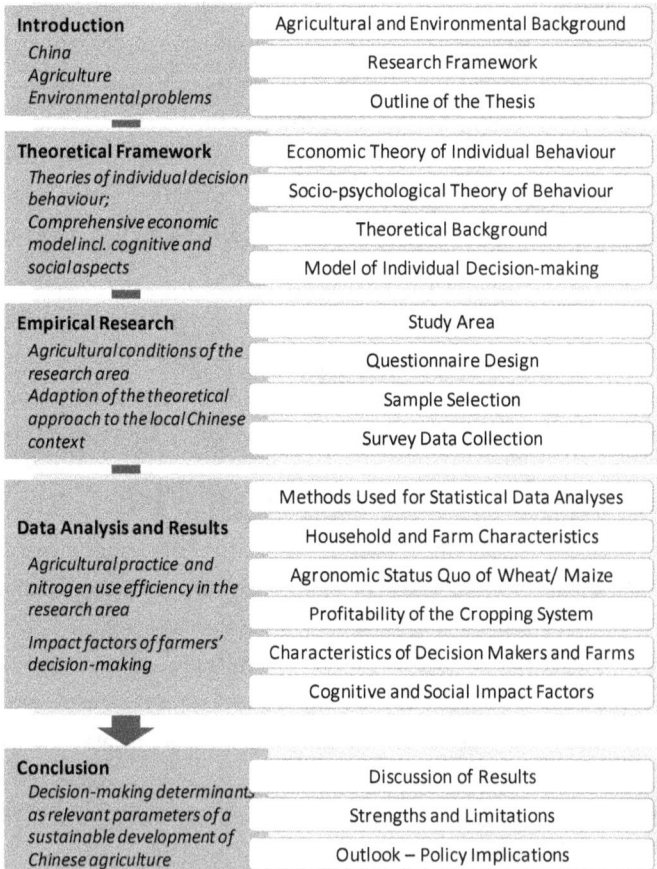

Introduction	Agricultural and Environmental Background
China	Research Framework
Agriculture	
Environmental problems	Outline of the Thesis

Theoretical Framework	Economic Theory of Individual Behaviour
Theories of individual decision behaviour;	Socio-psychological Theory of Behaviour
Comprehensive economic model incl. cognitive and	Theoretical Background
social aspects	Model of Individual Decision-making

Empirical Research	Study Area
Agricultural conditions of the research area	Questionnaire Design
Adaption of the theoretical approach to the local Chinese	Sample Selection
context	Survey Data Collection

	Methods Used for Statistical Data Analyses
Data Analysis and Results	Household and Farm Characteristics
Agricultural practice and nitrogen use efficiency in the research area	Agronomic Status Quo of Wheat/ Maize
	Profitability of the Cropping System
Impact factors of farmers' decision-making	Characteristics of Decision Makers and Farms
	Cognitive and Social Impact Factors

Conclusion	Discussion of Results
Decision-making determinants as relevant parameters of a	Strengths and Limitations
sustainable development of Chinese agriculture	Outlook – Policy Implications

2 THEORETICAL FRAMEWORK

Decision-making as an outcome of continuous mental processes generates a final choice, which is the basis for a particular behaviour. The mental processes are complex; thus, decision-making must be regarded from several perspectives.

From a psychological perspective, it is necessary to examine individual decisions in the context of a set of inherent needs. From a cognitive perspective, the decision-making process must be regarded as a continuous one, integrated into the interaction with the environment (group-thinking, social norms). Finally, from a normative economic perspective, individuals' decisions are concerned with expected utility based on rational assumptions (Kahneman and Tversky 2000).

The model of the *homo oeconomicus* combines different disciplines, hence, it can be considered in an interdisciplinary approach. In particular, Frey and Stroebe (1980), as well as Kirchgässner (2000) mention the concept of man and preferences in both economic and socio-psychological models. The concept is not understood anymore in a normative way, as explicit (expected) mathematical optimisation of means to a predetermined goal but rather as a positive approach to analyse the logic of human behaviour and the logic of economic argumentation (Marggraf 2008).

In modern economic interpretations, the *homo oeconomicus* interacts in a defined scope of action. Out of a given set of alternatives that result from the interaction of an individual's stable preferences over time and out of given restrictions, the individual decides between competing alternatives. The decision assumptions are made according to the following leading principals (*cf.* Marggraf 2008):

(1) Decision motivations are effected by self-interest.
(2) Decisions are constraint by problems of scarcity.
(3) Preferences are consistent and transitive. Behaviour changes are explained by the variations in restrictions.
(4) Rationality with regard to the calculus of utility maximisation is considered.
(5) Decisions are not regarded as individual case observations, but deduce from implied assumptions in general.
(6) Methodological individualism, *i.e* individuals' attitudes and incentive systems constitute the particular social system.

In the following, the economic model of individual behaviour is explained with its main theoretical assumptions (economic perspective). Critics are mentioned, as are the consequential alternative approaches that make the connection to social science, including those that deal with the effects of interaction with the environment on individual cognition. To conclude the theoretical framework, the cognitive hierarchy model is presented, focussing on inherent decision-making processes in detail (psycological perspective).

2.1 Economic theory of individual behaviour

In spite of criticisms and alternatives, the standard neoclassical model of rational behaviour is still the basis of many decision-making models that have been proposed in agricultural and environmental economics. Although over the years, advanced models have been developed and new courses set, the economic behaviour model rests on its main assumptions.

The economic model of individual behaviour presented is based on the approach of Kirchgässner (2000), who emphasises the methodological, individualistic approach, which already takes into account structural functionalist discussions. Additionally, modified theories are presented, in particular those considering social and cognitive motivations. Durkheim's (1961) social science approaches regarding individual behaviour make the connexion to Granovetter's (1973) structural emphasis on personal ties.

2.1.1 The economic model of individual decision-making

The economic model of individual decision-making is based on the rational axiom that people always try to maximise utility in general, or profit in particular, constrained by their scope of actions. This means they decide between different alternatives based on the available information. The decision situation itself is described by two elements: the individuals' preferences and the restrictions placed on them. The individuals' scope of action is restricted by such factors as income, prices and laws, but also by (expected) reactions in their social environment. According to Kirchgässner (2000), the individual need not have full information about possible choices, but must estimate the consequences according to expectations. Preferences derive from the intention of the individual. They reflect value positions in the socialisation process and are in principal independent of the actual possibilities of choice. Based on the preferences, the individual balances the advantages and disadvantages, well as the costs and benefits of various alternatives (Kirchgässner 2008). According to Kirchgässner (2008), individual behaviour is therefore (under the condition of uncertainty) still a utility maximisation and thus consistent with the concept of *homo oeconomicus*.

The original concept of *homo oeconomicus* is associated with the ideas of Adam Smith (1759), who suggests a sort of rational, self-interested, labour-averse model of man, while, at the same time, claiming that individuals have sympathy for the well-being of others. Nevertheless, micro-economists mathematise the assumptions of Smith's model. As will be seen below, the neoclassic theory has been criticised a great deal from various sides concerning the normative bias of the model (*cf.* Veblen 1898, Keynes 1930, Simon 1959). Many social and economic thinkers stress uncertainty and bounded rationality in the making of decisions, and it is often argued that perfect knowledge never exists. Alternative models of behaviour have been proposed modifying the traditional concept of the *homo oeconomicus* ('principles of bounded rationality and satisficing', Simon 1957; 'lexicographic preferences', Georgescu-Roegen 1966; 'habits and routines', Deaton and Muellbauer 1980; 'multiattribute utility', Keeney and Raiffa 1976; *etc.*) (*cf.* van der Berg *et al.* 2000). These approaches are grounded in a more comprehensive concept of man. Hence, the individual's intention to act is also determined by the person's scope of action that rather evolves competing preferences instead of having rational decision-making reasons available that apply to a group in general (Kirchgässner 2000).

In particular, economic anthropologists like Sahlins (1972), Polanyi (1944), Mauss (1924) or Godelier (1999) empirically demonstrate via cross-cultural comparisons that in traditional societies, decision making regarding the production and exchange of goods follows patterns of reciprocity that differ sharply from what the *homo oeconomicus* model postulates by its normative mathematical assumptions, neglecting the impact of societal norms. This substantivist point of view refers to social embeddedness, as well as to kinship-based ethics in traditional societies. Furthermore, new heterodox schools reject the basic utility maximisation assumption and argue for alternative understandings of how economic decisions are made and/or how human psychology works (Gabriel 2003).

2.1.2 Modified approaches including cognitive and social motivations

In modified formalist concepts of the *homo oeconomicus*, the maximisation axiom is no longer considered as optimisation on the basis of a given target function but instead in the sense of a systematic selection of certain known alternatives (Simon 1957; Becker 1967; Frey 1990; Kirchgässner 2000). Becker (1967) factored psychological elements into economic decision-making and insisted on maintaining strict consistency of preferences. Simon (1957) explained how people irrationally tend to be satisfied, instead of maximising utility, as generally assumed.

New behavioural economics approaches directly combine social, cognitive and emotional factors with economic decisions. The field is primarily concerned with the bounds of rationality of economic agents and therefore integrates insights from psychology with neo-classical economic theory (Kahneman and Tversky 1979). Some also assume a certain inconsistency in preferences ('fairness'; 'reciprocal altruism'; 'inequity aversion') (Fehr and Fischbacher 2002; Falk and Fischbacher 1999; Rabin 1994; Rawls 1971). Works on intrinsic motivation by Gneezy and Rustichini (2000) and on identity by Akerlof and Kranton (2000) allow agents to derive utility from meeting personal and social norms in addition to selfish consumption in particular.

Intrinsic motivations refer to the inherent traits of a person that allow him or her to take pleasure from a task itself or from the sense of satisfaction in completing or even working on a task. Intrinsic motivation occurs especially in public domains (moral and norm-based engagement). Experiments have shown that they are in dynamic relation to extrinsic incentives such as payments, which may even eliminate an individual's inherent intrinsic motivations through over-justification and resulting demoralisation (Deci *et al.* 1999). This so-called 'crowding-out effect' explains, among other things, why in some situations monetary incentives or regulations (punishments) are inefficient (Frey 1997). According to Akerlof und Kranton (2000), an individual's self-perception (gender roles, attitudes towards special activities, *etc.*)

can encompass decisions that contradict a rational utility calculation and that systematically influence economic mechanisms.

To sum up, in recent years, behavioural economists and social scientists have produced convincing evidence that an individual's selfish behaviour has limits. Intrinsically motivated fairness and norms of reciprocity, as well as a strong self-perception of one's own identity can also influence economic decision-making (Frey 2001). Thus, Kirchgässner's (2000) concept of *homo oeconomicus* does not contradict psychological considerations. On the contrary, socio-psychological concepts are compatible with the interpretation of the *homo oeconomicus*, because they are based on a similar idea of man (Frey and Stroebe 1980).

Thus, in this regard, the following section focuses the rationality of decision-making against the background of the individual's social setting.

2.1.3 Social embeddedness and the rationality of individual decision-making

Since the individualistic methodological approach of neoclassical theory does not regard social relationships as decision determinants, in 1895 Durkheim developed the collectivist approach deliberately as a counterpart to the individualistic theory. According to this approach, social behaviour can only be explained by the individual's social environment, and psychological, individualistic explanations are simply wrong (Durkheim 1961).

Nevertheless, according to Kirchgässner (2000), there is some overlap with socio-psychological approaches regarding the individual's behavioural intentions. Hence, an individual's intention can be explained by the influence of the social setting. Moreover, the recognised normative constraints and advantages of social cohesion are important to an individual's behavioural intentions, because the individual's utility maximisation then is related to the individuals' position within the society, too (Kirchgässner 2000).

In spite of Kirchgässner's (2000) explanations, the difference between the individualistic methodological approach and the collectivist approach of Durkheim (1961) remains. On the one hand, the methodological individualism explains societal processes of the macro-level by individual attitudes and incentive systems of the micro-level. Hence, once internalised, norms are followed according to the rationality axiom of individual behaviour. On the other hand, beyond internalised customs, habits and norms, social interactions also have an influence on an individual's behaviour as external forces (Granovetter 1985). Therefore, the social environment constraints an individual's decision, too. According to Granovetter (1985) the individual is embedded into systems of social relations. Thus, when making decisions, each individual has to cope with such factors as trust, conflicts, mutual adjustment, social and economic disorder and even social capital.

In this regard, Granovetter (1973) argues that it is necessary to analyse processes in interpersonal networks that provide the best bridge between the individual and social patterns, that is, how an individuals' decision behaviour is influenced by the forming of personal ties and other social and organisational phenomena on the macro-level. According to Granovetter (1985), human (in particular, economic) behaviour is embedded in social relationship networks, especially in premarket societies. Relying on personal ties implies effects of trust; the strength of trust and the degree of transitivity within personal networks informs an individual's decision. Thus, decision-making is influenced by the degree of social embeddedness or the position of the individual within the networks.

2.2 Socio-psychological theory of human behaviour

As in economics, there is a range of theoretical approaches for examining individual behaviour in social psychology. In the following, essential fundamentals are discussed that particularly focus on cognitive hierarchies in human perception processes. Afterwards, the cognitive hierarchy model of human behaviour proposed by Fulton et al. (1996) is described in detail since it serves as the basis for the empirical approach taken in this study.

2.2.1 Fundamentals of cognitive hierarchy models

Cognitions are mental processes, like decision-making. In cognitive psychology, human behaviour is defined as the result of the interaction between cognitive mental states and immediate social situations. Thus, the social nature of personality (people's values, beliefs and behaviours) is measured so as to understand the interactions of personalities within their social environment. Traditionally, emotions do not belong directly to cognitive process, since they are affective.

Two of the most famous theories are the theory of reasoned action (Ajzen and Fishbein 1980) and the theory of planned behaviour (Ajzen 1985). Both measure behaviour intentions as the highest order constructs in the cognitive hierarchy influencing the actual behaviour of individuals. According to these theories, behaviour intention depends on attitudes about the behaviour and subjective norms. Attitudes combine beliefs about the consequences of performing the behaviour and the individual's valuation of these consequences. Subjective norms are seen as a combination of perceived expectations from the social environment with intentions to comply with these expectations (Ajzen and Fishbein 1980). In addition, Ajzen (1985) extends these assumptions to cover the use of non-volitional behaviours in predicting behavioural intentions. However, fundamental values are not included in these cognitive hierarchy models (Sauer 2010).

Schwartz (1977) was the first to try to include values in his norm-activation model of altruism. According to this model, altruistic behaviour occurs in response to personal value orientations. These are activated by an awareness of adverse consequences and an awareness of responsibility. The theory was further developed by Stern and Dietz (1994), who link the value theory to the norm-activation theory by delineating a range of beliefs (personal beliefs to more focussed beliefs) about human-environment relations, their consequences and individuals' responsibility for their behaviour (personal moral norms) (Stern 2000). Since this model is limited to environmental behaviour and only focuses on some of the fundamental values (altruistic, egoistic and traditional value types), the cognitive hierarchy model described in Fulton *et al.* (1996) is better applicable to interdisciplinary topics outside of environmental psychology.

2.2.2 Cognitive hierarchy model of human behaviour

The social-psychological cognitive hierarchy model of human behaviour proposed by Fulton *et al.* (1996) explains to some extent why people may deviate from rational behaviour. Within the cognitive hierarchy model, cognitions are assumed to build upon one another, like an inverted pyramid (see Figure 2). Basic values are regarded as fundamental cognitions. They are not related to particular objects or situations but to positions in general. Values are deemed to be the basis of beliefs, specific attitudes and social norms, which in turn influence the preference for a particular behaviour and finally the actual behaviour (Fulton *et al.* 1996). It is assumed that cognitions increase with each hierarchical level and guide, as well as structure the individual's decision behaviour in a given situation (Homer and Kahle 1988). For example, two people who emphasise the same fundamental value can differ from one another regarding their basic beliefs, if the fundamental values are applied in different ways in their individual lives. Thus, the motivational goal of universalism, which emphasises equality and respect for others, may lead to the basic belief that all living things should be treated equally (strong focus on the natural environment), but if only applied to human beings, it will not exclude the use/ misuse of natural resources for the benefit of humans (Fulton *et al.* 1996).

Figure 2   **Cognitive hierarchy model of human behaviour**
(adapted from Fulton et al. 1996 and Sauer 2010)

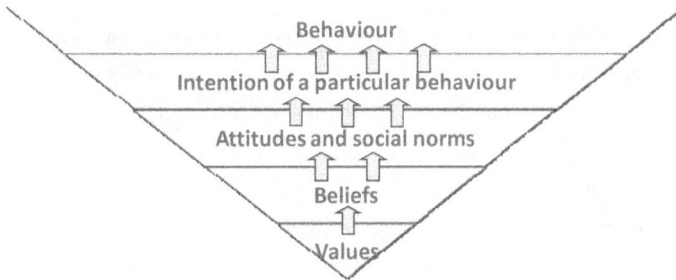

Thus, fundamental values represent the core of human cognition. They include ethical and moral positions, ideological and social aspects and aesthetic and intrinsic values. Therefore, regarded more broadly, they can also be considered as the core of social relations. They characterise a culture since they are imparted to societal members through daily exposure to customs, laws, norms, scripts and organisational practices that are shaped by and express the prevailing cultural values (Bourdieu 1972; Markus and Kitayama 1994).

Beliefs refer to the applicability of fundamental values to certain spheres of interest. They can be regarded as general attitudes towards relatively abstract objectives. Beliefs are not as stable as values but influence behavioural intentions through their impact on more specific attitudes (Fulton *et al.* 1996).

Specific attitudes and social norms are in turn directly related to particular objectives and behavioural intentions; they are attached to former experiences in certain situations. Specific attitudes and social norms show how mental functioning is related to cultural, institutional and historical context (Wertsch 1998). They are direct determinants of intended behaviour. Hence, cognitive modifications at that level are quite frequent and lead to real behaviour (Fulton *et al.* 1996).

Thus, the socio-psychological theories and concepts described have shown the necessity to integrate especially value positions and social norms or relationships into the economic model of individual behaviour. Due to this, and because the surveys conducted included these innovative aspects, in the following, concepts and theories on values and the socio-cultural concept of personalised relationship networks (*guānxi*) is introduced.

2.3 Theoretical background of selected decision-making determinants

2.3.1 Fundamental value positions

Behaviour is systematically and predictably influenced by basic values. According to current value theory, there is a universal set of basic values that are recognised in various human groups. Out of this set, each individual has value priorities or fundamental value positions (Schwartz 1994). A persons' inherent fundamental values predict his or her attitudes and choices; thus, they influence preferences and ultimately a particular behaviour (Strack *et al.* 2008). Moreover, values are imparted to societal members through daily exposure to customs, laws, norms and organisational practices that are shaped by the prevailing cultural value priorities (Schwartz 1999; Bourdieu 1972). Therefore, at an individual level, value priorities reflect the psychological dynamics of conflict and compatibility that a person experiences in daily life and society (Schwartz 1994).

Groundbreaking research on a conception of basic values has been conducted by, among others, Allport (1961), Feather (1995), Inglehart (1997), Kohn (1969), Kluckhohn (1951), Morris (1956) and Rokeach (1973). According to Schwartz (2005) the main features of a common value theory can be summarised as follows:

"- Values are beliefs. But they are beliefs tied inextricably to emotion, not objective, cold ideas.

- Values are a motivational construct. They refer to the desirable goals people strive to attain.

- Values transcend specific actions and situations. They are abstract goals. The abstract nature of values distinguishes them from concepts like norms and attitudes, which usually refer to specific actions, objects, or situations.

- Values guide the selection or evaluation of actions, policies, people, and events. That is, values serve as standards or criteria.

- Values are ordered by importance relative to one another. People's values form an ordered system of value priorities that characterize them as individuals. This hierarchical feature of values also distinguishes them from norms and attitudes." (Schwartz 2005, n.p.)

Nevertheless, most researchers focus on individual values; none of them classifies the substantive content of values. Following up Rockeach's idea (1973) to build value types systematically by reducing the vast number of values mentioned in literature to a smaller set of personality traits, Schwartz (1994) further developed the idea of classifying values. His approach is based primarily on the definition of values as "desirable transsituational goals" that vary in importance and serve as guiding principles in life.

Schwartz (1996) derived a comprehensive set of ten different motivational types of values (recognised across cultures) in order to distinguish the basic values – shown in Table 1 – from one another and coordinate them with each other (Schwartz 1994).

The structure of the value relations results from peoples' pursuit of certain value priorities. For example, achievement values of seeking personal success conflicts heavily with benevolence values enhancing the welfare of others. Contrarily, the persuit of conformity values are often compatible with benevolent values, because one strives to behave in a manner approved by one's close group (Schwartz 1994).

Table 1   Motivational value types in terms of their goals and single exemplary values that represent them (Schwartz 2005, modified table)

Value type	Definition	Exemplary values
POWER	Social status and prestige, control or dominance over people and resources	Social power, authority, wealth, preserving public image
ACHIEVEMENT	Personal success through demonstrating competence according to social standards	successful, capable, ambitious, influential
HEDONISM	Pleasure and sensuous gratification of oneself	pleasure, enjoying life
STIMULATION	Excitement, novelty and challenge in life	daring, a varied life, an exciting life
SELF-DIRECTION	Independent thought and action choosing, creating, exploring	creativity, freedom, independence, curiosity, choosing own goals
UNIVERSALISM	Understanding, appreciation, tolerance and protection for the welfare of all people and for nature	broad-mindedness, wisdom, social justice, equality, a world at peace, a world of beauty, unity with nature, protecting the environment
BENEVOLENCE	Preservation and enhancement of the welfare of people with whom one is in frequent personal contact	helpful, honest, forgiving, loyal, responsible
TRADITION	Respect, commitment and acceptance of the customs and ideas that traditional culture or religion provide the self	humble, accepting one's portion in life, devout, respect for tradition, moderate
CONFORMITY	Restraint of actions, inclinations and impulses likely to upset or harm others and violate social expectations or norms	politeness, obedient, self-discipline, honouring parents and elders
SECURITY	Safety, harmony and stability of society, of relationships and of self	family security, national security, social order, clean, reciprocation of favours

Thus, values relate to each other according to their major conflicts and conformity. Although the theory discriminates among value types, basic values are perceived as a continuum that can be mapped in a cycle (Schwartz 1994; Appendix 1).

Schwarz's value cycle (1994; 2005) identifies ten motivationally distinct universal values and four types of higher-order values. Openness-to-change values relate to the importance of personal autonomy and independence, variety, excitement and challenge. Conservation values relate to the importance of self-control, safety and stability in societal and personal relationships and of respecting cultural traditions.

Self-enhancement values relate to achieving personal success through demonstrated competence, attaining social status and prestige, and control over others. Self-transcendence values relate to protecting and enhancing the well-being of those with whom one has close contact, as well as the welfare of all people and nature (Schwartz 1992). It is assumed that every social group faces those values with a greater or less intensity and that they exist on an individual as well as a national level. Furthermore, the full set of value priorities can be related to other variables in an organised, coherent manner (Schwartz 1996). To demonstrate, a value structure averaged across the countries is shown in Appendix 2.

As shown in Figure 3, two dimensions structure the cycle like a coordinate system with reference to the major polar value oppositions: 'Openness to Change' to 'Conservation' (the 'Traditional axis') refers to the conflict between traditional stability and independent action; 'Self-Transcendence' to 'Self-Enhancement' (the 'Universalism axis') reflects the conflict between universal welfare and the pursuit of one's own dominance over others (Schwartz 1996). The two dimensions of the value positions facilitate theory building regarding the relations of the full set of value priorities with other variables (*e.g.*, behaviours) (Schwartz 1996; Strack *et al.* 2008).

Figure 3   Schwartz's universal value cycle (Schwartz 2005, modified)

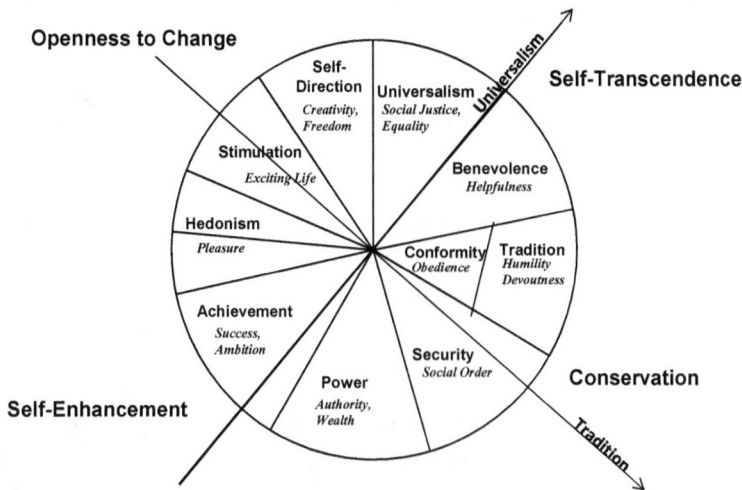

Note: Tradition is outside of conformity because the two value types share a single motivational goal. In conformity, self is subordinated to tradition, which is socially imposed (Schwartz 1992).

To sum up, Schwartz's approach of investing values can be used as basis for the cognitive hierarchy model. Since there is evidence that Schwartz' motivational goals are universal for all cultures and peoples, this approach fits also for the Chinese context. However, Schwartz' value survey has not yet been conducted for Chinese farmers in particular. The studies focussed either on Chinese students only (Matthews 2000), or on certain consumer groups or managers (Ralston *et al.* 1996). Hence, they do not fit for a general introduction that acts as referee for comparative assessments.

In order to make a preliminary classification, in the following, basic information about Chinese value positions are introduced by a literature review about Chinese values in general. In particular, Zheng and Cui (2008) provide results that can be used as fundamental background information.

Chinese value positions

According to Zheng and Cui (2008), Chinese fundamental value motivations are still influenced by Confucianism. Strong personal ties and close relationships are highly valued, and it is expected that people strive towards a harmonious society by maintaining these social networks. The individual is obliged to set up a good example by subordinating the self to the overall aims of the society. Thus, harmony is highly valued. And, since humans are regarded as part of nature, people also seek to live in balance with the natural environment (Zheng and Cui 2008).

Moreover, the Chinese highly value traditions and the life experience of the elderly whose achievements and benefits for the society are honoured by others using them to guide for their own decisions. In this spirit, people behave in a manner appropriate to their social role and status, which always overrides their own interests. Thus, social hierarchies are highly valued and involve privileges and obligations that are clearly defined based on social position (Zheng and Cui 2008).

Nevertheless, as Harris (2006, p. 8) points out, "the Chinese have a very instrumental view of the natural world". He goes on to observe that they seek satisfaction of immediate needs and short-term interests in order to aspire to economic security and welfare, from which in turn they expect social stability.

However, in spite of these basic Chinese value positions, since the society is in rapid transition, interactions with new values can also be observed. Since Deng Xiaoping's reform in the late 1970s, the Chinese – in particular the young generation and urban dwellers – place greater emphasis on individualism, entrepreneurship and materialism (Harris 2004). Although hedonism is traditionally frowned in China, such value positions continue to permeate contemporary Chinese society (Kwong 1994).

Referring to the cognitive hierarchy model, the concept of personalised relationships is introduced as it is a very important socio-cultural dimension in Chinse society.

2.3.2 Guānxi relationships – a socio-cultural dimension

The socio-psychological concept of cognitive hierarchy described by Fulton *et al.* (1996) stressed that – in addition to the fundamental influence of basic values and beliefs – social norms (specific attitudes towards certain objectives or behaviours) have a direct impact on behavioural intentions. Furthermore, modified economic approaches include social motivations, such as norms of reciprocity (Frey 2001) as well as social embeddedness (Granovetter 1985), among the concepts influencing individual decision-making; hence, these approaches also regard the community as a decision-influencing determinant.

This section focuses on *guānxi*, a typical and very dominant social phenomenon in China that constrains and guides individual behaviour according to objective, irrational and informal rules (Guthrie 1998). The overall explicit and implicit customary use and meaning of *guānxi* relationships influences interactions with other society members. Strong *guānxi* relationships maintain a person's acceptance and popularity, as well as his or her capacity to act. By disregarding the rules of such a behaviour, people become outcasts and, as a result unpopular and powerless.

Therefore, sociologists link *guānxi* with the concept of social capital; thus, they see it as a community-based value structure that is able to increase the benefit of the corporative associates. In this regard, Coleman (1988) suggests that social [network] capital conditions the development of human capital in a positive manner. It fills "institutional holes", especially in emerging economies (Bian 2002, p. 134). People with high social network capital are most active and are able to take advantage of the best opportunities. Even if they do not have a lot of human capital, they can make use of their ties to acquire missing information (Bian 2002).

However, utilitarian aspects are not the only function of *guānxi* relationships; cultural aspects matter, too. According to Goodwin (1999), there are inherent cultural differences in the ways people think and feel about relationships. In China, for example, Confucian doctrines and collectivism are indispensable socio-cultural elements of everyday performance. In particular, Hofstede (2011) highlights cultural dimensions, like Chinese society's long-term orientation and the high level of emphasis on collectivism by the Communist system, which goes along with loyalty and close commitment to ascribed groups. The maintenance of strong relationships consequently leads to low individualism. Furthermore, high levels of power inequality and wealth are ascertained in the study as the accepted cultural heritage of the social structure (Hofstede 2001)[7].

Review of different classification approaches

In the literature, *guānxi* has been translated with different terms. Some translate it simply as connection, social networking or special interpersonal relationship. Davies *et al.* (1995, p. 155) defined the term *guānxi* as "social interactions within the network place and its members in the equivalent of an infinitely repeated game with a set of people they know". Dunning and Changsu (2007) describe *guānxi* relationships as personalised relationship networks of influence. Thus, it is difficult to find a specific English definition (Hackley and Dong 2001), and the difficulties regarding the term suggest that *guānxi* is more than the Chinese word for personal networks or social capital, which also appear in other cultural contexts (Gold *et al.* 2002).

---

[7] Geert Hofstede conducted a comprehensive study of how values in the workplace are influenced by culture. In the 2001 edition, 74 countries and regions are listed. As a result, five cultural dimensions were determined that seek to differentiate among cultures. The dimensions are (1) Power Distance, (2) Individualism, (3) Masculinity, (4) Uncertainty Avoidance and (5) Long-Term Orientation (Hofstede 2001).

Several sociologists see *guānxi* as a distinctive Chinese phenomenon deeply rooted in Chinese culture and Confucian doctrines (*cf.* Bian 1994; Hwang 1987; King 1991; Bell 2000). According to the key concept of Confucianism, the self is realised in the social sphere; consequently, the society is relationship-based (Gold *et al.* 2002). *Guānxi* is traditionally understood as a network of familial obligations and sentiments of pseudo-familial ties (Bian 2002). Furthermore, the Chinese naturally use their social embeddedness rationally to satisfy their personal interests; in turn, they are obligated to assist others who are connected to them (Bian 1994).

Other researchers view *guānxi* as little more than a Chinese idiom of social capital and networks. They see it as a response to specific institutional and historical conditions that happen to exist in China and that in the long run become inextricably linked to the society (*cf.* Gold *et al.* 2002). Other factors that encourage *guānxi* today are the shortage economy and the weak legal infrastructure, which make networking and mutual trust fundamental parts of economic transactions and the use of *guānxi* a coping strategy for institutionally uncertain environments (Gold *et al.* 2002).

Based on these analyses and definitions, it becomes clear that several approaches slot into one another. Both the cultural and the institutional scholar can contribute to any discussion of *guānxi* relationships (*cf.* Gold *et al.* 2002).

At first glance, *guānxi* seems comparable with social capital. If the focus is on the generalised character as described by Bourdieux (1986),[8] persons who are linked support each other with resources. Furthermore, it is necessary to take into account the cultural roots of *guānxi*. While social capital is not naturally given and focuses on instrumental aspects in order to benefit from the interconnectedness, *guānxi* relationships attach more importance to the relationships themselves (Gold *et al.* 2002). Smart (1993), for example, mentions the intrinsic enjoyment of the on-going

---

[8] According to Bourdieu (1986), individuals' actual and potential resources are linked to create a durable network of more or less institutionalised relationships of mutual recognition. The members of this relationship network support each other with collectively owned capital. This social capital enables in turn a conversion to economic, political or symbolic capital. For Bourdieu (1986), social capital networks are not naturally occurring; rather, they are the result of an endless effort at institution.

personal relationship itself, creating a basis of trust. Hence, *guānxi* is actually based on mutual interest and mutual benefit. Giving favours, being indebted and being obliged to reciprocate are important characteristics of relationships built to last for the long term (Gold *et al.* 2002).

In addition, which aspects of *guānxi* one considers in detail depends on one's perspective. Viewing *guānxi* relationships against the background of social embeddedness, the focus lies on how decision-making is influenced by the interpersonal system of social relations that are determined by the strength of ties, trust, transitivity and so forth.

In terms of norms, *guānxi* relationships are regarded as internalised customs an individual has to cope with when participating in society as an accepted member. As a consequence, it is necessary to maintain of *guānxi* relationships, or strong ties. In turn, *guānxi* requires intrinsically motivated normative behaviour on the part of the individuals involved. Thus, the norms of maintaining *guānxi* relationships are already included in alternative concepts of an individuals' rational decision-making.

In the following description, the emphasis is on the constitution of *guānxi* relationships in order to explain the varying *guānxi* perceptions of individuals. Distinctive traits and cultural dimensions are discussed as well.

Description of *guānxi* relationships

The term *guānxi* itself consists of two Chinese words, *guān* and *xi*. *Guān* means "a door" and its extended meaning is "to close up" (Luo 1997). *Xi* means "to tie up" and can be extended to "relationships" (Luo 1997). *Guānxi* therefore means "pass through the door and get connected" (Lee and Dawes 2005). A person inside the door is regarded as "one of us" and can be trusted, whereas a person outside the door is regarded as a stranger and not to be trusted (Luo 1997). Hence, the term itself bears a cultural component in its meaning, too.

Guānxi ties are generally based on ascribed or primordial traits. They seem to occur naturally due to kinship, place of residence and achieved characteristics, such as attending the same school and having shared experiences (Gold *et al.* 2002). Such informal and intimate relationships are valued for what they are (Bian 2002)[9]. According to Lin (2001) the "instrumental action becomes the means and *guānxi* [building] becomes the end" (cited by Bian 2002, p. 118). Nevertheless, it is important to maintain and cultivate such relationships constantly over time (Gold *et al.* 2002). Thus, their very essence is also ambiguity and subtlety, which allows the persons involved discretion to define their relationship over time (Fan 2002). Compared to social capital, *guānxi* is less visible and less open.

From the perspective of universal moral principles, Fan (2002) distinguishes between "good *guānxi*" and "bad *guānxi*". Traditional *guānxi* relationships are perceived as good since the processes of giving favours and receiving benefits within a close cooperation are desirable. On the other hand, business *guānxi* is often regarded as bad since it is associated with making profit at the social cost of trust; favouritism and nepotism are the consequences (Fan 2002). According to Dunfee and Warren (2001), it also reduces social wealth, and Addison *et al.* (2008) pointed out that it benefits the few at the expense of the many. However, Fan (2002) also mentions that, whether good or bad, *guānxi* violates the principle of fairness and inherently discriminates against people outside the network.

Main traits of *guānxi* relationships

In addition to the above mentioned descriptions of *guānxi* relationships, a comprehensive study is offered by Luo (2000) and Dunning and Changsu (2007), who identified distinctive characteristics in order to explain different *guānxi* perceptions (see Table 2). Furthermore, they include the cultural dimensions of *guānxi* relationships and the functioning of *guānxi* as an alternative to formal institutions (*i.e.*, the instrumental social capital point of view). Since the latter is already covered in the socio-psychological approach of decision-making, the following focuses on the main traits of *guānxi* and its cultural component. Thus, the

---

[9] By contrast, there is also the business *guānxi* that is less emotionally-driven and more utility-oriented. It is rather a product of current political and socio-economic systems (Fan 2002), thus, closer to the social capital concept.

social embeddedness of the individuals is described and their behaviour according to the predominant traits.

Table 2   *Guānxi* traits (Dunning and Changsu 2007)

Traits	Description
UTILITARIAN	*Guānxi* is purposefully driven by personal interests.
RECIPROCAL	An individual's reputation is tied up with reciprocal obligations.
TRANSFERABLE	*Guānxi* is transferable through a third party as a referral.
PERSONAL	*Guānxi* is established between individuals.
LONG-TERM	*Guānxi* is reinforced through long-term cultivation.
INTANGIBLE	*Guānxi* is maintained by an unspoken commitment.

According to Dunning and Changsu (2007), *guānxi* is a utilitarian concept that binds two persons through the exchange of favours rather than through sentiment. It implies reciprocity, and since obligations tend to be seen as perpetual, *guānxi* is not necessarily equally reciprocal (Alston 1989). Indeed frequently, the exchange relationships tend to favour the weaker partner. Furthermore, *guānxi* is transferable to third persons if an intermediary feels satisfaction about his *guānxi* with both persons. *Guānxi* operates at the individual level. Interpersonal loyalty is given through trust, honesty, respect and social status (Davies *et al.* 1995), which is often more important than organisational affiliation or legal status in Chinese society. Due to its long-term orientation, *guānxi* is therefore also regarded as a stock of relational capital, which is to be conserved or augmented in times of abundance and plenty, but drawn upon in times of need. Lastly, *guānxi* is an intangible asset. People who share *guānxi* maintain an unspoken commitment. To disregard this commitment is to seriously damage respectability and social standings (Dunning and Changsu 2007).

The roots of *guānxi* are assumed to be in Confucianism.[10] Confucian doctrines are still present in Chinese life. In particular, the notion that an individual should be

---

[10] Confucianism is a philosophy based the teachings of Confucius, a Chinese philosopher of the 5th century BC, which gained in importance during the Han dynasty (BC 206 to AD 220). The doctrines cover social and political life and strive to achieve moral perfection through self-cultivation. Its main themes encompass (1) humanity and the ethics of reciprocity, (2) shaping rites in daily life, (3) filial piety and respectful subordination in certain hierarchical relationships, (4) relationships and associated mutual duties in the sense of an overall social harmony, (5) striving for the ideal of a

primarily a relational being and part of a communitarian social system encourages the Chinese to live in a social order and stability defined by role relationships between individuals (Dunning and Changsu 2007). The conceptualisation of *guānxi* takes this cultural motivation as the point of origin for its approach. Nevertheless, the authors also point out that the relationships vary across different cognitive systems and that *guānxi* depends on the institutional infrastructure of societies (Dunning and Changsu 2007).

Therefore, in addition to Luo (2000), Dunning and Changsu (2007) also draw attention to collectivism and power distance as the underlying cultural dimension behind interpersonal *guānxi* (see also Hofstede 1991; 2011) (see Table 3).

Table 3 **Cultural dimensions of *guānxi***
(Dunning and Changsu 2007, modified)

Traits	Description
COLLECTIVISM	Group taking precedence over the individual
POWER DISTANCE	Interdependency between unequal parties

Collectivism is a cultural dimension of *guānxi* because Chinese individuals are deeply embedded in a social relationship system that derives from traditional Confucianism, which emphasises harmony and groups that take precedence over individual dimensions (Dunning and Changsu 2007). Furthermore, the institutional infrastructure of the political and social system also influences the societal relationships. Due to the cultural and social meaning of collectivism and the individual's consequential social reputation, collectivism intervenes on the micro-level; "[...] the self in relation to the other becomes the focus of individual experience" (Dunning and Changsu 2007, pp. 332).

---

gentleman, *i.e.*, moral cultivation of the self, (6) rectitution of names and avoidance of social disorder, (7) governing by virtue and (8) meritocracy, i.e. studying and seeking knowledge to achieve honour, which brings wealth (Fung 1976). Most of the teachings have manifested themselves in the culture over time. Although they have been adapted to societal changes, they remain present in Chinese daily life to a greater or lesser degree.

Power distance leads to a stronger perception of *guānxi* because Chinese society and hence relationships within that society are hierarchically structured[11]. This is generally accepted as it is again based on a long-established Confucian order. The mutual fulfilment of roles, along with the corresponding obligations and shared trust, form the basis of the Chinese social system. Thus, there is a strong interdependency within asymmetrical relationships. Reciprocal balance results from favouring the disadvantaged, on the one hand, and gaining a good reputation for such behaviour, on the other (Dunning and Changsu 2007).

Finally, Dunning and Changsu (2007) also point out that *guānxi* is an alternative to formal institutions. It provides certainty and security, which makes up for deficiencies in economic and political life and also guides individuals to function in a desired manner through norms and values (Dunning and Changsu 2007).

2.3.3 Environmental attitudes in China

According to the socio-psychological model developed by Fulton *et al.* (1996), attitudes are influenced by people's fundamental value system. Since they influence an individual's preferences, they are also directly related to particular objectives and behaviour intentions. Within the context of this research, specific agri-environmental attitudes of overfertilisation are of particular interest. Since most literature about environmental attitudes in China is about the perspectives of urban people, there is no literature about the general perceptions of rural farmers or about their specific agri-environmental attitudes.

A macroscopic snapshot of different surveys concerning the general Chinese environmental awareness and associated behaviours concluded that most Chinese seem to have a very limited concern for environmental issues (*cf.* Weller and Bol 1998). They tend to aspire to a modern life-style connected with environmentally harmful status symbols (Harris 2004). In particular, poorly educated people in rural areas show less environmental awareness than urbanised people (Qing and Vermeer

---

[11] In Chinese philosophy, there are five traditional hierarchical relationships: (1) sovereign and subject, (2) father and son, (3) elder and younger brother, (4) husband and wife and (5) friend and friend. The rational justification of this social system is economic conditions (Fung 1976).

1999). However, given the Chinese Confucian tradition, there are still environmental values in China and this awareness is rising (Qing and Vermeer 1999). In particular, urban elites who are adversely affected by the severest environmental pollution, are increasingly complaining about the negative external effects and seem to be re-evaluating nature as a protectable good (Harris 2004). However, people usually care only about those problems that affect them directly. Thus, individuals' environmental concern is directed mainly towards issues that affect them at home, such as sanitation, drinking water and indoor pollution, but not towards issues affecting surrounding areas (Harris 2006).

Thus, since farmers are directly dependent on the natural environment and their *guānxi* networks, it seems indispensable to study their fundamental value priorities and agri-environmental attitudes. In order to solve the environmental problems in China and to cope with the country's societal changes, concealed beliefs and value motivations as well as decisive *guānxi* characteristics have to be uncovered. Only in this way is it possible to tackle environmental issues and the farmers' basic demands at the same time.

2.4 Comprehensive model of individual decision-making

Based on the theoretical background of the economic and socio-psychological approaches of individual decision-making, a comprehensive theoretical model has been developed. As the review of theories demonstrated, models often do not capture the full complexity of a concept. Nevertheless, the overall idea is to combine the economic model of individual behaviour with socio-psychological approaches by including fundamental values and attitudes as preference-forming variables. Moreover, the cultural dimensions of social life are included. In Chinese culture, the most essential characteristic are *guānxi* relationships. For desired behavioural changes, the cultural component is important. In addition to the individual orientation of fundamental values, it could be a decisive determinant in successful transformations.

The empirical model is based on hypothetical assumptions adapted to the research approach. Thus, the theoretical model is tailored to certain Chinese farmers' agri-environmental attitudes and their fertilisation behaviour. As a result, the model is designed (1) to detect relevant key determinants that might influence success in adopting newly implemented technology approaches through well-designed agricultural training and (2) to accurately predict farmers' reactions to external changes and policy initiatives.

Based on the economic model of individual behaviour the individual (and its socio-demographic starting conditions) states preferences for an intended and particular utility-oriented decision under the condition of offensive restrictions (Figure 4).

Figure 4 **Comprehensive theoretical model of individual decision-making with special attention to cognitive and social aspects (Author's illustration)**

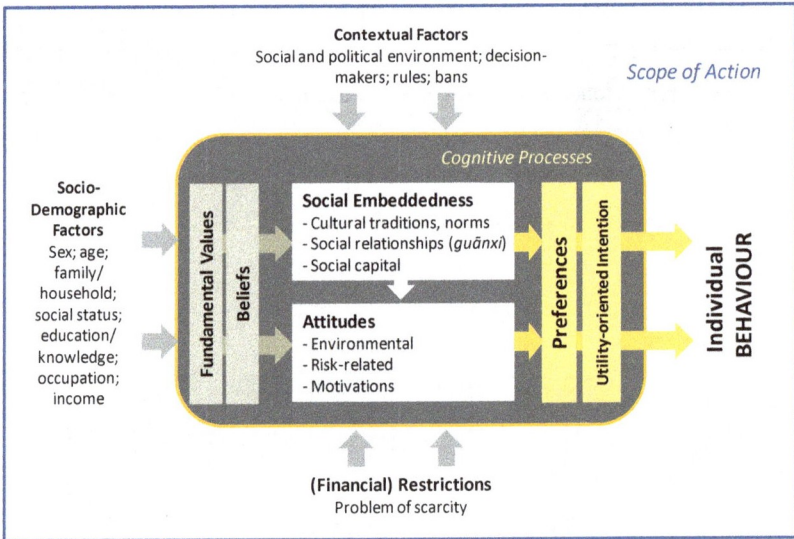

The individual's restrictions are, on the one hand, stable for all decision processes while only focusing on socio-demographic aspects and financial constraints. On the other hand, restrictions vary according to the particular decision situation. Furthermore, there are contextual factors, like the social and political environment, as well as rules and bans that define the scope of action, and various motivational aspects, like monetary incentives or promising future perspectives, that influence an individual's cognition. Thus, such external determinants must also be included into the decision-making model. Taking into account the socio-psychological approach, the model considers in particular fundamental value positions as a basis for general beliefs and specific attitudes, for example, environmental attitudes. It is assumed that basic socio-demographic aspects, like gender, age or knowledge, influence such inherent positions just as do contextual factors. Social embeddedness, including lived social norms, habits and traditional practices as well as network relationships and the resulting social capital benefits, build another decision-making determinant in this model. The model also encompasses the cultural component. It is assumed that this social component is affected by fundamental values and beliefs at the individual level by external conditions at the macro-level. Since cognitions are dynamic and not static, mutual influences exist between cognitions, external contextual factors and social relationship dynamics.

Combining the economic and the socio-psychological approaches, all the determinants build up stated preferences followed by utility-oriented decision intentions, the precondition for a definite behaviour.

3 EMPIRICAL RESEARCH

In order to verify the comprehensive model of farmers' individual behaviour, a quantitative farm household survey was conducted in Shandong Province, a major agricultural production area in China. The investigation focussed not only on the status quo for agricultural production and on the agri-environmental situation, but also on farms' production efficiency and productivity. Furthermore, the empirical research sought to determine what kind of determinants are relevant for Chinese farmers' agricultural and environmental decision-making and which determinants should be emphasised as key factors for behaviour change strategies. The findings were underpinned by open, unstructured expert interviews and results from group discussions in order to acquire additional information with regard to policy recommendations.

This chapter begins with a depiction of the study area. Geographical characteristics, socio-economic information and the state of the art of agricultural production describe the contextual situation that builds the framework for farmers' decision-making. Next, the questionnaire design and data basis is explained. The following section provides information about the sample selection and how the survey data had been collected.

3.1 Study area

The study area is Huimin and Shouguang County of Shandong Province; both are situated in the northeastern part of the North China Plain (NCP) (Figure 5).

3.1.1 The North China Plain

The NCP covers 320,000 km² and distributes to parts of seven provinces.[12] It is the major agricultural production base for wheat and maize in China (Kendy *et al.* 2003); thus, it is the most suitable region for the overall project aims.

---

[12] These provinces include parts of Anhui, Beijing, Hebei, Henan, Jiangsu, Shandong and Tianjin.

Figure 5   Relief map of China and the research area
(Map-of-China.org 2011, modified)

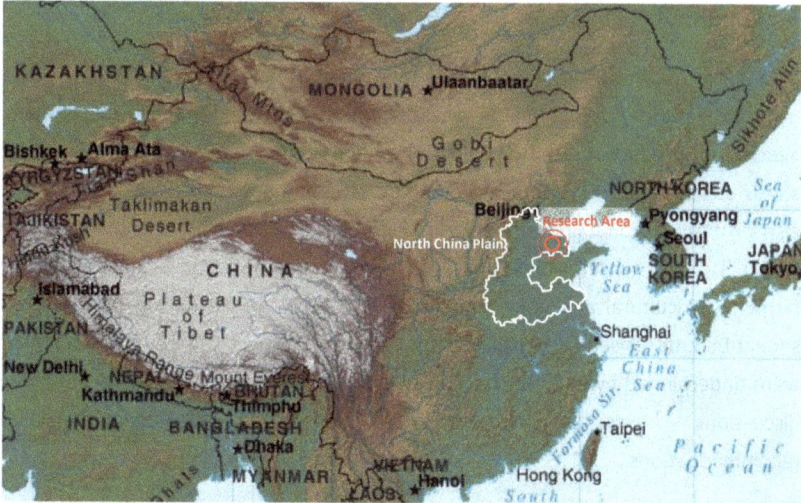

In the west, the mostly flat alluvial plain is enclosed by mountains; in the east, by the Yellow Sea. Three rivers flow through the NCP; the *Huai* River in the south, the *Huang* River (Yellow River) in the centre and the *Hai* River in the north, which is why the NCP is also called *Huai-Hai Plain*. These rivers deposit silt along their banks, replenishing the soil, which is beneficial for agriculture (Kendy *et al.* 2003).

The climate is typified by cold, dry winters and hot, humid summers. It is temperate, semi-humid and monsoonal. Annual rainfalls vary unpredictably by more than 30 percent from year to year. On average, precipitation is less than 500 mm in the north and 800 mm in the south. Furthermore, rainfall does not correspond with crop needs. Since a typical winter wheat/ summer maize double-cropping system needs 660 to 920 mm of water annually, groundwater irrigation has to be employed to counteract the deficit (Kendy *et al.* 2003). All together, the area constitutes nearly 40 percent of total national agricultural production. Half of the total wheat yields and about one-third of maize yields are produced in the NCP.[13] The remarkable

---

[13] South of the *Huai* River, rice is produced in crop rotation with summer maize. The hillier region of South China is warmer and more humid than North China and hence better for rice production.

outputs on the fertile arable land are accompanied by environmental problems due to higher production intensities, fertiliser input, extensive irrigation, *etc.* Furthermore, proceeding urbanisation and infrastructural development increase the pressure on land and cause an intensification of agriculture. Due to irrigation and overfertilisation, the NCP suffers from water shortages, pollution, and soil contamination (Kendy *et al.* 2003).

The research area is located in the lower reaches of the Yellow River, the administrative unit of Shandong Province (see Figure 6). Except for the hilly peninsula and the Taishan, Lushan and Mengshan Mountains in the centre of the province, the northwestern, western and southwestern parts belong to the NCP.

3.1.2 Socio-economic situation of Shandong Province

With about 95 million inhabitants in 2010 living in an area of 156,700 km², Shandong Province is very densely populated (610 inhabitants/ km²)[14] (National Bureau of Statistics 2011). Jinan City is the provincial capital. Shandong is one of the richer provinces in China. It maintains stable economic development through industrial manufacturing and agricultural intensification and has thus become a net inmigration province (UNESCAP 2000).

In 2010, the total growth rate of Gross Domestic Product (GDP) was about 12 percent (ranking third in the PRC behind Guangdong and Jiangsu). The primary sector records the slowest increase, with 3.6 percent (secondary sector: 13.4 %; tertiary sector: 13.0 %) (Shandong Bureau of Statistics 2010). The major force of this agricultural growth is the development of animal husbandry. In particular, meat, eggs and milk production are increasing steadily (Shandong Bureau of Statistics 2010).

However, this does not stem rural labour emigration. Rural living standards have increased and consumer supply has risen, even in remote areas. Thus, peoples' incomes do not stretch to meet the demands on them. Consequently, 47.1 percent of the labour forces live in urban areas; this is an increasing tendency. In 2010, the

---

[14] In comparison, Germany's population density is about 229 inhabitants/ km².

average disposable income of urban workers in Shandong Province rose by 12 percent over the previous year to about 2,200 EUR (19,946 *yuán*;[15] *cf.* the average urban household income of 33,691 *yuán*). In contrast, rural residents' per capita net wage income averages 760 EUR (6,990 *yuán*), less than half as much. This economic disequilibrium is a strong pull factor for urban migration (Shandong Bureau of Statistics 2010).

Figure 6   Research counties in Shandong Province (PRC)
(ChinaTouristMaps.com 2010, modified)

Because of regional disparities, families are disrupted. Many men migrate to find off-farm employment and contribute only a limited part of their time to farm activities; often they only supervise or return to help at peak periods, such as ploughing or to harvest. Thus, it falls mainly to the wives and grandparents who remain at home to take care of day-to-day farm work (Bossen 2000). Neither men nor women are eager to farm if other options are available (Bossen 2000).

The problem is that due to the household responsibility system (HRS), farmers are contracted as sharecroppers or tenant with the village corporation as landowner.

---

[15] *Yuán* RMB converted to EUR at an exchange rate of one Chinese *yuán* to 0.10867495 Euros.

Thus, each *Hùkŏu*[16]-registered inhabitant contracts land from the village committee in accordance with an officially defined size.

The land originally serves to secure families' subsistence. Nowadays, due to the growing population, the allotted farmlands have diminished to sizes that do not meet families' increased needs. Hence, farms often serve as retirement arrangements to secure the livelihood of elderly family members.

Furthermore, farms provide basic social and economic safeguards in times of urban unemployment or for day care of grandchildren whose parents have gone to work in urban areas (Fan 2008). Nevertheless, farm households are obliged to maintain their farms even though they expect low benefits. Those, who leave their farms uncultivated, often lose their land forever (Fan 2008).[17] In addition, in order to expand the farms, the plots cannot be sold or bought easily (Bossen 2000). Thus, in order to keep the land in the family, farm work is often done by older generations.

Furthermore, the *Hùkŏu* registration system disadvantages rural household members who migrate to urban centres. Without local *Hùkŏu*, farmers are not allowed to do certain jobs or receive any governmental supply of living necessities. For example, they do not receive housing subsidies, their children have to pay higher school fees and they are not eligible for social security benefits (Barning 2008; Fan 2008).

In spite of *Hùkŏu* restrictions, off-farm employment has become a major income source, increasing the social status of farm households. An estimated 40 percent of total rural income derives from off-farm activities. Nevertheless, there still are farm households that do not engage in any off-farm work (Barning 2008). In some cases, this can be explained by a lower level of education, on the one hand, and gender differences, on the other; both factors can affect access to off-farm employment.

---

[16] The *Hùkŏu* (household registration) system is the official system of residence regulation in China. Among other things, this registration is used to control the movement of people between rural and urban areas. People who live and work outside their *Hùkŏu* registration – thus, outside their regional boundaries – do not qualify for fixed social services, education, health care, employer-provided housing, etc.

[17] Currently, farmers' land use rights are limited to 30 years. The village collective holds the real power.

Furthermore, missing relationships (*guānxi* and social capital) may limit access to the urban labour market. In other cases, larger farm sizes (> 2 ha), which increase farmers' ability to live from their agricultural incomes, need the labour of the whole family; in such cases, human capital may well seem to be better invested on the farm itself (Somwaru *et al.* 2001).

3.1.3 Impact of agricultural regulations

In the course of grain self-sufficiency and lateron in 2004 with the focus on "The Three Rural Issues", China introduced a number of policies to benefit farmers instead of taxing them. Farmers now receive direct subsidies as well as subsidies for seeds and machinery purchases; this is intended to encourage grain production (*cf.* Appendix 5). However, since each province grants the subsidies in its own way, the incentives have had only minor effect on rural incomes. In total, subsidies and tax reduction equal only 1 to 2 percent of the average per capita rural household income (Gale *et al.* 2005). Thus, grain prices and off-farm income remain important pull factors for household economies.

3.1.4 Agriculture in the research area

Shandong Province produces a wide range of agricultural products. The dominant farming system of small-scale farmers in the alluvial northern and eastern regions is a winter wheat/ summer maize double-cropping pattern.[18] Cash crops like peanuts or cotton often extend the system, but have decreased in importance. Additionally, vegetables are grown in greenhouses, and wine production is carried out in the mountains. Furthermore, the province is popular for its poultry. In spite of good grain yields and subsidies, Shandong Province is on the way to concentrating more and more on labour-intensive food industries, like vegetable and fruit production, which are more profitable. Since labour is still cheap, agricultural companies produce 40 to 80 percent below international prices (Zhang and Dong 2002). Similarily, food quality has been developed to comply with export standards.

---

[18] Wheat is planted in autumn and harvested in late spring. Maize is planted in late spring and harvested in autumn.

In 2001, the provincial government started to reduce the traditional planting areas for grain and cotton. Since then, agricultural companies have increased and strengthened competitive products like vegetables, fruits and livestock, as well as floristry.

Table 4 shows the development in the growth rates and outputs of important farm products.

Table 4   Growth rates and outputs of agricultural products in Shandong Province (Shandong Bureau of Statistics 2010)

	Output in 2010 (in 10,000 tons)	Growth rate to previous year (%)
Total grain	4335.7	0.4
- Winter wheat (summer)	2060.0	0.6
- Summer maize (autumn)	2275.7	0.3
Cotton	72.4	-21.4
Oil	342.2	2.3
Vegetables	9030.7	1
Fruits	1438.9	1.4
Meat	704.7	3
Pork, beef, mutton	454.5	2.4
Poultry	238.9	4.1
Eggs	384.8	1.9
Milk	271.6	5.2

As a result of increased demand for high-calorie processed food products due to higher living standards, industrial meat, livestock and vegetable production is on the rise.

As will be seen below, small-scale farmers in particular are being confronted more and more with structural changes and political measures. The pressure on arable land is growing, and new production patterns, coupled with a lack of well-implemented special vocational training, are leading to increasing mismanagement by small-scale farmers, attempting to adapt to the new market situation. For example, several farmers in Jiangsu, who are just moving into the more profitable and highly promoted specialisation of melon production, suffered losses when the majority of their ripening harvests exploded. The destruction of their harvests was traced to the improper use of a plant growth regulator (Spiegel Online 2011). This is just one example of many that shows the dire consequences of the lack of agricultural and environmental knowledge on the part of small-scale farmers responding to new incentive programmes that do not meet the needs of farmers on their level.

After this general overview, the next section will deliver insight into the respective pilot counties that were chosen in terms of investing the research objectives.

3.1.5 The pilot counties Huimin and Shouguang

The study looked at small-scale farmers in Huimin and Shouguang Counties[19] (*cf.* Figure 6). Table 5 offers a comparison of production and the economy in the two counties and juxtapose that information with statistical data for Shandong Province as a whole.

Table 5 Huimin and Shouguang Counties in 2010
(Huimin Bureau of Statistics 2011; Shouguang Bureau of Statistics 2011)

	Huimin	Shouguang	Shandong Province
Total area	1,357 km²	2,072 km²	156,700 km²
Number of villages	1,282 (14 townships)	975 (9 townships)	
Population	638,000	1.04 millions	95 millions
Population density	464 inhabitants/ km²	492 inhabitants/ km²	610 inhabitants/ km²
GDP	11.598 billion *yuán*	47.03 billion *yuán*	39,416.2 billion *yuán*
GDP growth rate	14.9 %	14.2%	12%
- primary sector	- 1.2 %	- 5.0 %	- 3.6 %
- secondary sector	- 16.1 %	- 24.4 %	- 13.4 %
- tertiary sector	- 20.3 %	- 15.9 %	- 13.0 %
Rural per capita net income	6,626 *yuán*/ year	9,495 *yuán*/ year	6,990 *yuán*/ year
Urban per capita income	25,465 *yuán*/ year (wage*)	22,860 *yuán*/ year (disposable income)	19,946 *yuán*/ year (disposable income)

*It is assumed that wage income is gross income and not disposable net income; hence, the disposable net income will be lower.

[19] China's administrative division is hierarchically organised in provinces and autonomous regions in the first level, municipalities as well as Hainan in the second level and county-levels in the third. Advanced divisions are townships in the fourth level and villages in the fifth level.

Huimin is considered representative for ordinary intensive agricultural areas in the North China Plain, growing mainly wheat and maize in cropping rotation, whereas Shouguang is specialised in vegetable production. Other crops in Huimin are cotton, tree fruit, vegetables and mulberry trees for silkworm cultivation (Huimin Government Portal 2011).

In an area of 1,357 km², Huimin County has 1,282 administrative villages under the government of 14 townships and a total population of 638,000 people (Huimin Government Portal 2011; Huimin Bureau of Statistics 2011). In 2010, the county's GDP was 11.598 billion *yuán* (an increase of 14.9 percent over the preceding year), of which the primary industry has only a very low share, with 1.2 percent (secondary: 16.1 %; tertiary: 20.3 %). Table 6 shows furthermore, that traditional agricultural production (grain, cotton) is decreasing, while labour-intensive livestock production is increasing.

Table 6   Major agricultural products
(Huimin Bureau of Statistics 2011; Shouguang Bureau of Statistics 2011)

	Huimin		Shouguang	
	Output in 2010 (in 10,000 tons)	Growth rate to previous year (%)	Output in 2010 (in 10,000 tons)	Growth rate to previous year (%)
Total grain	53.31	-1.2	65.2	-0.9
Wheat (summer)	26.14	-1.3	31.8	-0.6
Maize (autumn)	27.27	-1.1	33.4	-1.2
Cotton	2.62	-16.0	1.9	2.9
Oil	0.68	-4.2		
Vegetables	110.46	-1.6	438.6	0.5
Fruits	13.16	6.9	11.0	-6.8
Pigs	23.5	34.3	37.9	5.6
Cattle	13	18.2	0.7	12.5
Sheep	13.6	4.6	9.2	5.7
Meat	5.52	11.5	13.3	13.7
Pork, beef, mutton	3.48	9.4		
Poultry	1.9	38.7	5.9	16.6
Eggs	7	27.3	2.1	0
Milk	1	11.1	1.3	30.0

The average rural per capita net income of farmers in Huimin is about 6,626 *yuán*/ year, and the average wage of off-farm workers nearly triple as much, at about 25,465 *yuán*/ year (Huimin Bureau of Statistics 2011).

In contrast, Shouguang has a population of 1.04 million people living in 975 administrative villages, divided into 9 townships (Shouguang Government 2011; Shouguang Bureau of Statistics 2011). Shouguang is much richer than Huimin. It is gaining in importance through its well-known and successful vegetable production.[20] For marketing reasons, there is a high grade of specialisation by farmers, with entire villages concentrating on producing one kind of vegetable only. Since vegetable production is more profitable, and agricultural production strategies as well as income sources differ from those in Huimin, the farmers of Shouguang County have higher average incomes. Thus, the rural per capita net income there may reach 9,495 *yuán*/ year. Compared to other counties, this is quite high.

In addition, Shouguangs' GDP is about 47.03 billion *yuán* – higher than that of Huimin County. The growth rate of both counties' GDP does not differ much, but the primary sector's share of the GDP growth rate in Shouguang is much higher, at 5.0 percent (secondary 24.41 %; tertiary 15.92 %) (Shouguang Bureau of Statistics 2011).

However, even in Shouguang, farmers grow wheat and maize in double-cropping systems. Still, these production lines are decreasing year by year to make room for more profitable livestock and vegetable production. The Statistical Bureau of Shouguang reported average yields of 454 kg/ *mǔ*[21] for wheat and 474 kg/ *mǔ* for maize in 2010; both yields had decreased by 4.8 percent compared to the previous year (Shouguang Bureau of Statistics 2011). This could stem from overfertilisation, but might also result from the fact that the best land for wheat and maize production was used for other agricultural production (for instance, vegetables

---

[20] In total, Shouguang exports about 500 different kinds of vegetables to Europe and the United States (Zhang and Dong 2002). The main vegetables species in which the county specialises are grown in greenhouses using intensive production methods.

[21] The Chinese area unit *mǔ* is equal to 1/15th hectare (~67 m²). In the following, the Chinese unit is used in addition to international standard units, since they demonstrate better the proportions in less industrialised small-scale agriculture and transformations do often not adequately fit to the context.

production) instead leading to an increase in average yield qualities in wheat/ maize cropping systems.

In spite of the agricultural and structural differences between Huimin and Shouguang, both counties stand exemplarily for the problem of overfertilisation in the NCP; so far, however, there are no statistical data available. In the following, fertilisation practices for wheat and maize production in the overall fertile NCP is reviewed.

3.1.6 Fertilisation in the research area

In the NCP, intensive winter wheat/ summer maize double crop rotation goes along with high nitrogen application rates per crop (about 588 kg N/ ha annually) (Zhang *et al.* 2004). Besides the disparities between regions and different crops, nitrogen application rates vary greatly among individual fields or households reflecting farmers' lack of instruction and a certain recalcitrance when applying nitrogen fertilisers (Ju *et al.* 2004). Because agricultural policy is focussed on food self-sufficiency, and mineral nitrogen manufacturing has been heavily government subsidised since the 1970s, nitrogen fertiliser use increased a dramatic 271 percent, and farmers experienced an increase of grain yield per acre of 98 percent. Especially in intensive agricultural regions of higher income, farmers do not refrain from using large amounts of fertiliser. However, today high nitrogen balance surpluses and the resulting nitrogen losses are causing serious pollution of ground and surface waters with reactive nitrogen (Zhang *et al.* 2004). At the farm level, recent studies in China estimated the loss of net farm income due to decreased yields at as much as 15 percent, which was caused by an overuse of mineral fertilisers (Buresh *et al.* 2004). These studies also suggest that farmers could reduce nitrogen inputs by as much as 30 percent without yield loss, resulting in an even higher income.

The empirical research described below gives evidence of agricultural production and fertilisation behaviour on the part of small-scale farmers of intensive wheat/ maize double-cropping systems in poorer Huimin and wealthier Shouguang Counties. Furthermore, cognitive aspects as well as agri-environmental attitudes and knowledge is analysed in order to draw a full picture of farmers' decision-making. A broader overview of several influencing determinants indicates possible to change training and extension systems for better implementation processes and policy incentives.

3.2 Questionnaire design

A quantitative farm household survey was conducted in intensive agricultural zones of Huimin and Shouguang Counties. In order to deal with the research objectives and to verify the theoretical model of farmers' individual behaviour, a broad questionnaire was designed providing the data basis. The questionnaire is divided into two parts. The first part is a general farm household survey of 1,380 households that, in addition to structural farm items and socio-demographic variables, focuses on project-relevant agro-economic questions about the agricultural production system (*i.e.*, yields, farm inputs/ outputs, costs, incomes, *etc.*). The second part was included in 420 of the 1,380 households. Its questions are designed to address the head of the farm household in particular. In the second part, social and cognitive variables are included alongside the rational profit-oriented decision-making determinants (*i.e.*, fundamental values, *guānxi* relationships, agri-environmental attitudes). The questionnaire aims to uncover farmers' inherent perceptions and attitudes towards social and environmental matters. The two survey parts can be matched up via personal identification numbers so that the individual farmers' socio-demographic variables, identified by the second part, can be correlated with their farm characteristics, elicited in the first.

The survey was designed in cooperation with our Chinese counterparts from the Chinese Centre for Agricultural Policy (CCAP).[22] Thus, questionnaire content and sample selection, as well as data collection, entry and processing are the result of numerous compromises and agreements. Hence, there are important deviations from standardised methodologies. These cooperative methodologies are described

---

[22] The cooperative partners from the CCAP were Prof. Dr. HUANG Jikun, Prof. Dr. HU Ruifa, Dr. JIA Xiangping and XIANG Cheng, with whom we worked closely. By "we", I refer to myself and, in particular, Dr. Holger Bergmann who was also involved in the cooperative exchange and survey discussions.

and discussed in detail in the following sections, in order to make clear the contextual framework of the study design.

3.2.1 Questionnaire composition

Since there were diverging research foci, we divided the questionnaire into two parts. The CCAP attached great importance to the use of their already often-examined functional design for the agro-economic section (part I) because they wanted to use the survey for comparison with other surveys. Constructive revisions to enhance the variables were marginally adapted; our counterparts maintained, based on their long experience in studying structural and agri-economic information in China, to have developed the survey method in an optimal way, to gain statistical information within the Chinese context.

Since this research focus is beyond the agro-economic information, an additional questionnaire (part II) was created that includes in particular social, cognitive and attitudinal questions. Since this part does not fall within the scope of our partners' discipline, they provided support regarding culturally and politically sensitive translations. However, the design was up to us. Despite sceptical remarks on the part of the CCAP mentioning the farmers' low level of knowledge and skills with respect to filling out and understanding the questionnaire, the sometimes abstractly formulated social and cognitive questions were given a trial. Moreover, most of the items included had already been tested in urban China (*i.e.*, value items, *guānxi* items).

In addition, the questionnaire was administered in two steps. This decision was taken for two reasons: first, the length of the questionnaire, and second, because agronomic data concerning the maize harvest should be surveyed directly after harvest time in order to acquire recent data promptly. Moreover, farmers do not have an accounting system, so if there were too much time between harvest and the interview, we would risk their having forgotten the exact figures.

The content of the survey is summarised in Table 7 according to the questionnaires attached in the Appendicies 11 and 12. A description of variables follows, subsequently.

Table 7   Questionnaire composition

	Questionnaire contents	Segment labelling
I AGRO-ECONOMIC PART	SOCIO-DEMOGRAPHICS *Household composition, age, sex, education, village position, off-farm work, house assets, etc.*	A. Roster
	GENERAL FARM INFORMATION *Location and infrastructure, cultivated land*	B. Transportation C. Land owning
	FARM TYPE *Planted crop varieties, livestock assets, handling of faeces*	D. Planting structure E. Poultry and livestock F. Faeces
	WHEAT/ MAIZE PLOT MANAGEMENT *Plot information, management, agricultural inputs, yields*	G. Plot- and field management
	FERTILISATION (on wheat/ maize plots) *Applied fertilisers, fertiliser and manure management*	H. Fertilisation management
	EXTENSION SERVICE EXPERIMENT (on wheat/ maize plots)	J. Extension service
	MATERIAL PROSPERITY	M. House assets N. Consumer durables
	FERTILISATION KNOWLEDGE	P. Open question
II SOCIO-PSYCHOLOGICAL PART	MAIZE HARVEST MANAGEMENT DATA *Harvest management data, yields*	G. Plot- and field management (maize)
	HOUSEHOLD INCOME *Income sources (share of crop income, remittances, etc.)*	1. Income group 2. Income composition
	FARM PERSPECTIVE	3. Future Plans
	DISASTER	4. Good/ bad yielding years 5. Disasters/ compensation 8. WTP compensation
	CUSTOMER/ PRICE POLICY/ MARKET	6. Customer
	COMMON PRACTICE *Decision-making on the production management*	7. Decision-making on annual production
	AGRI-ENVIRONMENTAL KNOWLEDGE *Support in fertilisation decisions* *Knowledge on agri-environmental pollution* *Information source agri-environmental pollution*	9. Decision support/ knowledge in fertilisation issues
	AGRI-ENVIRONMENTAL ATTITUDES *Agri-environmental responsibility* *Fertiliser reduction for the sake of the environment* *Fertiliser reduction and economic-risk perception*	10. Agri-environmental attitudes
	WTP ENVIRONMENTAL SERVICES *Clean drinking water, Waste water collection*	11. WTP environmental services
	GUANXI-TRAITS *Utilitarian, Reciprocal, Transferable, Personal, Long-term, Intangible, Collectivism*	12. Guānxi
	FUNDAMENTAL VALUE POSITIONS *Universalism, Benevolence, Conformity, Tradition, Security, Power, Achievement, Hedonism, Stimulation, Self-Direction*	13. PVQ 21

Note: Some segments of part I of the questionnaire contain variables beyond the agro-economic analysis of this research focus and were used only by our counterparts from the CCAP. Segments that refer solely to CCAP research were not used in this thesis; these segments are indicated by the use of grey lettering.

3.2.2 Description of variables

The SOCIO-DEMOGRAPHIC variables of all household members, like age, gender, education and off-farm income sources, give an overview of the household composition and the available physical and human resources that are responsible for the farm's economic capital. Division of roles and responsibilities among different family members – men, women, productive youth and the elderly – is determined by factors such as tradition and labour migration. Based on the status and respective duties of the farm residents, farm management decisions can be made. These decisions are in a large part influenced by on- and off-farm conditions. To sum up, socio-demographic variables describe the starting factor for the composed preferences leading to a household's utility-oriented decision-making.

GENERAL FARM INFORMATION like farm location and infrastructural variables are important for evaluating farms' access to market structures. Information about land owning and cultivated land are important reference figures, also with regard to future perspectives in the farms' expandability options. A farmer with secure tenure is much more likely to think of long-term production and conservation activities than sharecroppers or migrant labourers.

FARM TYPE variables describe the planting structure. They provide information about the nature and extent of the cultivated varieties, as well as any livestock assets and treatment of faeces. The information is valuable in order to estimate the current alignment and efficiency of the farm in relation to its agricultural income composition.

The detailed variables on WHEAT AND MAIZE PLOT MANAGEMENT contain plot information as well as agronomic data on the various production steps (ploughing, sowing, irrigation, chemical treatment, intertillage, harvesting and other management activities). This information gives evidence about the agronomic mode of production and incidental economic costs in these counties. They can be used for comparability with other regions and for efficiency calculations in order to detect mismanagement and improvement opportunities. Furthermore, data on family labour times are requested; such data suggest opportunity costs and the costs of hired labour and (technological) offsourcing of certain production steps. Finally, figures on the harvest outputs act as a referee for the total production efficiency in the management of the particular plot.

Agricultural land in this part is represented by the size of the largest plot. Since one of our research interests is grounded in optimisation calculations for a better nitrogen management system, the main plot exemplarily reflects the main production crops and related fertilising problems.

The FERTILISATON segment of the questionnaire seeks to analyse in detail the fertilisation management on the farmers' largest wheat and maize plot. Specific dates and items on the type, applied amount and NPK ratio of compound fertilisers are investigated in order to calculate the Nitrogen Use Efficiency on the plot. Furthermore, fertilisation times are asked to detect mismanagement regarding application time and frequency. Labour times and cost aspects shed light on fertilisation expenses and are also used for profit and opportunity cost calculations.

HOUSEHOLD INCOME variables provide evidence about the total household income. Income variables are surveyed in categories since it was argued that in general Chinese farmers would not tell non-natives how much they earn. Therefore, the farmers were asked to specify income shares in order to see how income is composed and what the main income source is. Income represents the main restriction in a farm household and the main constraint on decision-making. Hence, based on answers regarding farm management and the share of off-farm work, conclusions can be drawn concerning options for ameliorating the farmers' income situation. Furthermore, remittances from relatives and friends were investigated. The relative share on total income will also give evidence about the farm household's embeddedness in personal relationships and hence about additional financial support.

The variable FARM PERSPECTIVES points out possible future farm developments and the farmer's personal motivation to continue farming. It is adressed in a closed question with a given set of response parameters. Thus, if farmers state that they may rent out land and sell some of their animals in the next five years, they attach less importance to the farm and are on the way to giving up farm production, probably in the interest of more efficient off-farm activities within the family.

Continuing as they have up until now indicates a farmer's constrained opportunities to influence the current situation. If a farmer plans to start a new production line, he or she is striving to develop the farm in a more efficient way by focussing on different production activity, which seems to promise better profits.

Farmers' COMMON PRACTICE in agriculture, and hence their decision-making on the annual production programme, is measured by a given response set, too. By means of different decision criteria, farmer's strategic alignment of annual production management can be analysed. For example, a farmer may decide to plant the crop for which the best price is expected, for which the highest subsidies are provided or with which the neighbours have had success.

In the section on AGRI-ENVIRONMENTAL KNOWLEDGE, knowledge-based decision-making is measured by three question sets. The first set evaluates farmer's support sources in decision-making regarding nitrogen and manure management. The categories range from established habits and traditions to advice from relatives and friends and, at the other end of the range, to extension services, TV, or providers of agro-chemicals. The different items point out the quality of farmers' information, and thus their degree of agri-environmental knowledge. The second question set assesses farmers' knowledge concerning selected agri-environmental problems on a four-point scale (groundwater pollution caused by overuse of fertilisers, pesticide residues in vegetables) (*cf.* Vogel 1996). This will give an impression of the farmers' self-assessment of knowledge on environmental pollution. The results will also demonstrate their problem awareness regarding this topic since the answers will distinguish between farmers that have already recognised that their agri-environmental knowledge is insufficient. Farmers may feel well informed; however, in reality specific knowledge is marginal existent). The third question set deals with information sources on agri-environmental pollution of groundwater caused by nitrogen and pesticide overuse. The answer categories (multiple-response set) can be related to the knowledge stated in the preceding question and may thus discern the real quality of farmers' agri-environmental information. Thus, if information derives from agricultural extension training, it is assumed that it is of better quality than information from family members or traders. Furthermore, the question gives evidence about general sources and networks of knowledge influencing the attitudes and preferences of farmers and, thus, their behaviour.

The next questionnaire block addresses on AGRI-ENVIRONMENTAL ATTITUDES and contains items of different agri-environmental dimensions (foci). Two or three items measure the priorities of one focal point. Using multiple questions diminishes misunderstandings, and the effects of social desirability, because single questions on a cognitive issue cannot be formulated unerringly. The first question block deals with attitudes concerning general responsibility for reducing environmental pollution (government vs. individual responsibility) (cf. WVS 1990). The second block represents attitudinal dimensions related to the farmers' sphere of activity (for example, the benefits vs. the potential damage from agro-chemicals) (cf. Vogel 1996). The third concentrates on risk-related agri-environmental attitudes and farmers' consciousness of being burdened by environmental and financial problems (such as reduction of nitrogen use vs. economic security).

The variable WTP ENVIRONMENTAL SERVICES evaluates to what extent the farmer is willing to pay for the provision of clean drinking water or waste collection services. The responses give evidence of farmers' perception of environmental problems resulting from agro-chemicals and their willingness to change their practices in response. Furthermore, it is supposed that their willingness to pay would correlate with their income.

The section on GUANXI TRAITS contains 13 items (cf. Appendix 4). These express the characteristics described by Dunning and Changsu (2007). Each of the seven guānxi dimensions demonstrates its usefulness in predicting interpersonal relationship qualities of trust and commitment. The respondents' relative evaluation of these qualities provides evidence of their current perception of each trait and the importance they place on it.

Twenty-one verbal portrait items seek to measure farmers' FUNDAMENTAL VALUE POSITIONS, as expressed by Schwartz's (1992) ten universal motivational values. Value priorities and value conflicts among the personal orientations of different farmers were extracted and compared, as well as related to varying attitudes, guānxi orientations and other cognitive variables.

3.2.3 Question-forming and response-scaling techniques

Question forming and response scaling techniques were adapted to the various contents.

The production-oriented data were compiled by variables that will be necessary to calculate different production efficiencies. They should also deliver valuable statistical data for the cooperative scientists in our project on fertiliser management, extension services and crop management techniques. As such, the questionnaire design is functional and orientated towards practical goals, expressed in short metric variables. Most items are self-explanatory. They are organised into clearly arranged tables, without any further description. Since the formatting is not accessible for farmers who are not used to filling out such questionnaires and who think in their own categories and measurement units, it is up to the interviewer to get the information and data from the farmers in an interview. Thus, the interviewer filled out the questionnaires. Expenses are displayed in *Renminbi* (RMB) or in Chinese *yuán* (CNY),[23] the currency of the People's Republic of China. Amounts are measured in the common Chinese measurement unit *jīn/ mǔ*. *Jīn* is the weight measure for half a kilogramme (kg) and *mǔ* the surface area measure for 667 m² (≈ 1/15 ha). Since sometimes farmers' yield responses could also be in *dan* – a *dan* equals 100 *jīn* (≈ 50 kg) – or other local measurement units, conversion might be necessary and interviewers needed to pay attention to that, too.

Recommendations for best practises in questioning were addressed, but were not standardised. Interviewer bias as a result of leading questions or of incomprehensible or bureaucratic phrasing cannot be excluded, but is diminished through constrained answer categories and comparability.

In contrast with these relatively simple measureable ordinal and metric scaled items describing the farmers' agro-economic and socio-demographic situation in the first part of the questionnaire, the second part reflects, in principle, the literature reviewed.

---

[23] The exchange rate for the Chinese *yuán* is 0.105130984 Euro.

Ranking and scaled questions evaluate attitudes to certain topics through latent underlying variables. In order to define the socio-psychological variables, that is, the farmers' varying agri-environmental attitudes (16 items), their *guānxi* traits (13 items) and their basic value positions (21 items), multisited items were selected from Vogel (1996), Dunning and Changsu (2007), WVS (2007) and Schwartz (2001). These items identify the underlying behaviour generating dimensions of the divergent environmental concerns, knowledge or attitudes concerning the use of agricultural inputs and so forth. For example, items like the following can measure one underlying latent attitude and thus reflect farmers' attitudes towards chemical fertilisers: *"Commercial fertilisers and pesticides promote high quality products. Besides, they have no harmful effects"* and *"The groundwater burden resulting from the washing out of fertilisers is worse than many people imagine"*. In this example, the items express antipodal attitudes. This method has the advantage of mitigating acquiescence. Thus, respondents who agree with the first item are expected to disagree with the second item (*cf.* Schnell *et al.* 1999).

The selected items were randomly scattered throughout the topic related sequence of the questionnaire. In order to elicit "true" replies, the imposition of cognitive consistency is prevented by responding to a series of inverse items. The questions usually take the form of five-point Likert scales,[24] which range from 'strongly agree' (1) to 'strongly disagree' (5) and which are used to investigate self-assessment and attitudes on single items. The scale specifies respondents' level of agreement with a statement without using extreme response categories, so that the farmers are able to portray themselves in a more favourable light. Thus, farmers may evaluate according to any kind of subjective or objective criteria. Even in surroundings like China, where direct expressions of critical attitudes are shunned, the respondents have the option of answering in tendencies. Nevertheless, the more selective the items are, the better the underlying attitudes are measured (*cf.* Schnell *et al.* 1999). It is assumed that different underlying attitudes, or decision dimensions, form the bulk of determinants influencing the farmers' preferences.

---

[24] The Likert scale technique is named after the psychologist Rensis Likert (1932) who developed this interrogation method to measure attitudes (Burns 1997).

For the evaluation of fundamental value positions, Schwartz's (2006) Portrait Values Questionnaire (PVQ 21) was applied. This questionnaire was extracted from the European Social Survey (ESS)[25] and is based on the universal value survey of 1992.

Each of the 21 items expresses one aspect of the motivational goal of one of the ten basic motivational values, without clearly naming the values as the topics of the items. The items are composed as verbal portraits of different people to provide graphic evidence across cultures. For example, the following portrait describes a person for whom self-direction values are important: *"Thinking up new ideas and being creative is important to him. He likes to do things in his own original way."* For reliability, two items measure each of the ten values (three for universalism). The values from different motivational goals are intermixed throughout the questionnaire (*cf.* Appendix 3 and Appendix 12).

The scaling technique is similar to the Likert scale, but the six categories are organised along two bipolar dimensions that discern how similar the described person is to the respondent (Schwartz 2006). The respondents are asked to answer the question "How similar or dissimilar is this person to you?" Thus, they compare themselves with the portrait and rate on a six-point importance scale the extent to which they identify with the described personal trait, from 1 ('This person is definitely not similar to me') to 6 ('This person is very similar to me').

This technique is able to summarise the oppositions between competing values. It has the advantage that respondents do not need to discriminate among equally important values, nor do they need to compare directly values that appear incommensurate to them. Furthermore, this rating method measures the negative values of those people who have problems expressing that they have rejected certain goals (Schwartz 1994). In particular, in Chinese culture, negative responses are not articulated as such.

---

[25] The ESS is a biennial repeat multi-country survey covering over 30 nations. The survey aims to monitor change and continuity in a wide range of social variables, inter alia including the Schwartz's PVQ to evaluate human values. The first round was fielded in 2002/2003, the fourth in 2008/2009 (further information are available at http://www.europeansocialsurvey.org/).

3.2.4 Questionnaire adaption to the local situation

Due to the cross-cultural survey for the theory of value content and structure, the long version of the PVQ (40 items) was available in Chinese from Schwartz, so there is evidence about accurate translation and phrasing of the portraits.[26] Thus, the 21 items for the shorter PVQ could be easily identified and used for the interviews.

The other parts of the socio-psychological questionnaire sections were developed in English and translated into Chinese by a Chinese native speaker also fluent in English. Some sentences have been adapted to Chinese farmers' cultural context and were back-translated for accuracy.

Afterwards, the questionnaire was pre-tested with some farmers in March 2009. In cases where the interviewer recognised that farmers were unable to respond to certain questions, those questions were changed or better adapted to the cultural context and translations were improved.

Before the survey was carried out, 32 interviewers – university students from several Beijing universities – were trained in a special workshop dealing with questionnaire contents and methods for administering each part. The challenge was the need for different interrogation techniques in the first and second parts of the questionnaire. Whereas it was important in the first part to have the exact data in the right units, irrespective of questioning techniques, the sensitive social and cognitive questions in the second part required the interviewer to read the questions down exactly as written. If a respondent were to hedge or digress it would prove difficult for the interviewer to give hints without suggesting possible responses (Burns 1997). Furthermore, interviewers needed to maintain a certain sensitivity to the surroundings during the interview in order to avoid possibly biased answering behaviours (Schnell *et al.* 1999).

3.2.5 Research ethic

Since the survey was conducted in two waves, the two questionnaire parts had to be merged. For this reason and in compliance with questions that are tailored to a

---

[26] Translation by WANG Xiaoming in 2008

unique person's social and cognitive attitudes, the farmers interviewed during the first wave have to be the same as in the second wave. Thus, farmers had to be identified in order to contact them again for the second part of the investigation. Although it is against the ethics of research, research in China is stacked against the respondent's right of voluntary participation and confidentiality (see Burns 1997).

Thus, for the accomplishment of the survey, farmers were selected and later contacted by the village committee, who then expected them to participate. Hence, there was indirect social pressure for farmers to participate without their knowing what the consequences of non-participation might be.

Furthermore, detailed information on the interviewed person (name and contact details like telephone and mobile number) is registered on the first page of the questionnaire for retraceability. This is because our counterparts wanted to be able to clarify data misunderstandings or failures in the agro-economic data set or with regard to the experimental design. Furthermore, local bureaucratic administration requires such transparent procedures. However, the contact details enabled us to interview the same person a second time, enabling us to merge the two parts.

In order to comply with anonymity criteria for the data analysis, in both questionnaire parts, respondents were marked with personal identification (PID) numbers. [27] However, due to cost-intensive aspects, the social and cognitive questionnaire section was only applied for a smaller sample size of 420 farmers, so that not all respondents needed to be traced back by PID numbers.

Moreover, a general household code (hcode) was used for identification. Traceability to respective respondents was not important; thus, the data were independent of the respondents, since only agro-economic household data concerning the maize harvest were surveyed in the second wave (in some cases, by telephone).

---

[27] pPID = previous PID is the respondent of part I of the questionnaire; nPID = next PID is the respondent of part II

3.3 Sample selection

The quantitative farm household survey (including the intensive farmers' survey) in the two Counties of Shandong Province was conducted in September and November 2009.

The sample selection had to comply with the various research foci of the different disciplines within our overall project. Hence, the frame population was selected according to different criteria. Feature characteristics were of primary importance; then, (rudimentally randomised) snowball systems[28] were applied for the sample selection (Schnell et al. 1999; Diekmann 1998).

Since the actual research topic originated in the multidisciplinary Sino-German Nitrogen Project, the alluvial plains of Shandong Province were selected because of their intensive production of winter wheat/ summer maize and high nitrogen fertilisation rates. However, the selection of the pilot counties depended on more than the varying agricultural conditions. Existing relationships of mutual trust between the Chinese scientists from China Agricultural University (CAU) and local political and agricultural administrations had to be considered as well. Since our Chinese partners from CAU already had existing relationships with the Huimin and Shouguang County governments and local research centres to conduct their field experiments, the selection was up to these counties.

For the overall project and this research, agro-economic criteria (such as, data about the area per capita sown with maize and wheat) were important selection characteristics for the townships. Moreover, for the CCAP's experimental design, the still existent, but ailing agricultural extension systems were also important criteria.[29]

---

[28] Snowball systems are systematic selections of a special population affected by external constraints of the conditions in the research field. This means that, although our partners tried to randomise the sample, they had to adapt to the local (political) conditions and involve the administrative governments in the sample selection process. This approach most closely resembles the "snowball system" described by Schnell et al. (1999) and Diekmann (1998).

[29] The CCAP's overall study aim was to evaluate the impacts of various field technologies in reducing the use of chemical fertilisers (1) with or without minor yield loss and (2) with farm income maximisation. Furthermore, they wanted to identify sustainable extension modes to disseminate these technologies. The experiment was to combine technological treatments with distinct policy interventions within a randomised, stratified sample.

Since townships in rural China vary sharply in terms of farming structure, Township and Village Enterprises (TVEs), extension capability, public service, and so forth, pure randomisation might generate bias. Therefore, within the counties, the sample was stratified again, according to the townships' varying economic prosperity levels. The townships and villages would have been selected (almost) randomly, if it were not for interference on the part of the administrations.

Within Huimin and Shouguang County, 1,380 farm households were selected for the overall survey according to a sophisticated sample selection that complied with the different research foci and the budget constraints. The concept is laid out in Figure 7.

Figure 7   Scheme of sample selection (adapted from the CCAP, modified)

County I				County II			
Strata I		Strata II		Strata I		Strata II	
Township I (Experiment)	Township II (Control)	Township I (Experiment)	Township II (Control)	Township I (Experiment)	Township II (Control)	Township I (Experiment)	Township II (Control)
A B C D 15 15 - 15 30 30 30 30	A B C D 15 15 - 15 30 30 30 30	A B C D 15 15 - 15 30 30 30 30	A B C D 15 15 - 15 30 30 30 30	A B C D 15 15 - 15 30 30 30 30	A B C D 15 15 - 15 30 30 30 30	A B C D 15 15 - 15 30 30 30 30	A B C D 15 15 - 15 30 30 30 30

Village A: Training
Village B: Training + visiting
Village C: CAU pilot village
Village D: Control, i.e. business as usual, but possibly contaminated by neighbouring villages with special training or CAU plots
Village V: uncontaminated control villages having an existing extension system

Sample selection of the frame population:
2 counties x 4 townships x 4 villages = 32 villages

⇒   15 farmers in 28 villages = 420 farmers for intensive farmers survey (incl. socio-psychological part)
⇒   30 farmers in 32 villages = 960 farm households for experiments on technology adoption
→1380 agro-economic questionnaires

The main parts of the scheme are adapted from the CCAP's experimental design.

Villages in eight townships (four in each county) were selected according to two different strata regarding data on wheat/ maize planting areas[30] and the disposition of the village leaders towards participating in the survey (also a part of the experiment for which the CCAP needed the support of the local extension people). Finally, the frame population was selected by the village administrators who

---

[30] The figure of reference for the strata is an index of the area per capita planted with wheat and maize in the respective townships, built up by the CCAP based on several information of the local government.

provided lists with "relevant" farms according to their own estimation and criteria, out of which the CCAP randomly selected 30 farm households for their experimental design and 15 additional farmers for the intensive farmers' survey.

Both selections served as a basis for the project's agro-economic investigations. For the later intensive survey containing the sensitive socio-psychological questions, pilot villages that took part in CAU experiments were not included. Those villages had received scientific technology training and been subject to experimental field trials within the overall project in these counties and were therefore considered to have been "contaminated". Thus, in order to investigate farmers' decision-making, the sample size of 420 farmers was used. The selected farmers had not yet been biased by the experimental incentives, since the CCAP evaluated the adoption rate of the recommended technology after this baseline survey had been carried out. Thus, the status quo of the agronomic performance was investigated first.

The final sample selected according to the scheme is shown below in Table 8.

Table 8   Selected sample

Counties	Strata*	Townships	Villages	N
Huimin 惠民	Richer (1)	Sunwu 孙武	Dishangli 堤上李; Mazhou 马周; Xiaotun 小屯	160
	Richer (2)	Weiji 魏集镇	Siyang 四杨村; Yinhuangcui 引黄崔; Hanjia 韩家	167
	Poorer (3)	Hefang 何妨乡	Shenjia 沈家村; Zhanjia 展家; Bigu 毕顾	156
	Poorer (4)	Sangluoshu 桑落墅	Lijiejia 李界家; Dadaozhang 大道张; Shijia 石贾村	158
Shouguang 寿光	Richer (1)	Tianliu 田柳镇	Dongma 东马村; Xingsi 邢四; Sheli 阇梨	162
	Richer (2)	Taitou 台头镇	Daoyi 道一村; Nantaitou 南台头; Taiping 太平村	166
	Poorer (3)	Yingli 营里镇	Wujia 吴家村; Xinzhuang 新庄; Nanchahe 南岔河	168
	Poorer (4)	Houzhen 侯镇	Wangjia 王家村; Siqicang 四岐仓; Weijia 魏家	202

* Figures of reference for economic strata are economic per capita data on the net area sown with maize and wheat in the respective townships. The numbers reflect the relative order on a scale from 1=rich to 4=poor.

To conclude, the sample is a selection of defined farm households: economically diverse farms producing wheat and maize in a typical intensive agricultural area of the North China Plain, the alluvial plains of Shandong Province. According to the statistical data, Huimin and Shouguang are the extreme points of the statistical population of Shandong Province; the same holds true for the selected townships.

This kind of (randomised) stratified sampling method was conducted because such strata already existed within the research area. The two economic strata draw inferences about the selected counties that may be lost in a more generalised random sample. Thus, more efficient statistical estimates are possible that are – because of opposed strata – also transferable to other regions/ populations defined by the same characteristics (*cf.* Schnell *et al.* 1999).

3.4 Survey data collection

For agronomic and practical reasons, the survey data collection was conducted in two waves that were merged together according to the respondents' PID numbers. The first set of interviews was conducted in September 2009 after the wheat harvest (late May to early June) and contained the agro-economic questions (n=1380). The second set of interviews was carried out in November 2009, after the maize harvest. It involved a further 420 farmers who answered, in addition to a short agro-economic survey on their maize harvest data, a longer section containing agri-environmental and socio-psychological questions.

The mode of questioning was a standardised personal face-to-face interview. However, in part I, the phrasing of questions was not specified verbatim. Due to its focus on pure numerical and practical agro-economic data, objectivity and reliability were not negatively influenced, regardless of which person conducted the interview. In contrast, in part II standardised interrogation was required in order to avoid interviewer bias through subjective interpretation of cognitive questions or communicated stimuli towards certain socially expected "right" responses. In order to promote a relatively neutral interview technique, interviewers received special training before carrying out the survey to avoid (at best) distortion of results (Diekmann 1998; Schnell *et al.* 1999).

3.4.1 Interviewer training

The interviewer training contained an introduction to the questionnaire's composition and the research goals. Furthermore, certain questions and response documentation were explained and test interviews were conducted in role-plays.

For part I of the questionnaire, the interviewers were introduced to the relevant structural composition and data documentation codes, congruent to the table formatting. Most of the interviewers had never previously conducted a survey.

A particular training focus was the situation in the field (rules of conduct) and appropriate behaviour towards farmers. The main topics discussed, were how to contact farmers, possible problems with local Chinese dialects,[31] advice related to best practices and appearance in the field so as to forge good relationships between farmers and the interviewers. This is a very important issue since most of the questions were very detailed and farmers have all the information in their minds rather than recorded in any accounting system. Thus, interviewers were encouraged to motivate farmers to think clearly about their responses in order to acquire accurate data. If necessary, the interviewers were to check relevant information themselves, such as noting down nitrogen, phosphorus and potassium (NPK) content or names of fertilisers directly from the packages. Furthermore, the interviewers were asked to put their questions in a manner farmers could understand. If possible, they were to adapt their repeated question to the farmers' understanding. Hence, they had to know the agricultural practices, be aware of the local technical terms and units and check directly whether the farmers' answers were reliable. For this reason, particular agro-economic variables were explained in detail during training to avoid misunderstanding.

Regarding the socio-psychological part of wave 2, the interviewers were trained in questioning methodology in particular. The interviewers had no experience in asking sensitive questions in social surveys. Thus, response errors like social-desirability, the presence of third persons or the tendency to acquiescence ("yes-manship") were selected out as central themes. In particular, in Chinese culture and for less educated persons with less self-confidence, there is a tendency to assimilate to

---

[31] In general, the Chinese language refers to the Beijing dialect, which is the original language spoken by the predominant ethic group, the Han Chinese. Although Mandarin, the standard official form of the Chinese language is understandable to most of the Chinese, local dialects are broadly spread and spoken. In particular, among the rural population, dialects can be so distinctive that people from other regions or provinces have difficulties to understanding them, especially in southern China.

assumed expectations on the part of higher-ranking persons. Interviewers were therefore given strategies for dealing with non-response or non-opinion responses to items (see Schnell *et al.* 1999).

Among other things, verbal and nonverbal comments regarding disapproval of or agreement to responses were to be avoided during interviews. Furthermore, interviewers were to point out the anonymity of data analyses in order to encourage honest opinions (Diekmann 1998). Finally, no third persons (governmental staff, neighbours, other family members) were to influence the interviewed person through attendance, comments or further explanation.

Since Likert scales were used for the questionnaire design, literate farmers were encouraged to fill in the marks themselves. This would ensure better understanding since they could read the questions at their own speed. Furthermore, Likert scales require differentiating between the answer categories. Thus, it was very important that every item be answered and no question left out. The interviewers were encouraged to supervise this.

3.4.2 Questioning operation

The two-step interviews in September and November 2009 were carried out by 32 university students from CAU, who were selected to conduct each part of the survey in nearly two weeks. The village leaders were informed beforehand. Afterwards, they contacted the local farmers to ask them to allow time for the interview on the arranged day. Escorted by two experts from the CCAP, who organised the contacts with the local village leaders, the group was divided by county. The interviewers surveyed each of the selected households village by village according to the list provided by the local administrations. The respondents were offered a small incentive (soap and a towel) for their time and participation. Since most of the farmers were busy and had time constraints, the incentive was one way to increase response rates (Schnell *et al.* 1999). Part I of the interrogation took place at the farmers' homes or even in the fields.

The questionnaire took on average 40 minutes to complete. Since part II did not contain agro-economic questions, if village leaders agreed, farmers were gathered in one central place and interviewed individually. The part II questionnaire lasted on average 25 minutes.

In the evenings, the daily questionnaires were revised and cleansed immediately by the interviewers in order to increase the completion rate and diminish nonresponse errors. Thus, bad handwriting, calculation failures or wrong unit transformations were corrected; missing values and blanks were amended from memory or farmers were contracted again the following day, if necessary.

3.4.3 Operation errors – Item nonresponse

Due to reduced nonresponse or non-availability (social pressure) and immediate data cleansing following first data cleansing, the sample acquired was quite good, with 1,342 valid interviews for the total household survey (part I, 97 %) and 394 for the additional farmer interviews (part II, 82 %).[32]

In the questioning operation, the survey data included the potential for a number of response errors. There were several reasons why farmers might not report actual values. Since the interviewers were students and had mostly grown up in urban areas, most of them had lost any connection to agriculture. In some cases, misunderstandings arose because the interviewers did not understand what was meant by farmers' detailed responses to the questions. Most farmers had the habit of explaining their answers, even when just a figure was required. Sometimes it appeared that the interviewers had to dig deeper while asking further questions because the expected answer did not fit the farmers' perception and expression category of agricultural facts. It also occurred that respondents had too little knowledge of management details. Others had already quit wheat or maize production and thus caused unit nonresponse errors (Schnell *et al.* 1999).

In the socio-psychological part, some questions appeared too abstract for farmers. Regarding some items, farmers were more likely to try to please the interviewers than to express their own opinions, and often interviewers were not skilled enough to motivate the farmers to answer according to the required methodology.

---

[32] The realised sample is the sample size after first revisions and several following screenings and data cleaning.

Furthermore, it could not be guaranteed that farmers were not exposed to external influences by persons around them, while giving their response to the social and cognitive part of the questionnaire. In addition, some were impatient due to the length of the questionnaire, and interviewers were sometimes under pressure to finish the questionnaires due to their tight schedule and the fact a driver was waiting for them. Hence, several operation errors and biases occurred that had to be considered when interpreting the data.

3.4.4 Data entry

In order to generate a data matrix for statistical analysis, data entry was accomplished according to the questionnaire codes (see Appendix 11 and Appendix 12). Each column was allocated a certain variable and each line referred to a specific household (hcode) or farmer (PID). Different specifications of one variable were expressed in the codes entered into the matrix (see also Schnell *et al.* 1999). The programme use for data management and analysis was PASW Statistics 18 (SPSS 2009),[33] which is a common and well-established tool in the social sciences (Schnell *et al.* 1999).

Whereas we entered data from the smaller farmers' survey (n=394; part II) ourselves to avoid additional misunderstanding in data cleansing; data entry of the overall household survey (n=1,342; part I) was performed by a Chinese company in Beijing, co-workers of the CCAP. The two data sets were merged by using the PID numbers, so that a data set was produced for the survey as a whole. Since the Chinese company had not entered the agro-economic data in a two-dimensional matrix that would enable statistical comparison, the whole data set had to be transferred by an expert programmer to an SPSS/PASW-compatible data matrix. Due to continuing data cleansing processes on the part of the CCAP, changes went through the data set, so we continuously had to adjust our data matrix to the new version, which also made the data vulnerable to transformation errors, because the cleansing criteria were not always traceable.

---

[33] SPSS was called PASW (Predictive Analytics SoftWare) between 2009 and 2010. Then, SPSS was aquired by IBM. Release 19 is called IBM SPSS Statistics 19.

3.4.5 Data screening

Data were screened and cross-checked several times in order to identify obvious mistakes and unrealistic values. Preliminary work on data validation for part I of the questionnaire was done by the CCAP. Wild codes were eliminated, and the data set was checked for consistency (Schnell *et al.* 1999). If possible, errors were corrected into realistic values. Examples were falsely placed decimal points or data stated in units not used in the survey, for grain yields expressed as total yield rather than yield per *mŭ* as asked for in the survey. In such cases, yield per *mŭ* was calculated afterwards, if realistically possible.

In spite of such corrections, many data were not trustworthy and had to be rejected. Cases with high rates of obviously wrong or missing values were excluded from further analysis, including data from farmers who no longer had winter wheat or summer maize in their cropping systems.

When the two datasets were merged into one matrix, the problem emerged that 92 of the 394 part II farmer samples could not be traced to their part I samples. Some farmers who had been interviewed in the first wave had already left the villages for off-farm activities when interviewers came in the second wave; others could not be found in the fields during the second survey period. As a result, the sample size for analysing socio-psychological variables in combination with data from part I of the total questionnaire was reduced to 302.

4 DATA ANALYSIS AND RESULTS

For data analysis, various statistical methods are used. These are adapted to the hypotheses, presented in the theoretical chapter. Uni-, bi- and multivariate statistics provide tools and models that help interpret the surveyed data. The first subchapter introduces methods used for statistical data analysis. The following subchapters present the results of the analyses in sequence, responding to main topics addressed in the empirical approach of the research framework (cf. Chapter 1.2). As each subchapter simply refers to the statistical methods described in the introduction, the results of the analyses can be combined reasonably, and preliminary interpretations can be drawn immediately within each subchapter. The successive subchapters are organised logically: A descriptive overview of household and farm characteristics is followed by an examination of agronomic and economic topics relating to nitrogen overuse and farms' profitability and efficiency. Then, the cognitive and social dimensions of Chinese farmers are discussed, leading to the final multivariate structural equation model, which explores the structural linkages between economic, social and cognitive factors.

4.1 Methods used for statistical data analysis

This preparatory subchapter introduces methods used for statistical data analysis and pivotal calculations necessary to describe the Chinese farmers' current agricultural practice and economic situation. Calculations, such as the apparent Nitrogen Use Efficiency of farmers' fertilisation practice and the Standard Gross Margins are inevitable to evaluate the farms' production efficiency and the profitability of the cultivated crops or to estimate the dimension of particular cost factors.

The programme used to calculate the uni-, bi- and multivariate statistics was PASW Statistics 18 (SPSS 2009). Univariate statistics describe single variables in the sample through frequency counts, ranges (high and low scores or values) and arithmetic means with quoted standard deviations. Hence, results are descriptive and allow one to generalise the main characteristics observed and demonstrate tendencies of central distributions. By contrast, bivariate or multivariate analyses explain the relationships between several variables and draw conclusions concerning the relevance of respective variables for the research question.

As a rule, descriptive analyses give an overview of the sample, which is why they are described at the beginning. Since the data has been analysed for two different samples (the larger sample size for part I of the questionnaire and the smaller, but more intensive for part II), it is also important to differentiate between the two samples, each of which is described separately before the respective analyses are given.

4.1.1 Descriptive analysis

Descriptive statistics are univariate and applied for socio-demographic factors and structural agro-economic variables, once for the whole sample (*cf.* Chapter 4.2) and again for the smaller sample size in part II (*cf.* Section 4.5.1). The division is necessary, since just as with the agro-economic analyses and calculations of Chapter 4.3 and 4.4, the bigger sample size is advantageous and more reliable. The data qualify for comparison between the selected counties with their differing levels of economic prosperity and for comparison with other regional data from the literature. The analyses of the smaller sample size in part II concentrate more on the farmers themselves. Although descriptive analyses were also conducted of the household's agro-economic variables, farmers' socio-demographic factors and attitudes comprised the main focus (*cf.* Chapter 4.5). These basic data were then used as background information for the multivariate analysis, which was – due to data availability –conducted only for the smaller sample size (*cf.* Chapter 3.4).

The analyses provide frequency counts and indicate percentages as well as mean values and standard deviations as measures of variability and diversity. Ranges and quartiles are counted in the case of variables with smaller sample sizes or high standard deviations in order to show the variability of scores. Thus, reference points are provided in samples where most of the data show considerable variation (Burns 1997).

In order to verify the theoretical assumptions, socio-demographic variables (age, gender, education, *etc.*) are described, as are contextual factors such as structural data on the farm, the farm household and farmers' knowledge of fertiliser usage and groundwater pollution, as well as their sources of information.

Furthermore, descriptive univariate analyses of agronomic and agro-economic variables demonstrate the agricultural practice and allow further calculations of farms' profitability and fertilisation efficiency. For example, in order to review the surplus dimension of the farmers' fertiliser inputs, average wheat and maize yields are presented, as are the amounts of mineral nitrogen and manure that farmers apply annually. Furthermore, in order to estimate the efficiency of farmers' production lines, these data are related to the mean crop outputs and to ensured standard data from the literature in additional calculations (*e.g.*, see Nitrogen Use Efficiency and Standard Gross Margins calculations).

To sum up, the descriptive analyses in this research deliver insights into the observable scope of action within which farmers make their decisions. The analyses also demonstrate the apparent effects of farmers' behaviour, such as yields or applied mineral nitrogen amounts, allowing for the calculation of use efficiency and profitability. These agronomic and economic calculations are conducted before continuing the statistical data analyses by bi- and multivariate analyses, since this information uses observed manifest variables to describe farmer's agri-environmental behaviour. It is against the background of this agronomic and economic information that the social and cognitive decision-making variables are analysed. In particular, the apparent Nitrogen Use Efficiency calculated below describes the framing of the research problem since it is assumed to demonstrate farmers' nitrogen overuse.

4.1.2 Apparent Nitrogen Use Efficiency

The apparent Nitrogen Use Efficiency (aNUE) is computed in order to estimate the fertilisation efficiency of the farmers' crop production systems (Moll *et al.* 1982).

According to Moll *et al.* (1982) and Olson and Swallow (1984), in contrast to the aNUE, the total NUE is defined by Raun and Johnson (1999) as being the yield of grain per unit of available nitrogen in the soil (including the residual mineral nitrogen present in the soil and the fertiliser)[34]. Assuming a total NUE, the calculation always includes residual mineral nitrogen that may be leached through the soil into the groundwater, as well as gaseous nitrogen emissions to the atmosphere (Moll *et al.* 1982; Hirel *et al.* 2007). For total NUE, this is tolerated as negative external effects of fertilisation; otherwise, yield maximisation could not be achieved as such. However, although this method would have been better reflecting nitrogen loss to water, soil or air, more specific soil scientific experiments would have been necessary, which are beyond the scope of this study (Moll *et al.* 1982). Instead of such measurements, the available nitrogen in the soil was substituted for the applied mineral nitrogen rate in order to calculate the apparent NUE (Ebertseder *et al.* 2005; Moll *et al.* 1982). Thus, the aNUE is calculated by multiplying the grain yields by the nitrogen uptake of the crop and, dividing the result by the amount of applied mineral fertilisers.[35] At the optimal level of nitrogen supply, the aNUE reaches 100 percent.

$$aNUE = \frac{(amount\ of\ grain\ yields\ in\ t/\ ha)\ x\ (N\ uptake\ of\ the\ crop\ in\ kg\ N/\ t)}{applied\ mineral\ fertilisers\ kg/\ ha}$$

Whereas the yield is available as a stated variable, the applied nitrogen fertiliser rate had to be calculated from several variables in the questionnaire. Hence, for each fertilisation date, the share of nitrogen in each compound fertiliser applied is multiplied by the volume of that fertiliser. Then, all applied nitrogen amounts for one season were added to the relevant crop. The nitrogen uptake of the crop with the harvest was estimated by standard figures from KTBL[36] (2005). The actual nitrogen uptake might be more or less, depending on the amount of residue remaining in the field, which was not possible to account in the survey. Thus, 23 kg

---

[34] For cereal production, the average NUE ranges from 30 to 35 percent, but NUEs up to more than 50 percent are possible by precise farming and optimised fertilisation (Moll *et al.* 1982; Hirel *et al.* 2007).

[35] Organic fertilisers are included as total amount; the share of mineral nitrogen from manure is not calculated as such.

[36] Winter wheat (sum of yield product and residues; N-uptake: 23 kg N/ t); summer maize (corn including residues; N-uptake 25 kg N/ t)

N/t for wheat and 25 kg N/t for maize (dry matter) are assumed for the aNUE calculations (KTBL 2005).

In the following, the Standard Gross Margin approach is used to calculate economic problems resulting from an overuse of fertilisers. The method aims to demonstrate cost intensive production steps and less profitable production decisions in order to identify saving capacities, which could be convincing factors that might change or influence farmers' decision-making.

4.1.3 Standard Gross Margin calculations

In particular in China the Standard Gross Margin approach is a reasonable method to calculate the profitability of a crop planting system. The approach has the advantage to estimate direct costs, irrespective of the farm area and intensity of production, in particular since Chinese small-scale farmers often farm according to habits and traditions and do not include complex estimation of costs for their accountings.

The SGM is a widespread European standard measure for the profitability of different production systems. Opportunity costs can be deduced easily; moreover, the method is able to present comparable data for different scientific purposes. For example, variations of the SGMs can be calculated by including varying costs for land or labour (Lund and Price 1998).

Single-step Standard Gross Margin calculations are the simplest form of direct-costing calculations; here fixed costs are segregated from variable costs. On a lower hierarchical level, the output of an end product is examined along with its variable costs; this is the Standard Gross Margin. On a higher level, all other incoming costs are allotted to the net profit of the farm economy (Mußhoff and Hirschhauer 2010). In this research, only the SGMs of single production lines are considered; first, because the project primarily focuses on the wheat and maize cropping system with its productivity and efficiency and second, because all other costs (fixed costs, family labour income, *etc.*) are difficult to estimate in the Chinese rural farm household economy.

In economic terms, the SGM characterises the economic success, in this case, of the crop cultivation per acre. It is defined as the value of output from one hectare less the costs of variable inputs required to produce that output. The SGMs correspond to the whole production period (Mußhoff and Hirschhauer 2010). The formula is as follows:

$$SGM \ [€/ \ ha] = yields \ [€/ \ ha] - variable \ costs \ [€/ \ ha]$$

Hence, in this research, SGMs for wheat and maize production are calculated separately. The farmers' individual yields for wheat and maize are multiplied by the average defined crop price minus the respective variable production costs (*i.e.*, costs for ploughing, sowing, irrigation and fertilising, plant protection, intertillage, harvesting and other costs for employees and rented machinery). As the production costs were itemised in the questionnaire, they were converted into the unit *yuán* per *mŭ*, then summarised.

In order to estimate the farm's profitability while assessing opportunity costs for family labour, the stated family labour input in days respectively hours of work for each production step was added and converted into the unit hours per *mŭ*, assuming a daily agricultural workload of eight hours. Then, to see how opportunity costs change the crops' SGM, realistic hourly wage scenarios were calculated as estimates of costs and used for advanced calculations with the SGM approach.

Similar to the Nitrogen Use Efficiency, the gross margin indicates the efficiency of the nitrogen input to yield ratio, but additionally, it takes the factor price and product price into account. On the one hand, there is no doubt that yield and nitrogen input strongly influence the resulting gross margin. On the other, there might be other factors or common characteristics of more, as well as less successful farm households in crop cultivation.

Based on the results of the Nitrogen Use Efficiency calculations for farmers' stated fertilisation amounts and the direct cost calculation using the Standard Gross Margin approach, there will be evidence regarding the farms' profitability and efficiency. In order to continue the social and cognitive analyses in line with the theoretical approach, bi- and multivariate methods are again needed. Below, analyses of the attitudinal items will reveal inherent reasons for farmers' behaviour.

Hence, in particular, factor analyses are necessary to reduce the number of items to the condensed latent variables that constitute the underlying reasons for certain decisions.

4.1.4 Factor Analysis of agri-environmental attitudes and *guānxi*-traits

In order to explain human decision-making and other social phenomena, various social and cognitive items were taken in consideration to suggest possible latent determinants. Thus, the items set of agri-environmental attitudes was tested for certain underlying response behaviours, as was the set of *guānxi* items and fundamental values.

A Factor Analysis (FA) searches for common variations in responses. A new set of latent variables (or factors) is extracted from a set of variables that are assumed to belong together. Hence, the factor analysis is a structure-detecting methodology that reduces a larger number of variables to a smaller number of factors containing (almost) the same information and providing a more manageable number of variables than the original set. Thus, communalities are determined and remaining variables left unexplained as errors (*cf.* Backhaus *et al.* 2000).

Due to its structure-detecting character, FA is particularly applicable for building latent variables out of agri-environmental attitude items and *guānxi* trait items. In the case of fundamental value items, the Similarity Structure Analysis (SSA) is used instead in order to evaluate farmers' value position within the value cycle (for more information, see Section 4.1.5 below).

The results of the FA indicate patterns of thought in certain response behaviours. Each factor can be described based on the composed items and their theoretical design. The explorative extraction of latent variables from the statements sets provides condensed factors, which can be used to explain underlying perceptions of different response types[37]. The advantage is that the limited number of factors can be used for further analyses and prevent cross-loadings (*cf.* Backhaus *et al.* 2000).

---

[37] Exploratory Factor Analysis (EFA) is preferred to Confirmatory Factor Analysis (CFA). Although the indicator variables were indeed selected on the basis of a prior theory, it was assumed that the factors do not load as predicted due to the different cultural and social context.

In order to extract the factors, the axes of variation of the variables (here the variations on the measured Likert scales) rotate to a new set of orthogonal axes. The order of the new axes summarises decreasing proportions of the variation. Thus, each latent variable is assumed to account for covariance in a group of observed variables (*cf.* Backhaus *et al.* 2000).

The statistical quality criteria of factors are (1) the Eigenvalue, (2) the explained variance, (3) the Kaiser-Meyer-Olkin (KMO) measure and (4) the statistical significance (*cf.* Backhaus *et al.* 2000).

The Eigenvalue is a minimum value to be extracted and results from the correlation of the selected variables. Thus, the Eigenvalue measures the relative weight of the extracted factors; thus, it explains parts of the total variance. The Eigenvalue should be less than 1 (scree test[38]).

The total explained variance of all factors is directly linked to the method of extraction and also to considerations regarding the communalities (h^2), expressing the common factor variance as a proportion of the total variance. Since not all selected variables were used for the FA, h^2 is often less than 1 ($h^2 < 100 \%$).

The KMO measure is a measure of sampling adequacy of the data set and correlation matrix used for the factor analysis. The KMO measure ranges from 0 to 1. KMO > 0.6 is desirable.

Statistical significance is measured by the Bartlett's test of sphericity (χ^2). It assumes a normal distribution and tests whether there is cross-correlation between the variables. Thus, it determines whether the included variables are homogenous in their variances and whether the correlation matrix was qualified for factor analysis (*i.e.*, correlation coefficients of r > 0.7 have a better level of significance). The level of significance of the test statistic is at best σ > 0.05 (*cf.* Backhaus *et al.* 2000).

The reliability of the internal consistency of the single factors is tested by Cronbach's Alpha; α = 0.65 indicates a reliability of 65 percent, so that the higher the percentage, the more reliable the factor.

---

[38] The scree test is a graphical method of determining the optimal number of factors to be extracted based on their Eigenvalue.

As already mentioned, fundamental values are analysed by Similarity Structure Analysis (SSA) in order to compare farmers' value position with the universal value cycle described in the theoretical section. Thus, the underlying latent variables are known and will be the same as in theory, yet will differ according to the strength of their occurrence. The use of this methodology has been widely tested in the research of fundamental values since only comparison to the theory – which has been universally verified for all cultures – will allow substantiated interpretations.

4.1.5 Similarity Structure Analysis with fundamental value items

The objective of the Similarity Structure Analysis (SSA)[39] is to evaluate farmers' value positions within the value cycle. To this end, a two-dimensional spatial representation of the correlations among the 21 single values is examined. As fundamental values were investigated with a non-metric multidimensional scaling technique, it was possible to represent all the values simultaneously as points in multidimensional space. The distances between the points reflect the empirical relations among the values. Thus, the more similar two values are, the higher the intercorrelation between their ratings and the more similar their pattern of correlations with all other values (Schwartz 1994).

SSA is a variant of Multiple Dimensional Scaling (MDS), which was developed by Guttman (1968; *cf.* Borg and Groenen 2005). MDS requires similarity of opinions among the respondents. The questioning method is described above in Chapter 3.2 (Questionnaire design). The analysis is an exploratory ordination method that enables values to cluster around multivariate objects. At the same time, MDS avails itself of an analysis technique similar to FA; as a result, a matrix of Pearson correlations is produced between the items. However, FA is metric, whereas in most cases SSA is a nonmetric ordinal MDS procedure. Hence, defined results cannot always be expected since the represented spaces are of lower dimensional representation. Moreover, it is the distance between the vectors' endpoints that is

---

[39] Equivalently to Similarity Structure Analysis (SSA), some authors use the term Smallest Space Analysis (SSA). According to Borg and Groenen (2005), both terms describe the same geometric analysis model for testing hypotheses on correlations with multidimensional scaling method.

crucial, rather than the direction of the vectors (for detailed information, see Borg and Groenen 2005).

The formula for running the nonmetric MDS procedure was taken from Strack (2010), which was based on Schwartz's (1992; Schwartz *et al.* 2001) scaling technique but is more suitable for further analysis. The formula itself was determined by FA from the four rounds of the European Social Survey (ESS 2002-2008/9)[40] and includes weightings for each of the 21 ipsative value items[41] (Strack 2010). Based on this formula, the generation of two axes in the value cycle ('Traditional axis'; 'Universal axis') enables direct correlations.

According to the theory and as already designated by Schwartz (2006), SSA is most suitable for analysing fundamental value items. In value theory, it is assumed that the ten motivational value types presented are inherent to every individual, but at different intensities. Thus, SSA is a more appopriate tool than FA since the distance between the values is more meaningful than the generation of latent factors. Rather, the nonmetric multidimensional scaling technique maps items as points in a multidimensional space such that the distances between the points reflect the interrelations among the items. The more similar the theoretical conceptions of any two items are, the closer their locations should be in the multidimensional space.

Thus, SSA provides two-dimensional spatial maps of relations among values, but without partition lines. The a priori assignment of items to values guides the partitioning of the maps (Schwartz 2006). Since this kind of data clustering is used to assess relationships in a coordinate system with several axes (one for each variable),

---

[40] The European Social Survey (ESS) is a biennial multicountry survey that covers more than 30 nations and is designed to evaluate the interaction between Europe's changing institutions and the attitudes, beliefs and behaviour patterns of its diverse populations. The first round was fielded in 2002/2003; the fourth in 2008/2009. For further information see www.europeansocial survey.org/.

[41] Ipsation is defined through the subtraction of the mean personal agreement from each item. The ipsation of ratings is necessary to eliminate the high percentage of acquiescence that generally exists in importance rankings. Furthermore, ipsated scores give Eigenvalues, which show an impressive elbow in the scree test, the basis for extracting exactly two factors (see also Strack *et al.* 2008)

the analysis will show where the Chinese farmers' average value position is located in the general cycle.

In order to compare the fundamental value position of the Chinese farmers with farmers in other (in this case) European countries, the means of the value items of the Chinese farmers is compared to the means of the value items from a reanalysis of the PVQ 21 within the first four rounds of the European Social Survey (33 countries). This reanalysis is conducted according to Strack's (2010) formula. This is possible because of the proven replicability of the Schwartz' universal value structure in different cultures and because of the high quality of the questionnaire translations, with regard to culturally sensitive issues (Schwartz 1992; Strack *et al.* 2008).

Afterwards, correlations with the extracted latent *guānxi* variables and agri-environmental attitude factors are envisaged in order to test bivariate relationships as such. Then, the relevant variables for the structural equation modelling can be taken as decision-making variables for any manifest variable selected. Thus, the correlations will independently show, whether there is a relationship between cognitive values and social relationships or cognitive values and agri-environmental attitudes.

4.1.6 Correlations with the value cycle

Thus, the correlations of the generated *guānxi* factors and agri-environmental factors with the value cycle, or the two value axes, will demonstrate linear relationships between farmers' social and environmental attitudes and their value positions.

Correlations measure the degree of dependency between two variables, giving Pearson correlation coefficients r from +1 to −1. If r is near zero, there is no correlation. In order to assess the probability that an observed correlation has occurred by chance, one referes to the significance level p. If $p < 0$, a linear correlation exists; if $p < 0.05$, results are moderately significant; if $p < 0.01$, results are quite significant; and if $p < 0.001$, the results are highly significant. Since this does not indicate whether the relationships between the variables are positive or negative, the two-tailed test was applied (*cf.* Backhaus *et al.* 2000).

In addition to the correlation matrix, graphic charts represent the correlating variables within the two value axes. Thus, any correlation is an intersection of both axes with the value cycle. For example, a positive correlation of an item with both the 'Traditional axis' and the 'Universal axis', refers to a value position that is situated in the first quadrant of the coordinate system, *i.e.*, values of benevolence, tradition and conformity. The exact position depends on the particular numerical values.

Complex dependencies between several latent and selected manifest variables are then tested with a structural equation model including economic, social and cognitive variables. Since all variables used have previously been analysed in detail, this model will focus on their interdependencies and relationships with the aim of demonstrating the influencing determinants, including the inherent ones that are relevant for each observable decision.

4.1.7 Structural equation modelling of economic, social and cognitive variables

The final analysis uses causal structural equation modelling (SEM) in order to verify the relationships between variables that will help to prove the hypothetical assumptions of the theoretical model.

The variables used for the SEM are different and comply with the hypothetical model in Chapter 2.4 (Figure 4): On the one side are the manifest objective variables, such as household income and sociodemographic variables (gender, age, education, *etc.*), as well as the amount of applied nitrogen fertilisers and farmers' willingness to pay for clean drinking water; on the other side are the latent variables, which measure respondent's subjective attitudes and which in this model refer to their fundamental values, their *guānxi* orientation and their agri-environmental position.

The model approach uses the partial least squares (PLS) method. PLS combines path, principal component and regression analysis in a single operation in order to examine the relationships among the latent constructs in particular (Albersmeier *et al.* 2009). Moreover, the PLS method is especially suitable for very complex and explorative studies and has minimal requirements as to residual distributions and sample size (Chin 1998). The programme used was SmartPLS Version 2.0 (M3).[42]

The analysis of the SEM itself is conducted in two stages: First, the measurement model is evaluated to ascertain the reliability and validity of the measurement instruments. Then, the structural model of the relationships between the constructs is tested according to the quality criteria.

Since the measurement model reflects the relationship between manifest and latent variables, it is evaluated by examining in particular the individual item reliabilities, internal consistency and discriminant validity of the measurements.

Items are defined reliable when all factor loadings of the items on their respective constructs exceed at least the critical value of 0.6, or, when more than 60 percent of variance can be explained (Hair 1998). Internal consistency is evaluated using Cronbach's Alpha; if $\alpha > 0.6$, all indicator items belonging to a latent variable are reliable. According to Fornell and Larcker (1981), the indicator construct loading on a latent variable (composite reliability) is reliable with values exceeding 0.7. The last evaluation criterion for the measurement model is discriminant validity, which is evaluated by the average variance extracted from the contracts (AVE). The average variance shared between a construct and its items is good if the error variance is less than 50 percent (Chin 1998).

In order to avoid double loading and non-loading of the model, minor modifications are necessary. In this way, the item measurements demonstrate acceptable levels of fit and reliability. Hence, whereas the measurement model reflects the internal consistency between latent and manifest variables, the structural model describes causal relationships between the individual latent variables.

According to Götz (2004), the path coefficients are standardised regression coefficients which can be evaluated like beta weights (β), showing the direct effect of an independent variable on a dependent one in the model. They should reach at least 0.1 (Sellin 1994). Bootstrapping is applied to evaluate the significance of the

---

[42] SmartPLS 2.0 (M3) was developed by the Institute of Operations Management and Organisation of the University of Hamburg (Germany) (Ringle *et al.* 2005)

path estimates. The R-squared values show the quality of the extracted endogenous latent variables and their explanatory power (Backhaus *et al.* 2000). To determine the significance of the substantial construct and thus the impact of the exogenous variables on the endogenous variables, the effect size (f^2) is also tested. This measures the R-squared values with and without the influence of exogenous latent variables (total effects) according to the formula $f^2 = \frac{R^2 included - R^2 excluded}{1 - R^2 included}$.

The substantial constructs are significant with endogenous variables measuring $f^2 > 0.02$.

Subsequent to the evaluation of the measurement and the structural model, the reliable paths are explained and interpreted. The results yielded by these data analysis methods are presented below. Preliminary interpretations and explanations are given directly within the respective subchapters.

4.2 Household and farm characteristics

In order to arrange the results of the agro-economic data, a brief sample description and selected frequency analyses and calculations will give an overview of the farm structures and main household characteristics.

Table 9   Farm household characteristics

	Huimin		Shouguang	
	n=641	*Std. Dev.*	n=698	*Std. Dev.*
Household members	4.2	*1.4*	3.6	*1.3*
Cultivated farm land [*mǔ*]	8.4 (0.6 ha)	*4.7*	6.5 (0.4 ha)	*6.5*
Size of the biggest wheat/ maize plot [*mǔ*]	2.5 (0.2 ha)	*2.4*	3.4 (0.2 ha)	*2.8*
Family labour input on that plot [days/ *mǔ*]	4.7		5.4	
Livestock production [in % of farm household]	33.5		10.6	
Fowl [%]	17.7		45.9	
Cows [%]	52.6		14.9	
Pigs [%]	15.3		28.4	
Manure used on field [%]	93.1		76.0	
Manure sold [%]	1.4		10.7	

As can be seen in Table 9, the average farm household includes roughly three to four family members. The small-scale farms polled cultivate on average 0.5 ha land, of which 0.2 ha is used for wheat and maize production. In Huimin, other land is cultivated with cotton (78 %), mulberry (5 %) or poplar; in Shouguang, apple (24 %), tomatoes (17 %), cotton (15 %) and cucumber (7 %) is produced in addition to grain crops, whereas cotton is the cash crop mainly planted on pig plots. As explained above, the land itself is generally contracted from the village to each Hùkǒu-registered inhabitant. This is the case for 98 percent of the land use in Huimin and 90 percent in Shouguang. The remaining use rights stem from renting land or other contracts.

In Huimin 34 percent of farmers and in Shouguang 11 percent stated that they also keep livestock – mainly fowl, cows and pigs. In Huimin, the manure these animals produce is used almost exclusively for fertilising the fields. In contrast, in Shouguang some farmers sell some or even all of their pig or fowl manure.

The head of the farm household[43] is on average 50 years old, male (in more than 80 percent of cases) and has had more than seven years of education (cf. Table 10). Female heads of households were younger in both counties and usually less educated (cf. Noack et al. 2011). High standard deviations for years of education derive from the high percentage of farmers who have never attended school. Particularly in Huimin, this number is quite high (13 % overall and 27 % for female heads of households; cf. Noack et al. 2011). As a consequence, more than two-thirds of heads of the households work full-time on their farms, another entire 20 percent work part-time and more than 6 percent are employed in non-farming activities.

Table 10 Heads of the farm households

		Huimin		Shouguang	
		n=629	Std. Dev.	n=682	Std. Dev
Gender [% male]		81.7		93.3	
Age [in years]		49.8	10.7	51.4	10.1
Education [in years]		6.2	3.4	7.2	2.9
No education [in %]		13.0		5.3	
Labour time on farm [in %]:	Full-time	71.5		67.2	
	Part-time	19.7		24.0	
	Non-farming	6.2		6.9	

---

[43] The head of the farm household is the survey respondent who was qualified to answer the full questionnaire, that is the one who managed the farm. Of course, the term 'head of a household' might also refer to another, socio-culturally identified household member. Therefore, data concerning the head of the household are only used for the comprehensive agronomic part of the large survey. Data regarding the socio-psychological part refer to the respondent as an individual. The respondents in this smaller sample are described separately in Section 4.5.1.

Furthermore, there are highly significant positive correlations between the age of the heads of the households and the percentage of working time they spend on the farm. The older the family head, the more likely he or she is to spend a high percentage of working time on the farm; the younger ones, however, are more likely to have off-farm jobs. Also better-educated family heads are more likely to work part- or full-time in non-farming sectors. They work mainly in the same townships, but if labour migration occurs, farmers in Huimin are more mobile and even seek work in other counties. Most of them work in the engineering or construction sector (36.5 %) and other enterprises (22.1 %), others in wholesale and retail trade (9.5 %) or in transportation (8.7 %). The rest work as craftsman (7.6 %) and or in public institutions (4.9 %) (*cf.* Noack *et al.* 2011). Unfortunately, no data was available to measure the total household income; nor was it possible to ascertain the share of agricultural returns or income from other working activities or income from other household or family members.

4.3 Agronomic status quo of wheat and maize production

According to the overall aim of the project and as already described in the section on research framework and methodology, the agronomic part of this study focuses only on double crop rotations of winter wheat and summer maize, which is sweet corn.

Winter wheat is planted in late October and harvested by combined harvester in May in about 96 percent of the farms. Summer maize is planted by hand directly into the wheat residues from mid-May to early June. Ripe corncobs are removed from the plant manually from late September to early October. The corn stover is collected as fodder.

4.3.1 Achieved yields of wheat and maize production and nitrogen demands

Table 11 shows that on average the yields from both wheat and maize production are quite good in both counties when one takes into consideration that precision farming is not practised and that most work on these small-scale farms is manually by family members instead of by professional labourers or machines that accurately apply seeds, fertilisers or agro-chemicals.

Comparing both counties, the average yields were lower in Huimin than in Shouguang. Whereas farmers reach about 6 t/ ha of winter wheat in Huimin, more than 7 t/ ha was harvested in Shouguang. The same is true for corn. While in Huimin, not even 7 t/ ha were produced in 2009, farmers in Shouguang were able to harvest more than 8 t/ ha. Regarding standard deviations, the figures show large ranges. Maximum values expose extremely high yields and minimum values demonstrate great yield losses for some farmers, in particular in wheat production. Yield losses could be explained by the drought that occured at the peak of wheat season in February 2009[44] and certain sites were more vulnerable than others. The very high yield values result from calculations with very small plot sizes. Most of the plots are smaller than 0.2 hectare; 7 percent are even smaller than 1 *mŭ* (0.7 ha). Interviewees gave their agronomic figures in *jīn* per *mŭ*, making measure translations necessary. However, due to the very small plots, the labour, also the production intensity per *mŭ* is more precise.

Table 11   Achieved yields [in t/ ha]

	Huimin		Shouguang	
	Winter wheat *n=620*	Summer maize *n=622*	Winter wheat *n=655*	Summer maize *n=453*
Average yields	6.0	6.6	7.1	8.2
Std. Dev.	*1.2*	*1.0*	*1.2*	*1.0*
Minimum	0.5	2.8	0.5	1.8
Maximum	15.0	10.2	13.5	11.3
N uptake [kg N/ ha]	138.0	165.0	163.3	205.0
Annually N uptake	303		368.3	

Note: N uptake (crop products, incl. residues) winter wheat 23 kg N/ t, corn maize (dry matter) 25 kg N/ t (KTBL 2005)

---

[44] During the winter wheat production season 2008/ 2009 drought conditions developed over several months in northern China with about 11 million hectares affected (50 to 80 % below normal). Irrigation efforts and rainmaking technology tided farmers over until March, when the drought ended (USDA 2009).

Nevertheless, in order to produce such respectable yield amounts, sufficient mineral nitrogen and/ or livestock manure amounts had to be applied. The nitrogen demand is measured by the nitrogen uptake of the harvested crops and removed residues. For winter wheat, the nitrogen uptake is about 23 kg N/ t and for summer maize (sweet corn), it is about 25 kg N/ t. Related to the average yields produced, this would mean, for Huimin that from any fertiliser source about 138 kg N/ ha is needed to produce winter wheat and about 165 kg N/ ha to produce maize. Since the average stated and hence expected yields are higher in Shouguang, more nutrients are removed and the nitrogen demand is comparatively higher – at least 163 kg N/ ha for wheat and 116 kg N/ ha for maize production. In a winter wheat and summer maize double-cropping system, the nitrogen demands are added to an annual demand of 303 kg N/ ha in Huimin and not less than 368 kg N/ ha in Shouguang. Concerning these figures, it has to be mentioned that according to the KTBL (2005) any fertilisation demand is calculated only by the dry matter nitrogen uptake of the respective plants. Nutrient inputs from nitrogen fixation within the soil or nitrogen emissions to the atmosphere were not taken into account; nor were processes of nitrogen leaching or other volatisation of the applied nitrogen. Nevertheless, for this demonstrative and transdisciplinary purpose, the total average assumed figure for nitrogen uptake of dry matter with harvest removal fits.

In the following, farmers' fertilisation practice is analysed and evaluated. The information gained is helpful to deduce farmers' fertilisation knowledge from their practical performance. In addition, the analysis of farmers' management support reveals the quality of information used.

4.3.2 Fertilisation management – practice, knowledge and decision making

Information about farmers' fertilisation management gained by uni- and bivariate analyses of variables from the first part of the questionnaire describe the fertilisation practice. In addition, the frequency analysis and mean values are supported by explanations given by farmers during the group discussions, which was very helpful for interpretating the stated fertilisation behaviour.

In general, the results concerning fertilisation practices reveal that all the farmers surveyed fertilise their fields with chemical fertilisers. Bivariate analysis showed that the fertiliser types correlate significantly with the season during which fertilisation occured. Detailed univariate analysis of various fertilisation variables draws a closer picture of the farmers' fertilisation management.

In general, before sowing winter wheat in late October, farmers apply a base compound fertiliser of nitrogen, phosphorus and potassium (NPK) and a diammonium phosphate fertiliser (DAP). In some cases, urea is used in addition to or alternatively to NPK (see Table 12). Most farmers apply at least one more topdressing (urea) in the re-greening growth stage in March.

Base fertilisers for the subsequent summer maize production is applied directly after wheat harvesting, prior to planting the maize (often without tillage) in late May or early June, either with urea or NPK fertiliser; additionally 10 percent fertilise with DAP only. At the first leaf stage in August, urea, but also NPK, is applied as top fertilisation. Moreover, 14 percent stated that they also apply urea at the jointing or booting stage as a second topdressing.

Table 12   Most frequently used compound fertilisers at basic fertilisation and growing stage

	Huimin		Shouguang	
	Winter wheat	Summer maize	Winter wheat	Summer maize
Base	59 % DAP	40 % urea	46 % NPK	54 % NPK
fertilisation	25 % NPK	29 % NPK	31 % urea	20 % DAP
	10 % urea	25 % DAP	13 % DAP	11 % urea
Growing	91 % urea	78 % urea	93 % urea	42 % urea
stage		16 % NPK		36 % NPK
				12 % DAP

Note: Other nutrient fertilisers are rarlely used

However, ideally, a double-cropping system would require at least four fertilisations and a nutrient management that is adjusted to the nutrients available in the soils.

Frequency analyses showed in addition that some farmers fertilise with manure from poultry, pigs, cows or other organic residues from crop plants or even human excrement. Moreover, farmers and local extention officials stated in personal interviews and group discussions that farmers irrigate their fields with surface water or pump water from local wells. However, the timing of such irrigation is not up to the farmers themselves; they have to wait for the water channels next to their fields to be flooded. In Huimin, irrigation water comes from the Yellow River and is limited in amount. Thus, it is frequently impossible for farmers to synchronise fertilisation and irrigation, which does not facilitate good fertilisation management, even if knowledge were available.

Consequently, farmers' fertilisation management is restricted in many ways. They have only the nutrient information on the fertiliser packages and their routine practices. Due to a lack of agricultural training, that takes into account farmers' knowledge levels and their comprehension abilities, discussions gave evidence that some farmers are able neither to understand the effects of the respective nutrients in the fertiliser products nor to calculate the amounts that might comply with best practices. "What I need is a hands-on guide about fertilising; don't tell me what is N, P or K; just show me a card with simple information written on it, such as how much diammonium or urea I shoud apply" (Farmer 1, Shouguang, who was experiencing reduced yield output in spite of having attended fertilisation training organised by the CCAP). In fact, some farmers just complain about the fertiliser quality or ascribe respective fertilisation effects solely to the quality or applied amount of the fertiliser.

Since farmers cannot coordinate irrigation with fertilisation, the discussions gave evidence that most think the amount of fertilisers used determines the output. "[..] The amount of fertiliser I used last year is in strict accordance with the recommendation of the training class, so I think the recommended amount of fertilisation is not enough" (Farmer 9, Huimin who was experiencing reduced yield output in spite of having attended fertilisation trainings organised by the CCAP). In this context, several farmers emphasised their established practices and were afraid of reduced yields. "We often fertilise according to habit or to advice from others. You [the extension person] should specify what kind of fertiliser we should use because your recommendation is less than we usually apply" (Farmer 1, Huimin, who had not followed the recommendations given during the special training on the CCAP's experimental design).

Additional descriptive analyses of the smaller sample from the second socio-psychological section of the questionnaire regarding the farmers' annual production decisions (n=394) affirm that, in addition to farmers' own farming experiences (*i.e.*, yields from the last year) and basic production conditions, like crop rotations and prices, neighbours play a remarkable role in farmers' decisions (12 %) (Figure 8).

Figure 8   Decision-making determinants of farmers' annual production

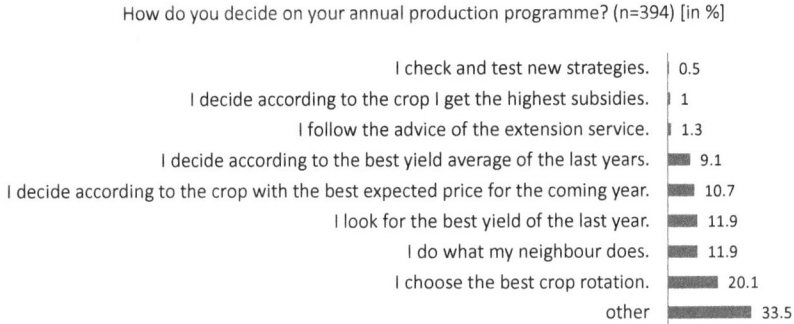

How do you decide on your annual production programme? (n=394) [in %]

I check and test new strategies.	0.5
I decide according to the crop I get the highest subsidies.	1
I follow the advice of the extension service.	1.3
I decide according to the best yield average of the last years.	9.1
I decide according to the crop with the best expected price for the coming year.	10.7
I look for the best yield of the last year.	11.9
I do what my neighbour does.	11.9
I choose the best crop rotation.	20.1
other	33.5

The graph also shows clearly that extension services have a negligible influence of just 1 percent, which coincides with the statements made by farmers in the group discussions. It was found that, due to failures they have experienced, farmers have difficulty following the advice given in extension trainings.

In particular, regarding farmers' decision-making support referring to their fertilisation management, nearly two-thirds of the respondents stated that their fertiliser management is based on established habits and traditions (see Figure 9).

Figure 9   Farmers' main support in nitrogen- and manure management

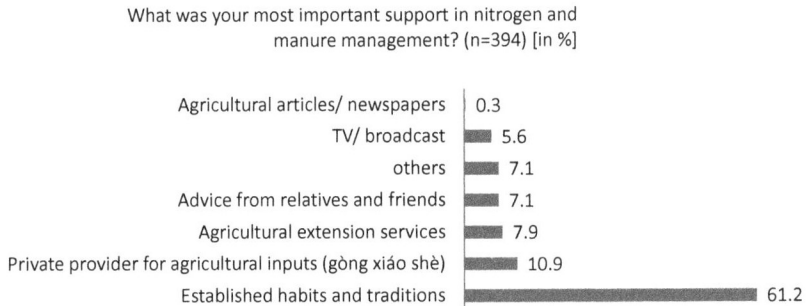

What was your most important support in nitrogen and manure management? (n=394) [in %]

Agricultural articles/ newspapers	0.3
TV/ broadcast	5.6
others	7.1
Advice from relatives and friends	7.1
Agricultural extension services	7.9
Private provider for agricultural inputs (gòng xiáo shè)	10.9
Established habits and traditions	61.2

The remaining gets their support from private providers (11 %) and/ or agricultural extension services (8 %). Again, about 7 percent rely on relatives and friends, while 6 percent get information from the media.

Thus, since detailed knowledge on nutrient processes is not available to them, farmers' fertilisation management is dominated by established habits and traditions. Nevertheless, farmers have realised over time that fertilisation is a success factor for profitable production. They would like to know more about the processes and impacts of fertilisers to increase its efficiency, but their decisions are influenced by uncertainty and missing know-how. Furthermore, they do not trust or follow the advice of the agricultural extension services since they have experienced reduced output after following this advice.

During the group discussion, farmers offered several explanations for this: (1) They did not comprehend the advice fully and were not able to follow it precisely; (2) their scope of action was restricted; for instance, external influences (*e.g.*, irrigation) were not within their power, resulting in extreme coping strategies based on farmers' own understanding of interrelationships; as in a consequence, (3) in accordance with the motto "the more the merrier", farmers applied more fertilisers, often at unfavourable growing stages. Furthermore, they continue to rely on other available – and, for them, more trustworthy – sources of information, which often did not align with best-practice knowledge.

The next section discusses the nitrogen amounts applied to the double-cropping system as a result of the fertilisation management farmers conducted based on their lack of knowledge and uncertainty about application practices, as well as risk-averse behaviours.

4.3.3 Dimensions of nitrogen overuse

In the first and second columns of Table 13 are the mean values and respective quartiles of farmers' applied nitrogen amounts in maize and wheat production, for the two counties surveyed. The mineral nitrogen amounts were calculated by adding of the nitrogen contents of all used fertiliser types (in percentage). The third column shows the mineral nitrogen amounts applied to the double-cropping system overall and results from adding the nitrogen amounts for both crops. The fourth column shows the estimated nitrogen amounts from organic manure applied annually. The estimate is based on the annual livestock inventory of the farm and the percentage of manure used on the fields: The entire annual amount of organic nitrogen in manure was estimated on the basis of the German system *Dungeinheit*.[45] The unit *Dungeinheit* (DE) takes into account the variations in nitrogen contents of different livestock excreta. Thus, it refers to the number and different kinds of animals stated in the survey. Since one DE contains 80 kg N and 70 kg P_2O_5, the DE of one fattening pig is, for example 0.14, which equals 11.2 kg nitrogen and 9.8 kg phosphorus per animal. Furthermore, the percentage of manure applied to the fields must also be taken into account since some farms also discard or sell the animal faeces to vegetable farmers or biogas plants and since we wanted to be sure that the amount applied on the fields is independent of the animal husbandry dimension.

Table 13   Annual applied nitrogen amounts and losses [in kg/ ha]

	Mineral N on winter wheat	Mineral N on summer maize	Mineral N on double crop system	Organic N [estimated]	Total N [calculated]		N losses [calculated]
Huimin	*n=312*	*n=308*	*n=620*	*n=177*			
Mean	264.6	274.1	**538.7**	**168.6**	**707.3**	→	**404.3**
Std. Dev.	*127.2*	*122.6*		*164.8*			
Quartile							
25	171.0	194.0	365.0	76.4	441.4		138.4
50	253.8	264.0	517.8	120.0	637.8		334.8
75	345.0	345.0	690.0	210.0	900.0		597.0
Shouguang	*n=208*	*n=245*	*n=453*	*n=34*			
Mean	185.4	194.3	**379.7**	**616.6**	**996.3**	→	**627.7**
Std. Dev.	*100.4*	*108.2*		*932.9*			
Quartile							
25	112.5	112.5	225.0	81.0	306.0		-62.3
50	153.0	171.9	324.9	195.4	895.2		526.9
75	232.9	252.1	485.0	746.3	1231.3		863.0

Note: For N uptake by the plants, see Table 11

The realisable sample size for organic nitrogen from manure application is comparatively small due to sampling problems and the resulting missing values

---

[45] The *'Dungeinheit'* was a key converter that is originally used in organic farming to determine the maximal stocking rate (1.4 DE/ ha) for different types of animals.

(n=211). Further calculations including nitrogen from organic manure are conducted using mean values instead of the individual cases. Being aware of the limitations, quartiles of mean values are used for different fertilisation scenarios to create an impression on the extent and variations of the total nitrogen amounts applied to the fields.

The total nitrogen amounts encompass mineral and organic nitrogen on the double-cropping system and the last column sums up the total nitrogen losses due to overfertilisation. It shows the total amount of fertiliser applied for the wheat and maize double-cropping system investigated, as well as the estimated amount of manure applied to the same fields, less the nitrogen uptake of the plants, which was calculated above in Table 11.

Table 13 shows that farmers in Huimin County apply about 30 percent more nitrogen from mineral fertilisers on the double-cropping system of wheat and maize production than farmers in Shouguang. If no additional manure is applied, the mean nitrogen fertilisation amount in Shouguang of 380 kg N/ ha nearly equals the nitrogen uptake by the harvested products (368 kg N/ ha; cf. Table 11). Thus, focusing only on the average figures, farmers seem to fertilise in a crop-adapted manner. Nevertheless, considering the high range of deviations and the information on farmers' management practice given above, the variation indicates that this seems to be a statistical mean value balancing the lower and upper average spikes rather than farmers' optimised strategy. However, in Huimin nitrogen overfertilisation from mineral fertilisers is more pronounced. Assuming the calculated nitrogen uptake of 303 kg N/ ha in Huimin County (cf. Table 11), a remarkable 235 kg N/ ha volatilises in the ecosystem, from mineral nitrogen fertilisation alone.

Taking into account the average figures for organic nitrogen from manure deposited on the fields through animal husbandry, the figures in Shouguang show higher statistical values than in Huimin since more livestock is kept in Shouguang. By adding the mean organic nitrogen values to the nitrogen values from mineral fertilisation, in Huimin there are total nitrogen values of 707 kg N/ ha, while in Shouguang there were 996 kg N/ ha; this in turn leads to considerable loss estimations of 404 kg N/ ha in Huimin and 628 kg N/ ha in Shouguang. Since nitrogen amounts from manure were estimated and added as mean values, any conclusions drawn from these figures must be cautious. However, if one examines only those scenarios involving lower organic manure application amounts (the lower 25 % of the average values), in Huimin, loss rates of more than 138 kg N/ ha are still found, equalling the nitrogen uptake of winter wheat in this region. In Shouguang, the standard deviations of manure application show greater variations; the lower 25 percent of the average actually demonstrates a nitrogen demand. However, the remaining nutrient depositions should be sufficient to cover this crop demand according to the soil sample results found by soil scientists from cooperating on our project.[46] In contrast, the upper 75 percent of average nitrogen losses indicate excessive environmental damage of 863 kg N/ ha.

4.3.4 Potential to increase the apparent Nitrogen Use Efficiency

Regarding the expected yield amounts and applied mineral nitrogen fertilisers, the apparent Nitrogen Use Efficiency of the crop system is estimated using the formula described in Section 4.1.2.

As in Table 13, the results shown in Table 14 refer to remarkable nitrogen losses, although these calculations do not include nitrogen from organic manure.

Table 14   Apparent Nitrogen Use Efficiency

	Huimin		Shouguang	
	Winter wheat n=620	Summer maize n=622	Winter wheat n=655	Summer maize n=453
Average yields	6.0	6.6	7.1	8.2
Applied mineral N	264.6	274.1	185.4	194.3
aNUE [%]	52	60	88	100

Note: N uptake (crop products, incl. residues) winter wheat 23 kg N/ t, corn maize (dry matter) 25 kg N/ t (KTBL 2005)

---

[46] *Cf.* research of our cooperative project partners Tobias Hartman and Prof. Dr. Torsten Müller from the Institute of Crop Science, University of Hohenheim, Germany, and Maximilian Hofmeier, Lisa Heimann, Dr. Marco Roelcke and Prof. Dr. Rolf Nieder from the Institute for Geoecology, Technical University of Braunschweig, Germany.

For summer maize produced in Shouguang, nitrogen fertilisers seem to be used efficiently (disregarding nitrogen being applied by manure, that is stated to be of higher relevance in Shouguang). Hence, the calculated aNUE in Shouguang is on average better than that in Huimin.

Furthermore, the results demonstrate a slightly better use efficiency in maize production. If nitrogen from manure were added, the aNUE would be lower still.

To conclude, the farmers' fertilisation practice is not very well adapted to the real situation, and there is still a given potential to conserve mineral nitrogen. It should be noted also that the higher aNUE does not diminish yields; instead, the yields in Shouguang are better than in Huimin.

Thus, applying less fertiliser will increase the aNUE while avoiding the risk of losing yield outputs. As for cost calculations, the next section focuses on the profitability of the cropping system and the potential for lowering the cost factor of mineral fertilisers in order to increase crop profitability.

4.4 Profitability of the cropping system

In order to calculate the profitability of the cropping system, irrespective of its area and intensity of production, the Standard Gross Margin (SGM) approach is useful. Frequency analyses of the production costs provide insight into the share of the particular cost units.

4.4.1 Standard Gross Margins of winter wheat and summer maize

Based on the data for the production cost components in Chinese agriculture, the Standard Gross Margins calculated are presented in Table 15. They show the profitability of the cropping system and make it possible to identify the main cost factors of the agricultural production. Nevertheless, the farm assets have not been valued in detail; Chinese farms are still family driven and thus based on traditionally grown structures with related problems in surveying the family assets and labour inputs. Therefore, the SGMs are calculated on cost components that are clearly definable in the Chinese cash-crop production process.

Another postulation is that the market return for maize as well as wheat is assessed according to guaranteed prices. China started to set minimum purchasing prices for grain, including wheat and rice, in 2004. When market prices are too low, the government buys wheat from farmers at this state-set guaranteed price, so that farmers will not suffer economic losses from growing grain (Xinhua 2009; People's Daily Online 2010). In 2009, this price for wheat was about 0.86 *yuán/ jīn* (≈ 198 €/ t) (Xinhua 2009; People's Daily Online 2010); for maize 0.88 *yuán/ jīn* for maize[47] (which equals ≈ 201 €/ t)[48] (MOA 2010). However, apparent market prices could have been much higher than the state's minimum purchase prices. Furthermore, local prices differ slightly due to transaction costs as well as transportation costs.

Table 15   SGMs of wheat and maize production

	Huimin		Shouguang	
	Mean	*Std. Deviation*	Mean	*Std. Deviation*
Winter wheat	*(n=620)*		*(n=655)*	
Yield [*jīn/ mǔ*]	797.8	*161.5*	945.6	*156.6*
Return* [¥/ *jīn*]	686.1	*138.9*	813.2	*134.7*
SGM** [¥/ *mǔ*]	**172.8 (258 €/ ha)**	*228.8*	**405.9 (670 €/ ha)**	*192.1*
Quartiles: 25	74.5		316.7	
50	202.4		430.7	
75	311.4		515.5	
Summer maize	*(n=622)*		*(n=453)*	
Yield [*jīn/ mǔ*]	879.1	*137.3*	1095.6	*134.0*
Return* [¥/ *jīn*]	773.6	*120.9*	964.2	*118.0*
SGM** [¥/ *mǔ*]	**582.8 (962 €/ ha)**	*165.3*	**814.2 (1343 €/ ha)**	*181.7*
Quartiles: 25	486.4		726.3	
50	590.8		832.4	
75	693.5		945.5	

*Wheat price 0.86 *yuán/ jīn*; maize price 0.88 *yuán/ jīn*
**Rents and family labour costs are not included for SGM calculations

The figures show that on average farmers in both counties make a profit with both crops. However, maize production is more profitable than wheat. This refers to the positive symbiotic effects that appear from the previously cultivated wheat crop in

---

[47] This is the average wholesale price of medium-class corn in major maize producing regions of China in October 2009. This meant a year-on-year increment of 9.6 percent.

[48] 1 CNY = 0.11 EUR

the double-cropping system. Due to data restrictions, SGMs for the total annual agricultural production in this crop rotation were not available. Nevertheless, some tendencies can be seen in the SGMs.

The average maize return and SGMs are lower in Huimin than in Shouguang. This divergence again reflects the different means of production in the two counties, which result in varying yields. In addition, the standard deviations indicate considerable differences between the counties. Minimum and maximum figures reveal that in some cases farmers in Shouguang seem to make both, high profits and high losses from farming. However, Shouguang farmers are, on average, better off than those in Huimin.

The next section will focus on the question of why farmers in Shouguang make greater profits. This will be explained by a closer look at their mean production as well as their factor cost components as reference figures for comparison. Special attention will be paid to their fertilisation behaviour, since it is assumed that farms' crop profitability is strongly related to farmers' excessive use of fertiliser.

4.4.2 Production costs of wheat and maize production

Mean values of the calculated production costs of winter wheat and summer maize are shown in Tables 16 and 17. The costs of the particular production steps result from calculations with associated cost variables.[49] For example, the costs for seeding are calculated as follows: The seed price is multiplied by the amount of seed sown on the total plot, then added to other expenditures (*e.g.*, machine costs and wages for employees) adjusted for plot size.

Similarly, fertilisation costs are calculated by adding the expenditures for each specific fertiliser type used by the individual farmer to other expenditures for rented machines or employee wages; the total is then, divided by the plot size. Finally, harvesting costs comprise costs for employee wages and machinery costs for combine harvesters.

---

[49] Family labour costs are not included in the calculation because among Chinese farmers, there is no generally admitted cost estimation for the work of family members.

Table 16   Winter wheat production costs [in ¥/ mǔ]

		Huimin			Shouguang	
	N	Mean	Std. Dev.	N	Mean	Std. Dev.
Ploughing	633	99.8	94.3	661	75.9	55.7
Sowing	631	69.2	45.9	633	33.3	18.0
Irrigation	591	53.8	39.4	646	63.9	36.6
Plant protection	623	15.3	12.6	6	7.4	3.8
Intertillage	24	40.8	12.2	5	27.0	14.8
Harvesting	602	57.6	17.7	451	51.9	17.1
Other costs	22	38.1	22.7	48	25.3	13.7
Fertilisation	617	228.2	117.7	585	225.9	110.2
Production costs*	633	**514.1**	109.8	661	**407.6**	150.4
		[848.2 €/ ha]			[672.6 €/ ha]	
Production costs** (means added)		*602.7*			*510.6*	
Fertilisation* [% of total prod. costs]		**44.4**			**55.4**	
Fertilisation** [% of added mean prod. costs]		*37.8*			*44.2*	

*Missing values replaced with zero
Notes: **Missing values replaced with means
a) Land rents and family labour costs are not included.
b) Since differentiation between non-occurring production costs and random missing values was not possible, both possibilities were taken into consideration for the comparative illustration.

Table 17   Summer maize production costs [in ¥/ mǔ]

		Huimin			Shouguang	
	N	Mean	Std. Dev.	N	Mean	Std. Dev.
Ploughing	625	14.5	20.1	455	12.1	15.3
Sowing	625	47.6	24.8	455	38.4	25.4
Irrigation	193	30.3	32.0	330	39.1	27.8
Plant protection	620	21.0	14.8	4	14.3	13.6
Intertillage	7	38.0	30.7	0		
Harvesting	8	49.5	15.3	110	56.6	21.0
Other costs	4	7.6	9.2	22	9.4	5.8
Fertilisation	414	148.0	77.6	150	171.2	85.4
Production costs	625	**191.3**	109.8	455	**149.6**	119.0
		[315.7 €/ ha]			[246.8 €/ ha]	
Production costs* (means added)		*356.4*			*341.1*	
Fertilisation [% of total prod. costs]		**77.4**				
Fertilisation* [% of added mean prod. costs]		*40.5*			*50.2*	

*Missing values replaced with zero
Notes: **Missing values replaced with means
a) Land rents and family labour costs are not included.
b) Since differentiation between non-occurring production costs and random missing values was not possible, both possibilities were taken into consideration for the comparative illustration.

Next to the calculations for the single production costs, the tables shows two different calculations for combined production costs. Due to doubts arising from interrogation and coding issues, it was not possible to differentiate between non-occurring production costs and random missing values. Thus, the tabular presentation takes both possibilities into account. For further calculations and considerations, boldface figures (missing values replaced with zero) are used. These are more realistic since it is reliable that for many families several cost components (intertillage, plant protection *etc.*) do not actually occur. Moreover, land rents and family labour costs are not included and machinery is not widely used among small-scale farmers. Hence, low numbers of cases do not allow calculations with missing values replaced by mean values.

However, in general, the results reveal that production costs for summer maize are somewhat more than one-third of the production costs for winter wheat (Huimin: 37 %; Shouguang: 36 %) (*cf.* maize calculations with missing values replaced by mean values, which reveal production costs for maize of roughly two-thirds those for wheat production – 59 % in Huimin and 67 % in Shouguang).

Irrespective of the calculation, the differences between wheat and maize production costs can be explained by higher ploughing and irrigation costs arising from the double-cropping system itself. Agronomic measures like ploughing and irrigation in times of drought are conducted only once or only at a certain time of the year, independent of the crop itself. For the investigation, the costs of these variables are ascribed to one crop only and are not allocated to both crops. However, despite this non-distinctive variable investigation, the higher expenditures for fertilisers are particularly noticable. For wheat, these are 35 percent higher in Huimin and 24 percent higher in Shouguang. Based on the nitrogen uptake by the plants (see Section 4.3.1), these differences are not justifiable since growing winter wheat would need lower amounts of mineral nitrogen than summer maize production.

While comparing the production costs, the table demonstrates that the major cost fraction is fertilisation. This is true for both crops. Fertilisers for maize cropping represent about two-thirds of all production costs, while this ratio is slightly lower in wheat, at nearly 50 percent. After fertilisation, the next-largest cost component in maize production for both counties is sowing, while for wheat it is ploughing in Huimin and irrigation in Shouguang. Furthermore, plant protection measures are more important in Huimin than in Shouguang. Intertillage as a production concept is rarely used in either area. Harvesting shows very divergent figures for wheat and maize. Maize was generally harvested by family labour in Shouguang to only a slight extent by hired labour. In contrast, wheat harvesting seems to have been contracted out and therefore, in most cases, is done by hired labour, which explains why this is reported as costs.

4.4.3 Family labour input

Moreover, family labour costs occur for the individual production steps. Depending on expenditures for employed labour that is paid together with the use of machines, the family labour can vary greatly. On average, farmers' own family labour input on one *mǔ* for the double crop production in Huimin averages 4.7 days a year and in Shouguang 5.4 days a year (days calculated by hours of workpeaks; *cf.* Table 18). For example, if one assumes daily agricultural work peaks of eight hours on wheat production in Huimin, 22.4 intensive working hours of family labour per *mǔ* is required in addition to the labour time of employed workers operating the rented machines and neighbourly help, which is widespread.[50]

Table 18   Family labour input for wheat and maize production

	Winter wheat		Summer maize	
	Huimin (n=617)	Shouguang (n=585)	Huimin (n=414)	Shouguang (n=150)
Mean [days/ *mǔ*]	2.8	2.6	1.9	2.8
Std. Dev.	6.0	4.7	1.6	2.1
Min	0.3	0.3	0.1	0.2
Max	125.8	77.3	19.4	14.3

Note: The variable day encompasses a working day with a workload of eight hours per day since respondents' statements were roughly estimated in "days" rather than in exact numbers of hours.

---

[50] By comparison, according to KTBL (2005), 9-12 hours/ ha are needed to produce wheat in a fully mechanised agricultural farm. Calculated in days/ *mǔ*, this is nearly a fifteenth of a family workcraft (*i.e.*, 2.7 % of the labour needed for winter wheat in Huimin).

For the entire double crop rotation, at least 37.6 hours per *mŭ* of family labour is spent each year for the agricultural production of small-scale farmers with low mechanisation in Huimin and Shouguang Counties. This is a quite high expenditure of time, when one considers that farmers' wheat and maize plots are on average three *mŭ*, while other crops or livestock account for a further three to four *mŭ* of land. Thus in total, for this time-consuming production, at least two labourers would be necessary. This is, also because the statistical evidence attests to the advanced age of the farmers and thus to their reduced capacity for physical labour. Nevertheless, these farmers also have no choice but to farm, and, as discussed above, the hours they work on the farm are not included in the estimated labour costs. Regardless, due to increased labour migration and the fact mentioned in Chapter 4.2 that in particular the younger household members are more likely to diversify the household's income strategy by off-farm jobs, farm labour will be scarce in future. A calculation of emerging opportunity costs for family labour will demonstrate the decreasing profitability of this production line, assuming increasing wages on the labour market in future.

4.4.4 Profitability development while assessing opportunity costs for labour

In situations of scarcity and in consideration of choices regarding efficiency, opportunity costs play a crucial role. Given today's economic prosperity and rising wages, the alternative costs of family labour time invested in farming instead of in other – better remunerated – employment should also be taken into consideration. Obviously, the value of the best alternative that is not chosen could be expressed in economic terms by assuming a realistic wage for off-farm labour in this region. Wages in China are increasing steadily due to the country's economic transition. As already pointed out in the description of the study area (*cf.* Section 3.1.2) the average disposable income of urban workers in Shandong Province rose by 12 percent in 2010. By contrast, rural wage incomes are less than half as much. According to Banister and Cook (2011), for 2008, the average compensation for employees in the manufacturing sector throughout China was estimated to be

1.36 USD/ hour.[51] This included an hourly wage of 5.25 *yuán/* hour for workers in Township and Village Enterprises (TVEs) and 10.74 *yuán/* hour for urban workers. Assuming eight working hours a day, 42 *yuán/* day could be earned daily in rural TVEs, 86 *yuán/* day in urban manufactures. The huge wage disparities depending on the regional disequilibrium allow calculations with diffferent urban wage incomes. In addition, Shandong is one of the richer and more industrialised provinces in China. Hence, these income figures are reasonable for scenario calculations in this province. In order to calculate the profitability of wheat and maize production in Huimin and Shouguang Counties, the opportunity costs for family labour input in wheat and maize production are calculated for paid wage scenarios of 40, 60 and 80 *yuán/* day.

The proposed rising opportunity costs for family labour stem from descriptions of the labour market in *The Economist* (2010), which estimated an annual growth rate of 20 percent for the manufacturing sector. Moreover, Banister and Cook (2011) observed a growth rate in labour costs from 2002 to 2008 of nearly 100 percent. However, no information is available about the future development of the SGMs; currently, agricultural inputs are subsidisied and fix market prices are guarantied. Therefore, scenario calculations with rising opportunity costs for family labour primarily base on current SGMs. It is assumed that in future, the SGM do not change significantly, as a national policy change towards free markets is not forseeable yet. In addition, the focus of this calculation is more on labour, as rural emigration is a crucial factor determining a farm household's profitability and income situation.

Table 19   Changes in SGMs if opportunity costs for family labour are included

	Winter wheat				Summer maize			
	Huimin (n=620)		Shouguang (n=655)		Huimin (n=622)		Shouguang (n=453)	
	Mean	*Std. Dev.*	Mean	*Std. Dev.*	Mean	*Std. Dev.*	Mean	*Std. Dev.*
SGM	172.8	*(228.8)*	405.9	*(192.1)*	582.8	*(165.3)*	814.2	*(181.8)*
SGM [40 ¥/ day]	60.4		301.3		504.9		702.1	
SGM [60 ¥/ day]	4.3		249.1		465.9		646.0	
SGM [80 ¥/ day]	-51.9		196.8		427.0		589.9	

Note: The SGM baseline does not include any family labour costs or fixed costs.

---

[51] Total compensation costs are 1.538 times the earnings for urban workers and 1.080 times the earnings for TVE workers (*cf.* Banister and Cook 2011).

Table 19 shows how opportunity costs change the SGMs, which remain positive. Assuming a current Chinese average off-farm labour wage of about 40 *yuán/* day, wheat and maize production is still profitable for small-scale farmers. However, if the opportunity costs of family labour are taken into account, its profitability decreases as potential off-farm earnings increase. At an urban wage level of 80 *yuán/* hour (*i.e.*, 100 percent increase in labour costs, which, according to Banister and Cook (2011), is possible in just five years and the current rate of economic development in China), wheat production itself is no longer profitable. Relatively high production costs combined with high family labour input and emerging opportunity costs make agriculture in this form economically obsolete.

Furthermore, opportunity costs are not restricted to monetary factors alone. Any other benefit that provides utility might also be considered. For Chinese farmers, there is obviously a social cost to be taken into account, since the general opinion is that prestige is lost by not having any employment other than farming. Since receiving benefits prevails over giving favours, social embeddedness might also be reduced by less influential *guānxi* relationships (see Section 2.3.2).

4.5 Characteristics of the decision-makers and their farm units

The preceding environmental and economic findings portray the farmers' current agricultural production and economic situation, revealing many problems that might be obvious. Thus, the question remains: Since economic objectives are not fully recognised or pursued, what other determinants influence the farmers' behaviour. Since the following analyses of farmers' cognitive and social determinants are based on the shorter, intensive survey, a brief overview of the farm household, its production lines and the farmers themselves is also provided below.

4.5.1 Respondent, household and farm characteristics

Based on the smaller, more comprehensive survey, the socio-psychological sample is characterised first (see Table 20).

The realisable sample is n=302, since in 92 cases both questionnaires (part I 'agro-economic' and part II 'socio-psychological') could not be merged via the personal identification (PID). Thus, only 394 questionnaires could be utilised for the analysis of the socio-psychological section (part II), and only 302 for the structural equation model presented in Section 4.6, which combines variables from both questionnaires.

The analyses are not divided according to the survey counties since a comparison was not initially planned for this research. Thus, conclusions are drawn only for small-scale wheat and maize-producing farmers in intensive agricultural areas of Shandong Province.

Table 20   Sample description

Respondent characteristics	N	Mean	Std. Dev.
Gender [% male]	302	70.2	
Age [in years in 2009]	301	51.6	9.8
Youngest respondent		29 years	
Oldest respondent		78 years	
Education [in years]	300	6.2	3.3
No education [in %]	35	11.7	
Full labour time on farm [in %]	301	85.4	
Part-time farm-work [in %]	33	11.0	
Farm characteristics			
Household members [figure]	301	3.8	1.5
Household income [yuán/ year]	302	17,368	13,522
Share of agricultural income [% of total]	297	60.3	31.6
Share of income from off-farm activities [% of total]	175	53.4	25.1
Farm size [in $m\breve{u}^{52}$]	302	7.5	6.0
Key data on wheat and maize production			
Size of the biggest plot [in $m\breve{u}$]	301	3.0	3.3
Wheat yields [kg/ ha]	270	6.7	1.1
Maize yields [kg/ ha]	302	7.3	1.4
Annually applied mineral nitrogen [kg/ ha]	277	245.8	123.9

According to the data presented in Table 20, a remarkable number of the respondents were female, were of advanced age (older than 50, on average), had had only six years of education and worked full time on their farms. Nevertheless, 11 percent already engaged in part-time off-farm work, too.

Moreover, detailed analysis shows that more than a third (38 %) attended school for less than five years; of these 12 percent received no formal education at all.[53]

---

[52] Cf. 1 mŭ equals 1/15th hectare (~67 m²)

Since farmers belong to the older generation, most of them (farmers aged older than 39) attended school during the Great Leap Forward and the Cultural Revolution, both of which were rooted in Mao Zhedong's communist ideology (1949-1976). During this time, the quality of Chinese education decreased dramatically because professional teachers had been systematically eliminated and teaching practices were designed to emphasis Mao Zhedong's ideology (CIA 1969).

Regarding farm characteristics, in general, 3.8 people live in a farm household. The respondents' average household income is about 17,400 *yuán* annually. About 60 percent of this derives from agricultural work. Although only 10 percent of the households live from agricultural income alone, these households do not have significantly higher or lower incomes. Possible reasons are the emerging missing values for off-farm income and/ or remittances received by other family members, which are often not considered off-farm income as such. The share of the total household income is on average 53 percent; however, only 11 percent of the respondents are engaged in off-farm labour. This demonstrates again the comparatively high profitability of off-farm activities and the high opportunity costs of farm labour. Furthermore, remittances from close relatives and gifts from good relationships make up 8.6 percent of the household income on average. Thus, agricultural income is not the sole basis of the Chinese farm economy. Other income sources are essential in farmers' coping strategy for maintaining the households' economic security, especially, since off-farm income is so lucrative.

Referring to the key data for wheat and maize production, the average production yields correspond with those of the larger sample, but the stated mineral nitrogen input is far lower. Thus, the smaller sample involves farmers that do not produce large nitrogen surpluses. The calculated demand would be 337 kg N/ ha, and the

---

[53] Following the political reforms of 1979, the quality of education improved, and the illiteracy rate decreased, reaching 7.5 percent in Shandong Province in 2009. This is slightly above the national average of 7.1 percent (National Bureau of Statistics of China 2010). Currently, primary education lasts 6 to 12 years. However, during the Cultural Revolution (1962-1974), socialist education was predominantly oriented on Maoist ideology, which led to a strong focus on labour instead of formal education. Thus, since education was largely tantamount to propaganda, even if several years of education could be proven, their quality cannot be considered comparable to several years of education subsequent to the political reforms.

stated applied amount of mineral fertilisers was just 246 kg N/ ha (organic nitrogen from manure not included).

It is against the background of this information that the following sections analyse farmers' underlying cognitive and social decision-making determinants. Farmers' source and level of agri-environmental knowledge is analysed in order to reveal the possible contextual scope for their decision-making, as it is assumed that, irrespective of their stated mineral fertiliser use and number of years of education, their actural knowledge level is quite low.

4.5.2 Agri-environmental knowledge

Since agri-environmental knowledge is measured by farmers' own perceptions, the following ratings are subjective valuations. Self-reliant farmers tend to state that they were informed, while those who relate their knowledge to broader contexts might feel less informed. In spite of that, farmers' own perceptions provide evidence about their needs. If respondents stated that they feel uninformed about a topic that is very close to their daily lives and affects their health, it implies that further information is wanted.

The findings presented in Figure 10 reveal that 60 percent of the total sample (n=394) have never heard of groundwater pollution caused by fertiliser overuse, and that only 24 percent feel informed about this topic.

Figure 10   Information about groundwater pollution due to overfertilisation

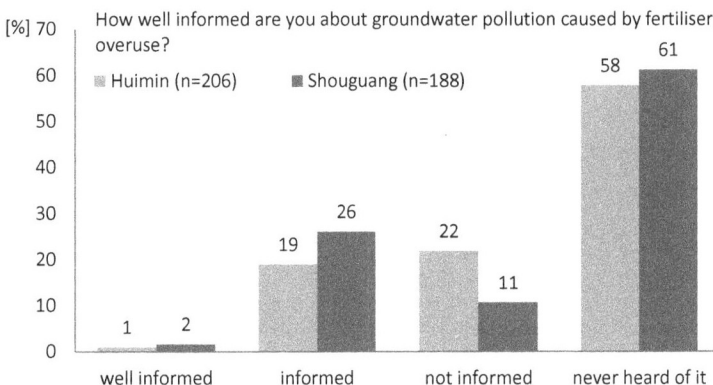

Divided by the two counties, it became obvious that farmers in Shouguang feel on average better informed than farmers in Huimin, even if more farmers in Shouguang stated that they have never heard of groundwater pollution due to overfertilisation. Thus, although farmers have been applying fertilisers for years, a remarkable number of farmers either have no information at all about the environmentally harmful consequences of fertilisation or feel insufficiently informed. In fact, only 1.3 percent, or five respondents, feels really well informed.

Figure 11   Agri-environmental information sources

Where did you get information about groundwater pollution caused by
nitogen overuse (n=117)?

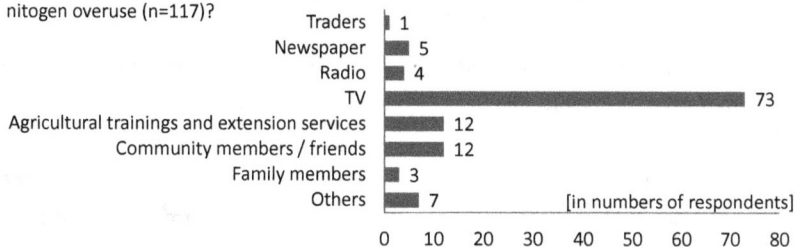

Source	Value
Traders	1
Newspaper	5
Radio	4
TV	73
Agricultural trainings and extension services	12
Community members / friends	12
Family members	3
Others	7

[in numbers of respondents]

0   10   20   30   40   50   60   70   80

Those people, who indicated that they have any information, mainly got their information from the public media, especially from television (62 %; *cf.* Figure 11). Other sources of information are community members and friends who also support farmers in their decision-making. Again, agricultural extension services have only a very slight influence on the farmers – about 10 percent (*cf.* Section 4.3.2).

In fact, (again) television has the greatest impact on farmers' agri-environmental knowledge about groundwater pollution. There is no evidence about the quality of the information gleaned from television, but the evidence indicates that this form of media is the most important information source concerning agri-environmental topics, regardless of how often farmers watch TV and what kind of programmes they see.[54] Moreover, the findings support the literature that agricultural extension services are not effective and comprehensive trainings do not exist.

---

[54] For instance, the Agricultural Channel of China's largest broadcaster China Central Television, CCTV-7, broadcasts agricultural information in particular, in order to promote agricultural development and to provide market information (CNTV 2011).

Regarding the fact that respondents in Shouguang feel better informed than farmers in Huimin, it is suggested that due to the export orientation of vegetable production in Shouguang County, farmers are more often confronted with inspection of critical values, such as nitrogen or pesticide residues. This in turn might lead to more knowledge transfer and information exchange regarding the negative environmental effects of agro-chemicals. There might be also an urgent need to adapt to official requirements in order to compete on the market; thus, the additional demand is, for the time being, covered by information from television.

4.5.3 General attitudes towards environmental issues

In the following, agri-environmental attitude variables are analysed by univariate description of selected variables, and a factor analysis is conducted in order to reduce the number of agri-environmental variables and condense information. The analyses give a brief overview of farmers' general attitudes towards different environment-related statements. On the one hand, the response dispersion of agreement and disagreement with selected statements regarding the various agri-environmental dimensions will show the variety of farmers' attitude alignments. On the other hand, the factor analysis condenses the different foci of the questionnaire block towards latent variables and demonstrates general tendencies indicating what may be of higher or lower importance to Chinese farmers. In this way, the perceptions underlying different response types will become visible. These results will later serve as background information for the latent variables emerging in the structural equation model.

In general, most farmers (n=394) agreed with the statement *"It is important to think about environmental issues."* Of these, 48 percent definitely agreed and 32 percent tended to agree. Only 5 percent disagreed, while the rest were indifferent. Those who agreed expressed that they value the environment as deserving protection in general, irrespective of any associated conditions. Although the question is phrased universally and abstractly, there were still 5 percent who did not agree. The position could be explained by different inherent value motivations, which might lead to more self-oriented topics of interest; this explanation is supported in subsequent sections.

In addition, 59 percent believe *"Farmers are the best protectors of the natural environment because they know best, what is good for the natural resources and therefore do not work against the natural environment"*. Only 18 percent disagreed with this statement, and 23 percent neither agreed nor disagreed. The statement refers to farmers who feel close to nature and their farming activities at the same time. Hence, they cannot imagine how their daily work is related to the harm of the environment. Unrestrained agreement with such a statement also indicates farmers' lack of knowledge since respondents who agreed seem to be not informed about the negative environmental effects of agriculture. Since there were also respondents who disagreed, there is evidence that there are also self-critical farmers who question their own farming behaviours.

However, the responses to the preceding statements are mirrored in attitudes towards the next question examined, revealing farmers' sense of responsibility.

In spite of the general opinion that environmental questions should be addressed, more than half of the respondents (54 %) agreed with the statement *"The government should reduce environmental pollution, but it should not cost me any money."* Agreement with this statement might also relate to the previous statement that farmers do not see themselves as originators of environmental pollution and hence, have neither a sense of guilt regarding their agricultural behaviour nor a resulting willingness to compensate for its consequences. Additionally, 18 percent were indifferent, and 28 percent (strongly) disagreed.

Thus, while the majority reject any financial involvement and accept no responsibility or emerging costs towards others (in this case the government), little more than a quarter of farmers feel any responsibility for environmental pollution or are willing to pay something for its reduction.

A detailed picture of farmers' environmental attitudes is provided by an additional analysis of all agri-environmental factors, indicating the latent variables and patterns of thought involved in certain response behaviours. The results are presented in the following Table 21, which in particular shows items that mainly focus on farmers' use of mineral fertilisers and the related environmental harm.

Table 21   Agri-environmental factors extracted

Factors	Variables	Agreements*	1	2	α**
ENVIRONMENTAL DISINTEREST / REJECTION OF ANY RESPONSIBILITY	Environmental problems are not related to my behaviour in fertiliser usage.	44.4	.782		
	I don't think about environmental aspects; I just do my work on the farm.	44.4	.715		
	Commercial fertilisers and pesticides promote high quality. Besides, they have no harmful effects.	45.1	.623		.604
	The groundwater burden from the leaching of fertilisers is overstated.	24.2	.551		
FERTILISERS SECURE THE AGRICULTURAL OUTCOME	If I stop nitrogen use in order to reduce harm to the environment, it would be too risky for the household's income.	46.6		.895	
	Stopping nitrogen use for the sake of the environment is too risky for the household's annual income.	73.1		.880	.750

*Cumulative agreements of the scale categories 'definitely agree' and 'tend to agree'.
**Cronbach's Alpha

Based on an Eigenvalue > 1, the Screeplot analysis shows an optimal number of two factors, and two factors were extracted successfully, verified with regard to the proven quality criteria: The KMO value for sampling adequacy exceeds six (KMO = 0.602). Moreover, the total variance explained is satisfactory, at 57 percent, since not all variables were used for factor generation. Then, the Bartlett's test of sphericity provides highly significant results ($\sigma = 0.000$), and the correlation coefficients exceed seven for most of the variables. In terms of internal consistency of Factor 1, two marginally lower correlation coefficients were accepted with regard to better Cronbach's Alpha values. Hence, reliability is proven for both factors.

While the content of the items describing Factor 1 – 'Environmental disinterest/ Rejection of any responsibility' – are focussed on environmental disinterest or even the rejection of any environment-related responsibilities, Factor 2 – 'Fertilisers secure the agricultural outcome' – describes that fertiliser use is inevitable to secure the agricultural outcome and is thus considered indispensable. Environmental harm is tolerated or even ignored by these two factors, because the question of the farmer's own involvement does not arise due to economic constraints or is rejected altogether.

As factors only reveal variables with similarly directed response behaviours, they do not make a statement about farmers' mean consensus with the factor. In order to get a rough idea of their mean consensus, the cumulative agreements are inserted to the right of the variables.

Referring to Factor 1, at first glance, the agreements and disagreements are not strongly set apart from each other. For the first and third statements, the percentage of agreements is slightly higher than that of disagreements. For the second and fourth, more disagreements are stated on average. For example the statement *"Commercial fertilisers and pesticides promote high quality. Besides, they have no harmful effects"* (third statement) is agreed with by 45 percent of the respondents and is disagreed with by 36 percent. The response dispersion demonstrates that there are two nearly balanced opposite attitudes towards commercial fertilisers and pesticides: Respondents who are convinced of the harmless quality of agro-chemicals and those who are more sceptical about their harmlessness. The response distribution of the second and third statements supports the latter, more critical group of farmers, but the disagreements (second statement 45.7 %; fourth statement 28.7 %) carry no weight for the latent variable; the difference in the second statement's response distribution is not high enough and the indifferent responses to the fourth statement outnumber both agreements or disagreements. Thus, overall, the factor expresses response dispersions that tend more to attitudes of environmental disinterest and a rejection of responsibility for environmental damage, although, for a majority of the farmers, environmental issues can indeed have meaning. To some degree, a rejection of the statements means that there is a sizable group that feels responsible for their behaviour, even if they do not know all the effects of their applied agro-chemicals, which could be caused by their stated knowledge gap and a resulting uncertainty regarding agricultural inputs.

Regarding Factor 2, there is greater agreement regarding the opinion that the application of nitrogen fertilisers is necessary to sustain the agricultural outcome and that less use would endanger family-wellbeing. For example, nearly two-thirds of the respondents think that *"Stopping nitrogen use for the sake of the environment, is too risky for the household's annual income"*, of which about 34 percent definitely agreed and 40 percent tended to agree (*cf.* 17 % (definitely) disagreed, and 9 % neither agreed nor disagreed). Hence, the majority knows about the benefits of fertilisers and deduce the economic risks of renouncing fertilisers, but they do not assess the resulting environmental impacts as significant. Only a small minority thinks that they can refrain from using fertilisers. This suggests that in these cases, agricultural activities were not as relevant for the household's annual income.

To conclude, most statements related to the two factors reveal that farmers have had positive experiences with nitrogen fertilisers and that, in large part, their family's economic well-being takes precedence over the environment in determining their behaviour, which can be characterised as risk-averse.

Taking into account farmer's risk-averse behaviour regarding economic issues, in the following, farmers' economic situation is contrasted with possible threats from nitrogen leaching. Thus, farmers' perception of the pollution status of their drinking water quality is considered against the background of their economic situation in contrast with the economic value of a clean environment as such, which is, given farmers' stated agri-environmental attitudes, less highly valued than their economic security.

4.5.4 Perception of water pollution and the monetary value of water quality

Based on the literature and on findings by our project partners in the natural sciences, it is clear that the groundwater, thus, also the wells for drinking water in the research area are heavily polluted. This is caused – among other things – by farmers' fertilisation behaviour and the resulting leaching of nitrogen into surface and groundwater resources.

Due to awareness of their poor agri-environmental knowledge, farmers were provided with additional information regarding groundwater pollution and the resulting problems for human health before asking them directly about their willingness to pay for the provision of clean drinking water. Emerging costs were another central theme that had to be covered.

Finally, farmers were asked to make a hypothetical decision as to whether they would continue to consume the untreated water, which is free, or whether they would be willing to pay a certain amount (out of a set of given alternatives) for better water quality. In this way, each selected a price that indicates the value that person places on clean drinking water. At the same time, they made a statement about their personal perception of groundwater pollution and the perceived risk dimension for their family's health emanating from that pollution. In this way, since the respondent's WTP is constrained by the household's financial resources, the expected utility of the clean water is evaluated. Thus, farmers stated willingness to pay demonstrates, first, farmers' perception of risk emanating from their currently untreated drinking water and, second, their valuation of clean water itself, either for the environment or for their health, taking into account their household income.

As shown in Figure 12, the findings reveal that more than two-thirds of the respondents (76.2 %) would pay something for the provision of clean drinking water. Almost 24 percent do not expect to receive higher utility from treated water.

Figure 12   **Willingness to pay for clean drinking water (n=302)**

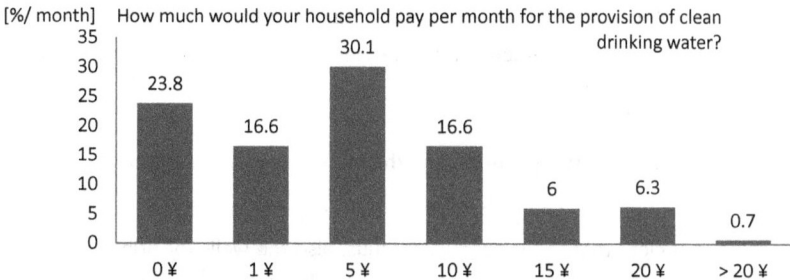

Based on the given set of alternatives, it became clear that the respondents are in general willing to pay even more than the minimum price. Most of them stated that they would pay 5 *yuán* per month. Given that the average household income is about 17,400 *yuán* per year, this is only 0.4 percent and does not affect farmer's financial situation at all. Even 20 *yuán* per month is not a high price (about 1.4 % of the household's income). The fact that there are also respondents who would to pay more than the scale offers shows that there seems to be a demand for water treatment among certain people, even at a higher cost. Thus, on the one hand, the problem of water pollution is indeed recognised and evaluated as harmful for human beings, while, on the other, some farmers do not want to pay anything for their water since they are of the opinion that their drinking water is clean and not affected at all by any harmful pollution.

General explanations about water quality were also provided during the group discussions. For example, in Huimin County, the local official stated that tap water comes from wells that rely on water from the Yellow River. Different farmers described it as "dirty", "smelly", "a little salty", also of a "yellow colour". Farmer 2 also relates this to the growing pollution. Farmer 9 even stated that "fertilisation is related to the deterioration of [water] quality" and others (Farmers 2, 4 and 7) agreed and added sewerage and breeding animals as additional negative influencing factors. By comparison, in Shouguang County, domestic and agricultural water is from different sources. Whereas agricultural water is from local wells, drinking water is pumped from somewhere else because irrigation water had become saltier and dirtier than in former times. Regarding the quality of their drinking water, they have the impression that this is still clean. While asking the farmers about the reasons for the decline in the quality of agricultural water, most of them do not have any idea, two relate it to flooding (Farmers 5 and 6) and one to the salty texture of the aquifers (Farmer 2). None of them agreed that excessive fertilisation could be the reason.

Since this research focuses not only on the agri-environmental knowledge and other observable decision-making determinants but also on cognitive processes, the next section analyses farmers' fundamental value position as the basic motivation for the constitution of preferences.

4.5.5 Farmers' fundamental value orientation

The portrait value items on the questionnaire survey farmers' fundamental value orientation. A re-analysis of the items seeks to compare the Chinese farmers' mean value position with the universal value cycle. The Similarity Structure Analysis offers a better interpretation of the results, since comparative values are used.

Table 22 shows farmers' mean ipsative value position on the value axes. The axes were calculated by multivariate Similarity Structure Analysis (SSA) according to Strack's formula (2010), weighting each of the individual 21 value items (*cf.* Section

4.1.5). The standard deviations derive from maximum and minimum values and indicate the variance between all the farmers' mean value positions.

Table 22   Farmers' value position on the value axes

	Minimum	Maximum	Mean	Std. Dev.
'Universalism axis'	-2.64	3.06	-0.03	0.92
'Traditional axis'	-1.89	2.44	0.32	0.74

listwise deletion; n=394

Supplementary to the data in the table, the scatterplot in Figure 13 illustrates in detail the denotation of the mean values. The dots within the coordinate system of the two value axes show exactly where each farmer's value position is located in the value cycle. The blue cross marks the mean value. Since the value cycle is transferred into the coordinate system corresponding to the value axes, it provides evidence about the farmers' most important fundamental value orientation. Thus, the farmers' value position is calculated as the mean of the 10 opposite values that emerge from weighting the 21 fundamental value items surveyed (cf. Section 2.3.1).

Figure 13   Chinese farmers' value position within the value cycle

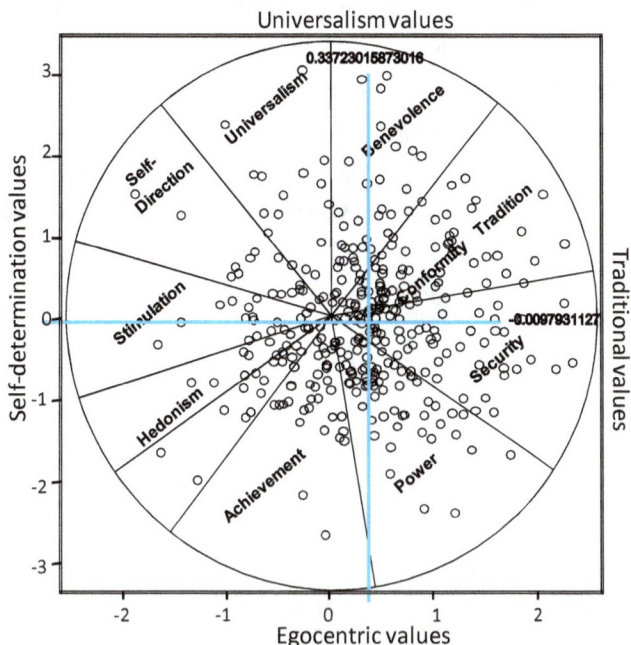

The results show that Chinese farmers' mean value position is located in the fourth quadrant at the boundary, close to the first quadrant. Compared to the value cycle, this is the area of security values, which are close to the conformity and power values on the traditional value axis. According to Schwartz' (1994) interpretation of the fundamental value types within the continuum of the value cycle, Chinese farmers emphasise on the subordination of self in favour of socially imposed expectations. Existing social arrangements give certainty to life. Furthermore, conformity and security emphasise protection of order and harmony in relations. The close power values stress overcoming or avoiding the risk of uncertainty by controlling relationships and resources (Schwartz 1994).

For a comparative interpretation, the meanings of the value items from the SSA of the European Social Survey (33 countries) was transmitted to the SSA mean of the Chinese farmers' value items. The results are shown in Figure 14.

First, regarding the countries in the ESS analyses, it is evident that – using Inglehart's term (1997) – the countries are aligned in a post-materialist/ materialist order.

Comparing the distribution of the countries with the Cultural Map of the World Values Survey created by Inglehart and Welzel (2010; Cultural Map *cf.* Appendix 6) makes it clear that Northwestern (Protestant) societies are indeed closer to universal, self-determining fundamental values, which are comparable to the Cultural Map's self-expression values. The former communist USSR countries of Eastern Europe are more traditionally and egocentrically orientated. Hence, surviving materialist values are more relevant for them. Catholic European countries fall in between. According to Inglehart (1997), societies emphasise post-materialist values (open and universal self-expressing values) if the need for the economic and physical security linked to survival is satisfied.

Comparing European countries with the Chinese farmers' value position within the value cycle, the graph shows that Chinese farmers are positioned centrally, exhibiting both, materialist and post-materialist values. However, they focus more on traditional values than most European countries, which is similar to the former communist countries of Central and Eastern Europe. In particular, within Chinese culture, maintaining traditional social order and the security of their families is of primary importance, including politeness and the concept of face saving in the context of a harmonious society (Zheng and Cui 2008).

Figure 14   Chinese farmers' value position compared to European countries

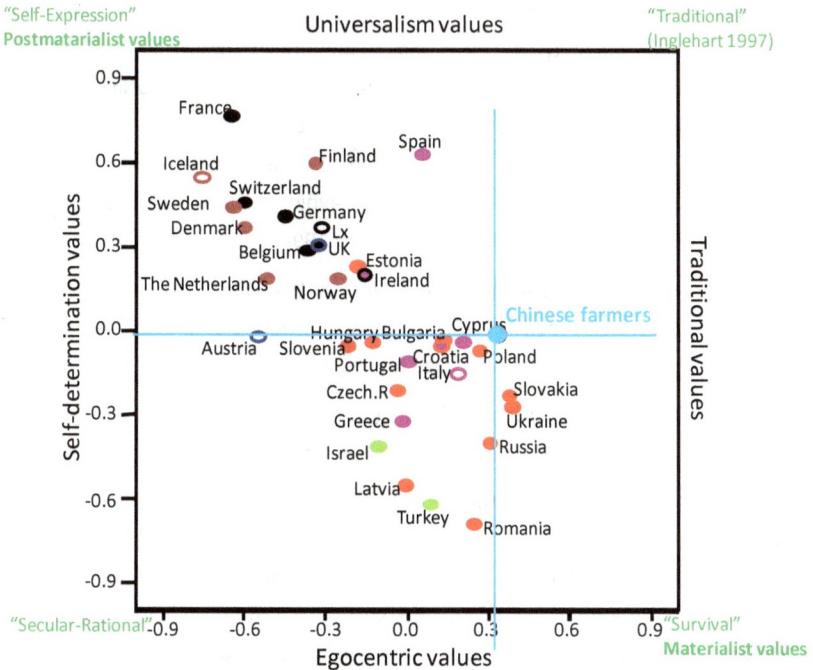

Source: Data of European Countries from the ESS (2008) 2002-2008, 33 nations in four rounds.
Effect size: eta ~.35, ∅ r ~.00; Formula of the value axes according to Strack 2010, supplemented by Inglehart's (1997) axes labelling of the Cultural Map (in green colour).

Since Chinese farmers do not represent the Chinese population as such, but demonstrate an occupational category in a selected region, the findings of Knafo and Sagiv (2004) provide further relevant information regarding the average value orientation of certain occupational environments.[55]

---

[55] The research also used the PVQ 21, but was conducted for Israeli workers; there is no evidence about Chinese workers. In spite of that, often small farmers tend to have higher scores for conservative and traditional values. Due to their economically deprived living conditions, they hold to their habits and traditions in a risk-averse manner. Modern value influences are rare, and open-minded values lead to insecurity and instability. This hypothesis is supported by Inglehart's (1997), explaining the materialist orientation with reference to scarcity and survival values.

Thus, according to them, the conventional work environment (to which farmers belong) creates the most traditional and conservative value orientations, compared to other occupation categories, such as investigative, artistic or enterprising work environments (*cf.* Appendix 7). Therefore, it is not remarkable that Chinese farmers' value orientation tends towards traditional values rather than those of the average population.

In contrast to Northern and Western European Countries, the Chinese farmers focus less on post-materialist universal and prosocial altruistic value positions. Thus, the problem of scarcity as well as survival concerns, which promote risk-averse behaviours, are of greater relevance. However, compared to the former communist countries, Chinese farmers have a higher universal value orientation, which might be influenced by traditional Confucian values, such as group harmony, and collective values (see also Zheng and Cui 2008).

Nevertheless, a shift in values towards secular-rational – thus towards success and influence-orientated values and away from universal values – is supposable, especially given that the ESS has already shown similar value changes among communist-imprinted countries like Russia, Romania, Ukraine, Slovakia (ESS 2010) (see also Appendix 8).

Furthermore, Zheng and Cui (2008) also pointed out that the society is in rapid transition and that interactions with modern and less universal values are exerting an increasing influence on the Chinese traditional focus on Confucian ideals.

In order to gain information concerning the interrelationships among farmers' fundamental values, farmers' alignment regarding their *guānxi*-relationships were also correlated with their various agri-environmental attitudes. Above, factors were generated from the respective item sets in order to determine the response facets. The condensed information is better suited to correlations with the value axes since factors can be more easily distinguished from one another than can individual items. Furthermore, a dimension reduction of *guānxi* and agro-environmental attitudes is useful for constructing latent variables for the subsequent structural modelling.

4.5.6 Traits of farmers' *guānxi* relationships

A factor analysis (FA) calculates the various facets of farmers' underlying *guānxi* traits. On the one hand, the results reveal additional information about informal systems and personal networks that farmers identified as relevant to their agricultural practice and decision-making (*cf.* Section 4.3.2). On the other hand, the results are used for further calculation, since the goal of a FA is to detect latent structures and since condensed item information is most suitable for correlations.

The results are set out in Table 23. Based on an Eigenvalue > 1, the 11 items load into four factors, which are able to explain 56.8 percent of the variance. The overall Cronbach's Alpha for 13 *guānxi* items was 0.55. Furthermore, the Kaiser-Meyer-Olkin (KMO) measure of sampling adequacy indicated that the FA is reliable based on its correlation matrix (KMO = 0.68). Given the multidimensional nature of the *guānxi* construct, the assumption of non-correlation among the items is unlikely. As a result, a varimax rotation method was used to identify the underlying factors that best explained the *guānxi* traits. According to Bartlett's test of sphericity, the variables are defined as significantly homogenous in their variances, and no cross-correlations occur between the latent variables. Moreover, based on the correlation coefficients, there is internal consistency, although the first two factors reveal marginally lower correlation coefficients since Cronbach's Alpha is based on good factor reliabilities.

The factor definition is as follows: Factor 1 is 'Collectivism', as all the items were identical with the cultural dimension of collectivism from Dunning and Changsu (2007; *cf.* Section 2.3.2). The items indicate that the group is superior to the individual. Moreover, within a group, harmony is defined such that group interests prevail over individual interests. As such, Confucian doctrines of harmony and communitarianism are highly valued and important for farmers' social relationships.

The other extracted factors 'Personal Ties', 'Utilitarian' and 'Navigating Relationships' are – in concordance with the literature – also particularly notable characteristics of *guānxi* (*cf.* Section 2.3.2). The factor 'Personal Ties' describes the person-focussed, long-term and intangibly reinforced orientation of *guānxi* relationships, which are created by nurturing and managing good contacts through personal commitment.

The exchange of favours and benefits comprises the 'Utilitarian' factor. This factor is motivated by primarily personal interests and rational considerations since individuals expect to benefit from their relationships. The last factor, 'Transferable', refers to navigating relationships within social networks. This trait is preferred for broadening the individual's scope of action. Interestingly, all items describing 'Reciprocity' were not directly extracted by the factor analysis. As such, the respondents' *guānxi* is not primarily dominated by reciprocal obligation, which leads to the assumption that *guānxi* is not exclusively instrumental in nature.

Table 23   Traits of farmers' *guānxi* **relationships**

Factors	*Guānxi* items	1	2	3	4	α*
COLLECTIVISM	I put group harmony above my own opinion.	.891				
	It's fair that group interests prevail over individual interests.	.883				.739
	Where work is concerned, I like to work in a group.	.541				
PERSONAL TIES	A personal connection is developed and reinforced through personal care and commitment.		.734			
	In my network of contacts, people depend on one another.		.714			.607
	People should help one another; you never know when you might need their help.		.641			
	A personal relationship with others is part of daily life.		.545			
UTILITARIAN	It is fair that people benefit from their network of contacts.			.883		.704
	It is natural that I do favours for my network of contacts and that they do favour for me.			.844		
TRANSFERABLE NAVIGATING RELATIONSHIPS	My limited contacts do not matter; my contacts are able to introduce me to their networks.				.871	.623
	I can make use of my contacts' contacts as long as I have a good relationship with my contacts.				.789	

*Cronbach's Alpha

In the following, the extracted factors will be correlated with the fundamental value orientations in order to provide evidence about the cognitive reasons for attitudes towards the alignment of social relationships and environmental perceptions.

4.5.7 Correlations between fundamental value orientations and *guānxi* traits

The correlations were conducted between the two extracted value axes and the factors related to *guānxi* traits. Two-tailed Pearson correlations showed that the *guānxi* traits were traced to fundamental values (see Table 24). The overall factor of all the *guānxi* traits ('*Guānxi*') correlates significantly with the universal value axis, but is not affected by the traditional value axis. Thus, there is evidence that *guānxi* is mainly influenced by universal value orientations. Traditional stability or independent actions ('Traditional axis') do not play a role in the concept.

Table 24   Correlations between universal value axis and *guānxi* traits

	Collectivism	Personal ties	Utilitarian	Transferable	*Guānxi*
'Universalism axis'	.154**	.136**	-.051	-.200**	.257**
'Traditional axis'	-.091[+]	.145**	.089[+]	.035	.019

**p < 0.01; *p < 0.05; [+]p < 0.1

A breakdown into single factors highlights the different value weights in the farmers' general formation of *guānxi* relationships, which explains the underlying value motivations for the respondents' focus on a respective *guānxi* trait within his or her personal relationships.

For clarity, the correlations are visualised as dots in a graph of both value axes that also point out the universal value motivations of the value cycle that underlie the axes (Figure 15). Although not all dots refer to highly significant values for both axes (*cf.* Table 24), the figure promotes a better understanding of the meaning of the correlation results.

The correlation analysis reveals that the factor 'Collectivism' correlates positively with the universal value axis to a significant degree and slightly negatively with the traditional value axis. Farmers with a strong focus on collectivism in their personal relationships are more influenced by universal values, like harmony and social justice. In the scatterplot, in addition to the negative correlation with the traditional value axis, a tendency towards more self-directive or self-determining values is observable.

Figure 15   Chinese farmers' *guānxi*-trait factors within the value cycle

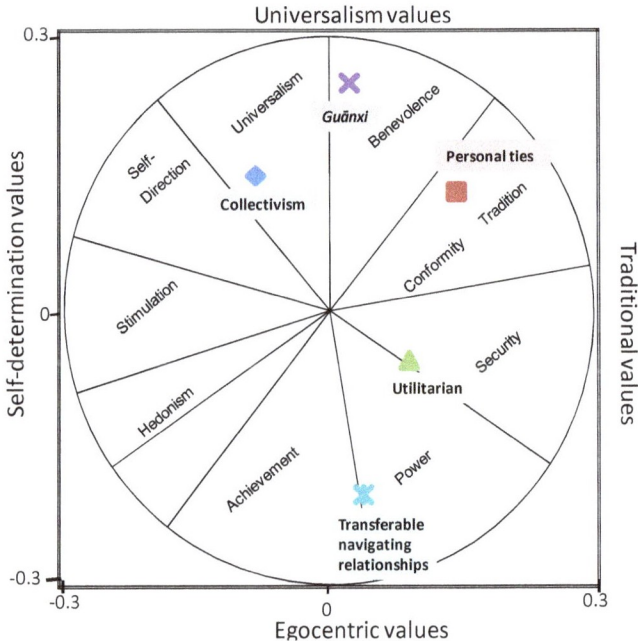

Similar, universal value motivations influence 'Personal ties' within the *guānxi* relationships, but with a stronger alignment with traditional values. The factor also correlates significantly with the universal value axis but as well significantly on the other axis with traditional values like loyality and trust, which are still relevant for personal ties.

Since this trait is the most significant one, the related statements describe the most distinctive *guānxi* characteristic. Personal ties motivated by universal values are of importance for farmers focussing on tradition; whereas collectivist bonding is guided mostly by universal values. Cultural traditions or self-determined values are of less importance for collectivist behaviour within *guānxi* relationships. Nevertheless, the findings show that collectivistic *guānxi* relationships are more likely to be preferred by self-determinist farmers and relationships emphasising personal ties that are targeted by traditional, conformist farmers.

Fewer universal values, but more self- or family-centred and traditional security values shape the 'Utilitarian' factor, which is characterised mainly by the exchange of favours and the pursuit of security for personal requests. However, this factor does not correlate significantly. Only the traditional value axis shows a slight tendency towards security values, thus, expressing the utilitarian character of relationships for the traditional value family welfare. The not significant but nevertheless, egocentric orientation on the 'Universal axis' reflects the inherent conflict between universal values in general and the family-oriented, non-universal duties necessitated by the everyday realities of farmers' live.

The factor 'Navigating relationships' shows the highest numerical values on the 'Universalism axis' towards egocentric values (negative correlation), as this characteristic is practised in order to acquire new personal relationships for greater influence, higher achievement and increased social power that is, for individual benefit. The findings are not significant for the 'Traditional axis', which lead to the conclusion that, independent if self-determinist goals such as hedonism or achievement or of traditional motivations, farmers seek to transfer relationships within the social network in order to enlarge their power and achieve success.

Before examining the findings of the structural equation model (referring to the impact of cognitive and social determinants on environmental attitudes and behaviour; Chapter 4.6), correlations between value orientations and environmental attitudes are tested to explain the interlinkage of certain cognitive value orientations with agri-environmental attitudes.

4.5.8 Correlations between fundamental value orientations and environmental attitudes

A bivariate Pearson's correlation of the value axis with the two agri-environmental factors and the meaningful statement describing the importance of environmentally-friendly activities was conducted to measure significant relationships (see Table 25).

Table 25 Correlations between universal value axis and *guānxi* traits

	Fertilisers secure the agricultural outcome	Environm. disinterest/ Rejection of responsibility	"It is important to think about environmental issues."
'Universalism axis'	-.185**	-.176**	.261**
'Traditional axis'	.148**	.166**	-.119*

p*** < 0.1; **p < 0.01; *p < 0.05;

The results show that the more farmers agree on the importance of environmental issues, the more likely their value orientation is to be universal and the less likely it is to be traditional. Farmers' agreeing with the statement "It is important to think about environmental issues" tend to be more open to changeing the harmful situation of public goods, even in a more self-directed way that deviates from the conservative social order. In contrast, farmers who agree that the 'Fertilisers secure the agricultural outcome' – thus, those who value agricultural inputs above environmental attitudes due to their risk-averse value-orientation show less concern for universal values and tend to focus more on securing their household's well-being through conformist values. The situation is similar for the factor 'Environmental rejection of responsibility', which gives priority to traditional and achievement values. Moreover, due to its underlying conformity and conservation values, this factor does not include openness values to changing habits, either.

Again, the correlations are illustrated in a graph to show the precise points of intersection at which the attitudinal factors intersect with the universal value cycle (Figure 16).

The statement "It is important to think about environmental issues" is, as expected, located opposite the other two factors. The negative correlations between the single statement and the two contrasting factors confirm that they are opposed attitudes. According to Schwartz's theory (1996), the more distant any two values are, the more antagonistic are their underlying motivations.

Hence, on the one hand, farmers who agree with the pro-environmental statement are driven by universal values. They like to live in harmony with nature. A tendency towards more self-directive values is supposed. Traditional values of influence in order to yield to the social order are of less importance than enhanced and self-stimulating value orientations.

On the other hand, farmers who favour high input agriculture and economic security without regarding their negative environmental impacts are located in the egocentric and traditional value area of power and security. There, mainly conservative values related to social order, control and public reputation, as well as familial well-being, play an important role.

Figure 16   Chinese farmers' agri-environmental attitudes within the value cycle

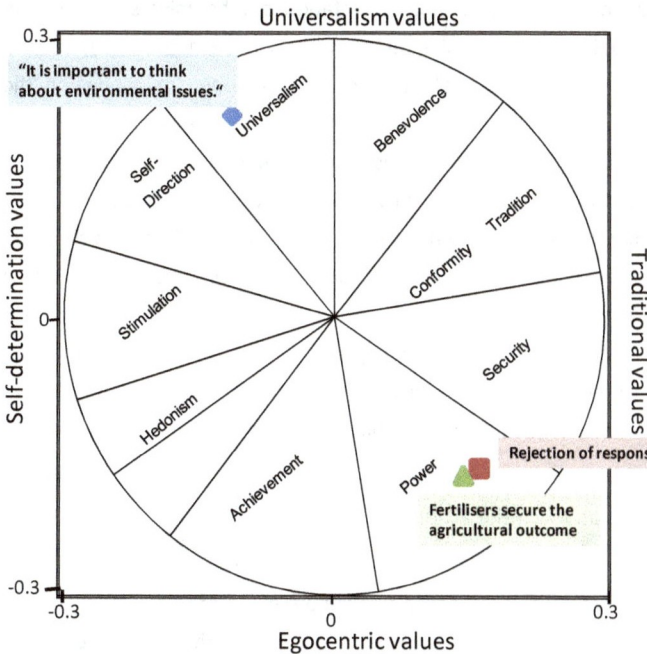

Having confirmed the different correlations of cognitive values with social and environmental attitude variables validates both, the factors previously extracted and the interdependencies between certain factors.

In the following, the bivariate analyses conducted serve as a basis for the modelling approach used to analyse the paths between these hypothetical decision-making factors in order to explain farmers' behaviour from a socio-psychological perspective.

4.6 Impact of cognitive and social factors on farmers' decision-making

In order to verify the relationships between variables that are relevant to prove the hypotheses assumed for the theoretical model described in Chapter 2.4 (Figure 4), a structural equation model (SEM) was conducted by the partial least squares (PLS) method.

After an evaluation and description of the model, the results are presented in three subsequent sections, adressing the model's various constructs.

4.6.1 Evaluation and description of the PLS model

The evaluation of the measurement model reveals the quality of the relationship between manifest and latent variables.

The results of the PLS modelling demonstrate item reliability since all factor loadings of the items on their respective constructs exceed at least the critical value of 0.6 (*cf.* Appendix 8).

Moreover, the assessment of the measurement model shows moderate Cronbach's Alpha values, which measure internal consistency (*cf.* Appendix 9). A plausible explanation for the low construct reliability is the small number of items from which the Cronbach's Alpha is derived. Even with an insufficient number of items, there is still internal consistency, especially since the individual item reliability as well as the figures for the composite reliability reach quite good values of more than 0.7. Furthermore, discriminant validity is satisfactory with an AVE in nearly all cases higher than 0.5.

The relationships between the individual latent variables are described and illustrated in the structural model. Bootstrapping yielded significant results for the path coefficients as presented in Figure 17. The questionnaire items used for the model as well as the scale direction of the variable are depicted in Appendix 8.

The SEM diagram corresponds to the theoretical model of decision-making assumed in Chapter 2.4, but focuses on cognitive processes influenced by socio-demographic factors and financial restrictions.

Thus, the first construct describes the influences of manifest variables on respondents' fundamental value position; household income and socio-demographic aspects (here: age, gender and education) from the preconditions for each decision-making process. These paths serve mainly as tools to describe the decision-maker for data interpretation. Apart from this scope of action, in theory, the two value axes ('Universalism axis' and 'Traditional axis') provide the starting construct for the cognitive path model.

The second construct describes farmers' *guānxi* orientations. Instead of four factors being extracted from the factor analyses in Section 4.5.6, only two of them were reliable for the path model. These two factors (one describing the utilitarian *guānxi* trait, the other one the collectivism trait) were generated from the same items as in the FA, which produces reliable results. Items that load positively on the LV 'Utilitarian' describe farmers' preference for utilitarian *guānxi* relationships. In contrast, negative loadings describe farmers' maintenance of morally motivated relationships. Positive loadings on the second *guānxi* LV, 'Collectivism', affirm the preference for collectivist relationships, while negative loadings refer to individualistic relationships. The *guānxi* constructs correspond with the theoretical assumptions conceptualised based on the fundamental value variables as well as on the manifest variables (socio-demographics and household income).

The third construct of cognitive processes comprises environmental attitude variables, unfolding different latent agri-environmental positions. The items loading on the construct are not similar to the factors extracted by the factor analyses, but the content conveys a very similar underlying message, for which the names for the LVs are the same as for the FA in Section 4.5.3. In favour of the discriminant validity – that is, the grade of divergence between the various constructs – and in favour of the significance of the path coefficients, some items cross loading with other LVs were removed from the model. This is usual for cognitive path models questioning cognitive indicator items, since these do not provide distinctive responses. Thus, both, fundamental value positions and social orientations affect such attitudes.

Furthermore, external variables, such as the influence of income and socio-demographic variables, are confirmed. However, these load primary on social and cognitive variables and show no correlation with environmental attitudes.

Finally, the different constructs are supposed to operate on the amount of nitrogen fertiliser applied and on farmers' willingness-to-pay (WTP) for clean drinking water, representing individuals' observable behaviour or behavioural intention in order to verify the theoretical model (*cf.* Section 2.4).

Regarding the quality of the SEM, the share of total explained variance is very weak ($r^2 < 0.19$). This implies a very low linear relationship indeed, but does not mean that there is no other causal relationship. It just shows that the influence of the selected items is low.

Moreover, regarding the quality of the substantial cognitive construct, the results show significant values with each endogenous variable measuring an effect size of $f^2 > 0.02$ (Appendix 10).

Thus, the structural model verifies the tentative impact of social and cognitive factors since some paths suggested in the theoretical research model can be confirmed; however, the model still needs to be extended in further studies by better explaining items and variables.

In the following three sections, the findings of the model concentrates on verifying of the assumption that individual differences in behaviour or agri-environmental attitudes relate to core aspects of personality and social disposition (*cf.* Section 2.4).

The results focus on the various factors directly influencing farmers' agri-environmental attitudes (Section 4.6.2), the various aligned reasons for farmers' fertilisation behaviour (Section 4.6.3) and the diverse decision motivations for farmers' WTP for environmental goods (Section 4.6.4).

Within each of the following sections, the respective relevant paths are explained and obvious interpretations directly linked to the paths are presented. A more comprehensive interlinkage of the model results follow in Chapter 4.7, explaining the individual differences of certain fertilisation-related behaviours and attitudes using social and cognitive determinants.

Figure 17   PLS Model of farmers' decision-making determinants

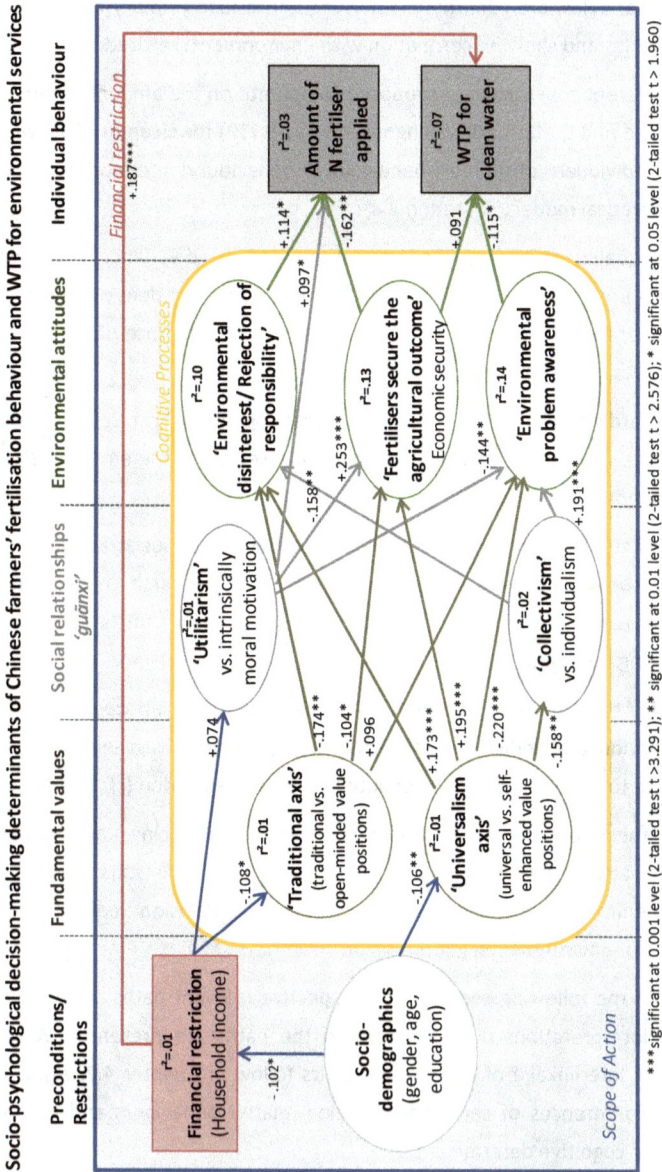

Socio-psychological decision-making determinants of Chinese farmers' fertilisation behaviour and WTP for environmental services

Preconditions/ Restrictions | Fundamental values | Social relationships 'guānxi' | Environmental attitudes | Individual behaviour

Financial restriction

Cognitive Processes

Amount of N fertiliser applied $r^2=.03$

WTP for clean water $r^2=.07$

'Environmental disinterest/ Rejection of responsibility' $r^2=.10$

'Fertilisers secure the agricultural outcome' Economic security $r^2=.13$

'Environmental problem awareness' $r^2=.14$

'Utilitarism' vs. intrinsically moral motivation $r^2=.01$

'Collectivism' vs. individualism $r^2=.02$

'Traditional axis' (traditional vs. open-minded value positions) $r^2=.01$

'Universalism axis' (universal vs. self-enhanced value positions) $r^2=.01$

Financial restriction (Household income) $r^2=.01$

Socio-demographics (gender, age, education)

Scope of Action

+.187***
+.114*
+.097*
-.162**
+.091
-.115*
+.253***
-.158*
-.144**
+.191**
+.074
-.174**
-.104*
+.096
+.173***
+.195***
-.220***
-.158***
-.108*
-.106**
-.102*

*** significant at 0.001 level (2-tailed test t >3.291); ** significant at 0.01 level (2-tailed test t > 2.576); * significant at 0.05 level (2-tailed test t > 1.960)

4.6.2 Factors influencing farmers' agri-environmental attitudes

Regarding the factors influencing farmers' various agri-environmental attitudes, the majority of the factors suggested in Figure 17 have an impact on attitudes related to *'Environmental problem awareness'*. The most important effect on this variable can be seen to derive from fundamental values, from *universal positions* (-.220***) in particular; *open-minded* values slightly confirm a tendency (+.096). *Collectivism* (+0.191***) and intrinsically *moral guided social interactions* (-.144**) are further decisive constructs that also reflect the high involvement of societal topics against the background of Confucian doctrines. Socio-demographic factors as well as household income act as indirect independent variables so that especially *female farmers* who are also *less educated, younger* and/or *more affluent* than the sample average (*cf.* respondent characteristics in Section 4.5.1, Table 20) are more likely to apply to this described construct and thus tend to agree with pro-environmental statements.

Important determinants of the attitude construct *'Fertilisers secure the agricultural outcome'* are *self-enhancing* (+.195***) and *traditional value positions* (-.104*). Regarding the influence of the social environment, there is a strong path dependency from *utilitarian societal interactions* (+.253***); thus, it seems that farmers whose preferences are guided by utilitarian issues focus more upon their agricultural outcome than farmers whose decision-making is intrinsically morally motivated. The financial background of utilitarian and self-enhancing farmers, who are – according to the socio-demographic data – expected to be *male, older* and/ or *better educated*, is slightly determined by a *worse income* situation. Thus, traditional value positions include also the great importance of the family and its security, which has priority above all in critical monetary situations.

The third agri-environmental construct, which describes *'Environmental disinterest'* combined with *'Rejection of any responsibility'* regarding negative environmental effects due to overfertilisation is also directly influenced by *self-enhancing* (+.173***) and *traditional* fundamental values (-.174**); thus, the socio-demographic precondition of the respondents tends to be similar to the construct just described (*older male, better educated* farmers of *lower income*). However, regarding the social component, *individualists* are more likely to agree with such attitudes than collectivist respondents (-.158**).

Pro-environmental attitudes characterise a smaller group of comparatively better-off, open-minded farmers *(cf.* mean data for socio-demographics). Although social relationships are highly valued in this group, its main traits do not correspond to the traditional concept of *guānxi* due to modern influences. Primarily, these farmers revitalise environmental values, while simultaneously establishing intrinsically morally motivated relationships; utilitarian aspects are of less importance. Their high universal and social consciousness entails a preference for collectivist thinking. Although collectivism is not understood in the traditional sense, close bonds are essential and crucial to survival within the current socio-political system. The decoupling of traditional concepts and the rejection of egocentric, utility-oriented relationships enable members of this group to espouse pro-environmental attitudes based on their altruistic values and intrinsically morally relationships.

In contrast, with regard to the other two agri-environmental constructs, both are strongly driven by self-enhancing values and, to a lesser extent, by traditional values. The generally older respondents are primarily family-centred and focus more on their own advantage; this emphasis is also enforced by greater financial restrictions.

The difference lies in the respondents' definition of social relationships: Farmers who deny any environmental responsibility do not rate their social relationships highly; they tend to act as individuals who do not like to operate for the collective's aims. Since rural areas are increasingly affected by the modern influences of migrant labour, farmers' fractured social structures are increasingly characterised by individualist attitudes towards social relationships. This, in turn, leads to unilateral, shortsighted decisions to use agro-chemicals, while, in response to economic pressure, ignoring environmental damage to the immediate, not very prestigious agricultural environment. This group must be distinguished from those farmers who, despite certain environmental problem awareness, are led by their poorer economic situation to grasp at any solution which will lead to a better quality of life. In general, the latter group has not yet exhibited preferences for the natural environment but, rather, for urban lifestyles. In contrast, better-off farmers live in keeping with their current situation; thus, they focus more on their social and immediate natural environment.

Farmers who emphasise economic security and who are thus primarily economically risk-averse in their attitudes towards over-fertilisation but not averse to environmental issues, rely on their established *guānxi* relationships. They expect benefits from *guānxi* while relying on traditional concepts and utilitarian traits. In addition, respondents might hold attitudes that mitigate a self-enhanced attitude orientation, since risk-averse attitudes tend to accompany traditional values. Thus, such farmers subordinate environmental harm to economic security.

To sum up, in particular older farmers of low income experience value conflicts between universal values of living in harmony with the natural environment and traditional values of family safety. Given today's comparatively low farm incomes, family welfare is primarily achieved through self-enhanced egocentrism. Depending on their value position, these farmers may accept a certain environmental responsibility or not. Since most of the older farmers also experienced even greater financial hardship during the Cultural Revolution (Egri and Ralston 2004), in the end, self-enhancing value positions have been consolidated, promoting risk-averse attitudes towards economic security among older farmers.

4.6.3 Decision determinants of farmers' fertilisation behaviour

Referring to the observed fertilisation behaviour, the model in Figure 17 shows significant influences on the variable *'Amount of nitrogen fertiliser applied'* from both latent agri-environmental variables being influenced by self-enhancing and traditional values and agreed with predominantly by older, male and/ or, on average, poorer farmers. Furthermore, the utilitarian *guānxi* trait is directly associated with fertiliser usage.

The path of the LV *'Fertilisers secures the agricultural outcome'* (-.162**) loading on the variable that measures the amount of fertiliser applied reveals that the more farmers fear decreased harvest outputs, the more fertiliser they apply. The path of the LV *'Environmental disinterest/ Rejection of responsibility'* (+.114*) reveals that farmers who have no environmental responsibility at all, apply less nitrogen fertiliser. A third path is identified from the LV describing farmers' preference for *'Utilitarian'* relationships (+.097*) that gives evidence that farmers whose social relationships stem from utilitarian motivations also tend to apply less fertiliser. Thus, the reliance on traditional *guānxi* traits leads to less nitrogen fertiliser use. In contrast, *'Environmental problem awareness'* – that is having a pro-environmental attitude – has no effect on the amount of nitrogen fertiliser applied. Moreover, household income does not directly influence fertilisation behaviour, either, but asserts its influence indirectly through the social and cognitive LVs in between.

Thus, farmers, who tend to use even more nitrogen fertiliser than required hold pro-fertiliser attitudes, when they are driven by self-enhancing values that result from low-income levels and utilitarian relationships. This behaviour is also motivated by traditional economic achievement intentions to secure the family's living standard. Moreover, important utilitarian *guānxi* traits play a remarkable role in the final decision. Here, the loading is both, indirect on the attitude variable 'Fertilisers secure the agricultural outcome' and direct on the manifest variable, *i.e.* the fertiliser amount applied.

In contrast, farmers driven by individualist and self-enhancing values without environmental sensibility, who just work on their farms and do not feel responsible for the environmental burden from nitrogen surpluses, use less mineral fertiliser on their fields. They are thus, solely more strongly influenced by their self-enhancing achievement values and the traditional intention to act in the family's economic interest. Furthermore, they are less influenced by advice from their social network as they tend to be more individualist. This opens them to a more rational evaluation of costs and benefits, but – given that community members and friends spread relevant agricultural information – ends with their being less informed about agricultural issues due to their weaker social bonds (Section 4.5.2).

While these two paths affect fertilisation behaviour, the results also show that there is no significant relationship between farmers' environmental problem awareness and responsibility and their fertilisation practices. In general, environmental problem awareness was supported by very open-minded universalists, and their socio-demographic background runs contrary to that characterising the other constructs. Nevertheless, these findings show that even younger people with good networks and intrinsic social relationships do not have the knowledge to recognise how their cognitive disposition might relate to their behaviour. This also supports the assumptions resulting from the preceding paths analyses that, in general, farmers with different values and varying social and financial justifications value the environmental good positively, but do not connect it with their own agricultural behaviour.

4.6.4 Motivation for farmers' WTP for environmental goods

Regarding farmers' *'Willingness-to-pay for clean drinking water'* in particular (see Figure 17), this construct shows highly significant effects from farmers' *'household income'* (+.187***). The higher the income, the higher the respondents' WTP for the added value of an environmental good.

Regarding the environmental attitude variables, higher WTP are reported by farmers of a more distinctive environmental understanding (*'Environmental problem awareness'*; -.115*). Conversely, heads of farm households who hold attitudes loading on the LV *'Fertilisers secure the agricultural outcome'* tend to have a low WTP for environmental services or even none at all (+.091). These farmers focus primarily on the economic security of the household and do not evaluate the negative environmental effects for the health of their family resulting from too much fertiliser use. Thus, the added value of a provision of clean drinking water is considered marginal.

No correlation was found between attitudes related to the LV *'Environmental disinterest/ Rejection of responsibilities'* and WTP. Taking into account the preceding findings, this group comprises both farmers with a higher WTP because they recognise the added value and farmers who believe their drinking water is clean and as a result, have no understanding at all of the environmental damage caused by residues of agricultural origin.

To sum up, the explorative model shows that cognitive and social factors have a direct influence on farmers' environmental attitudes and also – in accordance with the economic theory of human decision-making – on the definite behaviour that results from the preferences.

The results show promising tendencies and thus allow carefully drawn conclusions that might be helpful for agricultural training recommendations, challenging the current agricultural paradigm of increased food production in China and moving towards more sustainable agricultural practices. Thus, before going on to the conclusion and a final discussion, the following section focuses on the results presented and reveals the possible impact of different cognitive and social determinants of decision-making behaviour for adapted agricultural training approaches.

4.6.5 Relevance of cognitive and social decision-making determinants for better adapted agricultural training approaches

In closing, in accordance with the socio-psychological model, the results give evidence that, next to socio-demographic and economic preconditions and restrictions, fundamental value positions and the Chinese *guānxi* relationships shape the farmers' agri-environmental preferences. Both are relevant determinants for farmers' decisions and have to be taken into account in optimised training approaches seeking to increase the apparent Nitrogen Use Efficiency. For the intended behaviour change, there is a need for individually adapted incentives to accompany emerging dynamic societal demands.

The results of *guānxi* and the farmers' information sources reveal the necessity to address and exploit the existing social (*guānxi*) networks through systematic infiltration with persuasive agricultural information conducted by carefully selected and trained contact persons. In order to meet the challenge of enhancing sustainable agricultural production, it is indispensable for future policy recommendations (measures and instruments) to reveal the determinants of agri-environmental decision-making.

There is evidence that wealthier and younger people are more likely to change their behaviour. The more open farmers are and the better they are embedded into a social network, the more their relational capital will reinforce any advanced knowledge imparted through agricultural training. Farmers' social group and especially their behaviour type promise at least a structural change from the current agricultural paradigm towards better balanced and more sustainable solutions.

Furthermore, self-enhancing and better-educated farmers of living in worse financial conditions can be convinced by training that focuses on added values and stimulates farmers' pursuit of their own achievements. Although most of them already belong to the older generation, they have the desire to act in their families' economic interest; thus, they would be disposed to change their behaviour if it would benefit their families. Presuming the training is effective, an increased aNUE hence, less mineral nitrogen fertilisation, would show them, first, the positive effects on the state of their soil and water and, second, improved agricultural income since they would have lower fertilisation costs and, thus, save a noticeable part of their agricultural expenditures (*cf.* Section 4.4.2).

In addition, urban demands have found their way into the farm households and have already evoked changes in conservative and traditional values and social concepts. Self-enhancing, individualist orientations are increasing, and farmers no longer focus only on cross-linking with others. They are also driven to do all that they can for their own benefit. Hence, even training methodology has to focus on the added value that results from the positive environmental effects; however, it must also emphasise the benefit of multifunctional services in agriculture. To this end, creative rural development schemes have to be promoted and subsidised in order to give farmers incentives to be engaged; these schemes must encourage farmers to act independently and courageously and to be open to new ideas. On this way can they be motivated to avail themselves of new forms of agricultural services.

Finally, the results explain the different inherent motivations of farmers, such as why most of them rely largely on uncertain agricultural information sources (*cf.* Section 4.5.2) instead of drawing on extension services that they evaluate as less trustworthy, especially since the people offering these services are neither embedded in nor informed about farmers' daily lives and agricultural problems. The results imply that extension workers should be reliable persons who are well established in the farmers' community and who serve farmers fulltime (see also Hu et al. 2009).

In addition, farmers act as individuals with regard to the welfare of their families, thus, they should be treated like individual decision-makers, as well. If extension workers convince them with arguments that clearly relate to their individual situations, they will change their behaviour and use the optimised treatments according to their individual preferences.

This last results section has already preliminarily broached the relevance of cognitive and social decision-making determinants for better adapted training approaches that stay close to the socio-psychological model. The following chapter will build on these results and initial considerations for training to draw comprehensive conclusions.

5 CONCLUSION

Taking all the results together, it is clear that there are various reasons for nitrogen overuse by Chinese farmers in Shandong Province; these have been summarised and discussed on the basis of individual appearing decision-making determinants. The theoretical research framework, in particular referring to the comprehensive model of individual decision-making, has provided evidence for the conclusions drawn.

Subsequently, the section on strengths and limitations will mention the various restrictions placed on researchers (especially foreigners) in China. In this regard, great effort was invested to devise acceptable items and to adapt the survey to the existing conditions. Moreover, little relevant English literature was available. Therefore, much of the discussions and interpretations were original and thus set an initial benchmark for future researchers.

Hence, in the end, this work has presented policy implications that were deduced from the study results and that refer to continuative research topics supporting more sustainable and environmentally sensitive agricultural practices, while simultaneously pointing out that progress will not be made without a holistic approach being adopted.

5.1 Discussion of results

China's agricultural development and efforts to achieve self-sufficiency in grain production have caused significant negative environmental effects at escalating external costs. As mentioned in the introduction (Chapter 1), in particular, nitrogen fertilisation is a fundamental problem. Since the economic reforms of Deng Xiaoping in the late 1970s, farmers have experienced an increase in yields due to the introduction of subsidised chemical fertilisers. And indeed, the agronomic results reveal that the yields of the small-scale farmers surveyed, who plant about half a hectare, are quite good for a double-cropping system. Nevertheless, as expected for farmers in this intensive agricultural production area, the current chemical nitrogen fertilisers applied reach amounts exceeding the annual uptake by the plants.

Mineral nitrogen amounts, applied annually on intensive wheat/ maize production systems, total on average about 540 kg N/ ha are in Huimin County (*cf.* Section 4.3.3). This leads to nitrogen losses leaching into the environment of more than 200 kg N/ ha, causing excessive pollution of the groundwater and soil as well as a reduction in farmers' yields and profitability (*cf.* Chapter 4.3 and Chapter 4.4). In the long run, this development is contrary to Chinese government policies: first, advancement of the "The Three Rural Issues" (self-sufficiency in agriculture, the development of rural areas and improvement of farmers' economic situation) and second, mitigation of the perpetual environmental deterioration (*cf.* Introduction Chapter 1.1).

Evidence from the theoretical model of decision-making

In order to enhance sustainable production in Chinese agriculture, the thesis is mainly about agri-environmental decision-making by the main actors – the Chinese farmers' –within the given context. By taking into account the economic as well as social and cognitive determinants of farmers' nitrogen overuse in Shandong Province, a comprehensive analysis of farmers' individual preferences was conducted with regard to successful training approaches and better implementation of policy measures.

In this connection, the telling introductory citation from James Duesenberry (1960, p. 233) offers an essential concept worth bearing in mind when considering the results:

> "Economics is all about how people make choices. Sociology is all about why they don't have any choices to make." (Duesenberry 1960, p. 233)

Even though Duesenberry (1960) references deterministic sociological approaches in these opposing sentences, the middle course between them bears a grain of truth. This research provides evidence that individuals' decision-making process derives from their cognitive and economic constitution in connection with their social and natural environment as well as their own agency. Thus, social and cognitive determinants, such as the Chinese concept of *guānxi* relationships and certain value positions, expand rational economic deductions through empirical interpretation as well as specific attitudes. Rational profitability aspects and efficiency arguments are not crucial factors, in particular, since the postulation of stable preferences and unbiased beliefs are also empirically problematic (Hedström and Stern 2008). Moreover, a person's rational decision-making is based on individual preconditions, such as the person's education, age, living conditions and future perspectives; also, decisions originate within a scope of action that is defined not only by economic restrictions, but also by contextual factors, such as the current societal processes and political developments in China described in the introduction. Hence, farmers' economic decisions are embedded within a broad political agenda and close social relationships.

Thus, concerning the question posed at the outset – why farmers do not apply less fertiliser when the nitrogen saturation level has clearly been exceeded and it can be assumed that they would be able to save the extremely high fertiliser production costs – an answer can be found in farmers' socio-demographics, in particular their agri-environmental and technical knowledge.

Technical knowledge and other socio-demographic factors

In general, farmers' fertilisation knowledge was evaluated as very low (*cf.* Section 4.3.2). Farmers lack knowledge in fertiliser types, their mode of action and the best application times. Particularly, their management is not adjusted to the nutrient demands of the respective growing stages; in fact, farmers tend to adapt to external factors, like the availability of irrigation water.

Moreover, since the household and farm characteristics delineated in Chapter 4.2 show that the majority of the practicing farmers are of advanced age or female, while men and, in particular, the younger generation are employed off-farm, agricultural work remain to be done by those who have no other option than to work in this low-prestige sector. Thus, the motivation to farm is low, they have not had any vocational training and most of them just farm according to established habits and their experienced perception "the more the merrier" (*cf.* Section 4.3.2).

The little information some of them have about the harmful consequences of nitrogen surpluses seeping into the soil and aquifer comes mainly from television. Agricultural extension services do not come to the fore or provide agri-environmental knowledge (*cf.* Section 4.5.2). Often, the agents are tied up with better paid jobs. In addition, Huang *et al.* (1999) confirmed that they are non-credibly concerned with farmers' individual problems.

Thus, the problem is that, without specific knowledge and effective trainings, farmers would not be aware that overfertilisation results in less efficiency and in less profitability. As shown in Chapter 4.3, large amounts of chemical nitrogen are applied, resulting in low use efficiencies, even without including organic nutrients from manure. So it is assumed (based on plot-specific analysis by our project partners) that the real depositions in soil and aquifers would be much higher.

Taking into account the principles of decision-behaviour delineated at the beginning of Chapter 2, it can be assumed that, if farmers were aware of their substantial fertiliser overuse and the related high production costs demonstrated in Chapter 4.4 and simultaneously low fertiliser use efficiencies, their individual decision-making would be different, depending on their individual preferences and the economic constraints they face. Hence, in line with the theoretical model described in Section 2.1.1, farmers' considerations would adjust to the additional information in a rational way and new decision alternatives would be available, such as the reduction of fertiliser costs and the resulting savings in economic resources (*cf.* Section 4.4.2).

Contextual conditions and (financial) incentives

Regarding the impact of knowledge on distinctive individual decision-alternatives, production-related differences have been assessed in detail for the two selected counties, Huimin and Shouguang, with reference to different contextual preconditions and (financial) incentives.

The differing agricultural practices and levels of prosperity described in Chapter 3.1 (Study area) and the Chapters 4.2 to 4.4 (Analysis results) describe the economic and societal driving forces influencing farmers' technological knowledge. Of course, regional disparities also derive from geographical conditions, like soil textures and access to irrigation water; however, the results reveal differing contextual situations, such as a differing economic and agricultural regional development. As described in Section 3.1.5, farmers' scope of action is therefore defined by different production and economic policies, off-farm labour opportunities, sales markets, and so forth.

Whereas in Huimin the development options in the agricultural sector are limited (GDP growth rate of 1.2 %), in Shouguang County the vegetable market in particular flourishes (GDP growth rate of 5 %) and, with it, the secondary sector (*cf.* Section 3.1.4, Table 5). Thus, human capital (even in rural areas, as can be seen in the increased per capita income in those areas) is strengthened by involved technical advice on statutory requirements for agricultural practice as well as by regular inspections of threshold values for pesticide and nitrogen residues in vegetables, as practiced in Shouguang for export production.

Regional effects and the cultural practice of information chaining via *guānxi* networks in turn stimulates mutual exchange regarding best management methods, from which the whole region profits (*cf.* Sections 4.3.2 and 4.5.6.) Thus, the logical deviation of regional effects is confirmed by results revealing that farmers rely strongly on information from their social relationships, so that any knowledge input is diffused throughout the network.

Nevertheless, because of farmers' low specific knowledge and initial economic position, they are afraid of taking any action that might reduce yields. As a result, they are basically sceptical and risk-averse regarding any recommended reduction in nitrogen use for fertilisation. As already discussed, in general, advice from extension agents is not considered trustworthy. Thus, farmers would rather consult other farmers with whom they have a relationship (*cf.* Section 4.3.3) or farm according to their traditional habits and personal experience (*cf.* Section 4.3.2).

As mentioned above, the agronomic analysis presented in Chapter 4.3 and the profitability calculations presented in Chapter 4.4 reveal reasons for the differences in economic prosperity and agricultural practices between Huimin and Shouguang Counties.

Farmers in Shouguang achieve better yields and also have a better apparent Nitrogen Use Efficiency. Excluding organic manure, the average total amount applied annually exceeds the nitrogen uptake by the plants by only 11 kg/ ha; in Huimin, this is 236 kg/ ha, which is to more than two-thirds above the amount the crops need. Thus, because organic manure from livestock is applied in addition to chemical nitrogen fertilisers, although farmers fertilise much more effectively in Shouguang, there is still potential for reducing the amount, and the need to conserve fertiliser in Huimin is all the more urgent.

From an economic point of view, the Standard Gross Margins demonstrate in turn a substantially higher profitability for both crops in Shouguang. The breakdown of production costs reveals that fertilisation represents the most cost-intensive expenditure (*cf.* Section 4.4.2).

There is evidence that better educated and better-off farmers are more concerned about their agricultural production since there is a higher benefit expected from the promising and more profitable trade market structures. Thus, structural conditions provide an incentive to acquire specific agricultural information. Due to the better motivation, technical knowledge seems to spread more via informal networks. Moreover, it is possible that the extension system also functions more effectively in China's major vegetable production base.

However, what are the (contextual) parameters of relevance?

Parameters of relevance

As been seen, specific knowledge and education as well as motivational incentives matter. It has been suggested that farmers could make higher profits if they were to optimise their fertilisation practices. They just need to recognise at least the economic effect and learn the details of fertiliser usage.

For instance, comparing both counties, detailed results regarding the production costs reveal that the expenditures for summer maize fertilisation are higher in Shouguang than in Huimin, even though the total production costs are lower in Shouguang (*cf.* Section 4.4.2). Thus, assuming that farmers in Shouguang have a higher level of fertilisation knowledge, they might invest in more expensive fertilisers (possibly of higher quality). Moreover, since they have higher household incomes, farmers in Shouguang might also invest in machinery use and employed labour. If so, farmers adapt their means of production to their financial situation.

This in turn opens a discussion on the Chinese land tenure system and argues for larger farm sizes, which would increase profitability per *mŭ* and maximise efficiency through more precise farming as a result of machinery use.

Furthermore, regarding other expenditures, farmers in Shouguang spend less for all items except irrigation and fertilisation. Their practice seems to be more efficient (possibly more professional) because they recorded better coeval yields. In addition, costs for plant protection were indicated only in Huimin County. Thus, it is obvious that farmers in Huimin have more problems with plant diseases, which can be traced back either to differences in environmental conditions or again to their poorer agricultural knowledge and less effective farming methods.

In addition to the production costs mentioned above, opportunity costs for family labour occur because off-farm work is becoming more and more profitable due to China's increasing economic development and prospering labour market (*cf.* Banister and Cook 2011, Section 4.4.3). Thus, with decreasing farm profitability, agricultural work loses out to off-farm income activities. The incentives to work in the primary sector continue to decline, diminishing the possibility of a sustainable future for rural agriculture.

As evidenced in Shouguang, better-off counties with higher average farm household incomes and higher growth rates in the rural areas, use the alternative of employing subcontractors for selected agricultural production steps. This has the advantage that better technology is used and professionals are assumed to have more specialised knowledge of the technology. Furthermore, the "landowner", or the person who owns the user rights, is able to work off-farm, earning additional wages. Thus, increasing opportunity costs require technological progress and bigger plot sizes for better profitability and also farmers or subcontractors who are willing to continue to farm. As mentioned above, this takes for granted secured landowner rights so that farmers have a long-term perspective and hence the motivation to advance agricultural change sustainably.

Moreover, it requires knowing about farmers' motivational goals, their attitudes and their habitual behaviours in order to facilitate policy measures that prompt self-motivated behaviour change.

Attitude-based decision-making and underlying socio-psychological determinants

On this note, the results reveal that, in general, farmers' attitudes towards environmental issues are quite superficial (*cf.* Section 4.5.3). Due to farmers' low environmental knowledge and the fact that they have little to no information about the detrimental external effects of overfertilisation, they are torn between the added value of agro-chemicals and their altruistic Confucian attitudes towards nature. In principle, they can not imagine how their positive experiences with agro-chemicals could be related to environmental harm. Thus, as argued by Harris (2006, p. 8), farmers' "instrumental view of the natural world" prevails, since long-term impacts cannot yet be assessed and immediate gains for the households are more highly valued in times of scarcity.

A broader picture is provided by farmers' willingness to pay for the provision of clean drinking water (*cf.* Section 4.5.4) – a matter – that is directly related to their and their family's health, but also the household's income. Indeed, at least a quarter of the respondents seem to be convinced that their drinking water poses no harmful pollution threat eminating from their drinking water. Since the payment investments proposed are relatively low compared to their average low income, and two-thirds of the respondents stated that they would pay only a low amount of money (on average 0.4 % of household income), the majority of the farmers seemed indifferent. On the one hand, they do not know much about the health risk posed by contaminated drinking water and they want to be sure their drinking water is clean; also, because some had even recognised a decline in water quality compared to former years; on the other hand, farmers' do not want to pay much, in keeping with the generally stated opinion that the government should cover environmental costs (*cf.* Section 4.5.3). Thus, they are willing to pay an incentive for initiating measures that will make them feel more secure.

Thus, depending on cognitive positions, the results revealed that farmers either do not question the use of agro-chemicals at all, or they think more carefully about their use due to indications of environmental pollution and a developing environmental problem awareness, mainly evoked by the public media (*i.e.*, TV; *cf.* Section 4.5.2).

Nevertheless, as the model (*cf.* Figure 17, Section 4.6.3) has shown, the amount of fertiliser applied depends on agri-environmental attitudes rather than on household income. Positive attitudes towards agro-chemicals and the conviction that the household income must be secured influence the decision on the amount of fertiliser to apply. The money available within the household has no direct impact. Thus, farmers' attitudes, which emerge from inherent socio-psychological variables and experienced contextual factors, are more important for agricultural decisions than the household income itself. This again confirms the quality of the theoretical model and reveals, on the other hand, the problematic initial position that fertilisers are not questioned at all and that financial incentives alone will not solve the problem of nitrogen overuse.

In contrast, the model also revealed that farmers with a certain environmental problem awareness do not apply less mineral nitrogen. They do not seem to have the knowledge to link their behaviour to environmental problems. Thus, vocational knowledge about agri-environmental processes is indispensable since farmers' recalcitrance is a main driver of the failure of good agricultural practices.

As has been shown, farmers' lack of knowledge concerning fertiliser issues is a decisive determinant for why farmers neither fertilise efficiently nor behave rationally regarding their profit orientation by applying less fertiliser. However, this inability to use their own understanding is balanced by farmers' reliance on social relationships. Thus, farmers who are interested in advancing their agricultural practices emphasise their *guānxi* relationships. Simultaneously, farmers who are disinterested in agri-environmental issues tend to be more individualistic (*cf.* Figure 17). This means that, in general, farmers' specific dispositions can be distinguished according to their divergent inherent value motivations and the directions of their social relationships, as was assumed for the empirical approach of the research framework described in Chapter 1.2. Thus, for individually adapted training approaches and incentive-oriented recommendations, it would be effective to draw on social and cognitive determinants since they are relevant for farmers' decision-making.

Breaking down the determinants that resulted from the survey, this means that traditional Confucian values and personal relationships are still of importance for Chinese farmers and their decisions. Conformity and security values are predominant and highly valued in terms of complying with the social order in harmony and overcoming the risk of uncertainty by controlling relationships and resources (*cf.* Schwartz 1994). Nevertheless, since the traditional Chinese culture in particular has experienced drastic socio-political and economic changes, value positions are in transition.

Effects of a society in transition

According to Inglehart (1997), fundamental cognitions always reflect the socio-economic conditions of childhood and adolescence. Furthermore, Schwartz and Sagie (2000) stated that, in times of socio-economic insecurity, conservation and self-enhancement values are emphasised, whereas societal security results in more openness to change and self-transcendent value motivations. The findings in Section 4.5.5 reveal that there is a trend towards more materialist values or secular-rational values, to use the term Inglehart and Welzel (2010) proposed in their World Values Survey. Hence, universal and traditional value positions give way to instrumental or self-enhancing hedonistic and achievement value positions, and farmers slowly begin to detach themselves from their Confucian traditions, although recent policies have started to promote the old doctrines again to countervail resulting social tensions emerging from societal change (Zheng and Fewsmith 2008). Thus, the development of farmers' fundamental value positions is a consequence of China's opening economy and society as well as of farmers' insecure future perspectives in light of all the ongoing political measures, in particular for the low-prestige agricultural sector.

The findings are also supported by Egri and Ralston (2004), who found that younger generations of the Social Reform Era (1978 to present) were significantly more open to change and self-enhanced, but also less conservative and self-transcendent than older generations, who experienced the Republican Era (1911 to 1949). The Republican Era was characterised by extreme poverty and political instability and culminated in the 1945 civil war. Hence, Confucian doctrines, like benevolence, propriety, respect for social hierarchies and commitment to collective aims, predominanted. In the following 15 years of consolidation, this traditional order was displaced by the state and the Chinese Communist Party providing economic and political stability. The Cultural Revolution (1966 to 1976) finally discredited cultural traditions by setting new ideological values, like equality, conformity and self-sacrifice for collective interests (Egri and Ralston 2004). As recently as the Social Reform Era, which started in 1978 with Deng Xiaoping, Egri and Ralston (2004) identified an emphasis on individual achievement values, materialism and entrepreneurship. Moreover, Confucian ideas of a harmonious society were brought back into official favour, influencing the generation that grew up with the newly arising economic growth and prosperity.

Thus, against the background of these socio-economic and political developments, it becomes evident that the value position of most farmers of 40 years and older was formed during the Cultural Revolution Era, thus in times of economic insecurity and political instability as well as of cultural breakup. Only the younger generations' value position was influenced by the Social Reform Era. Nevertheless, one has to be aware of relying upon such generalisations, since the socio-economic situation in the rural areas is still worse than that in urban areas, which are characterised by economic prosperity and greater well-being (*cf.* Chapter 3.1, Study area).

Hence, overall, farmers' value positions have changed less than those of urban dwellers. Still, the tendency described above accounts for increased value influences from urban areas among labour migrants (*cf.* Section 4.5.5).

Impact of modified social relationships

This tendency is also true for Chinese farmers' *guānxi* relationships since, according to the cognitive hierarchy model of Fulton *et al.* (1996), social norms and relationships are influenced by individuals' fundamental values (*cf.* Section 4.5.7).

Thus, although *guānxi* is a very important component of Chinese culture, traditional value orientations are becoming less important for farmers' personal relationships; only universal or self-enhancing value directions come to the fore.

It is no longer essential for *guānxi* traits to have underlying traditional or open-minded values; it matters only that certain *guānxi* traits are still useful, as was traditionally the case. Thus, *guānxi* is becoming increasingly instrumentalised for individual benefit and is used less and less for the benefit of one's associates.

This means, in the long run that farmers' reliance on their *guānxi* networks to cope with knowledge deficiencies in agriculturally optimised technologies is not guaranteed. Instead, egocentric self-determining values increasingly dominate the traditional universal ones, and collectivism and personal ties dwarf culturally-established elements, which, while indeed indispensable for farmers' everyday performance, are not intrinsically honestly motivated in the same way, as was true for the original Confucian-based concepts that served to preserve the harmoniousness of society as a whole (*cf.* Section 2.3.2). Therefore, the correlation with the value cycle demonstrated variations in *guānxi* traits when they are compared to the original concepts described in the literature. Today, the utilitarian traits of *guānxi* and the aspect of navigating relationships are, against the background of the underlying value motivations, more associated with making a profit. These results support the thesis of Fan (2002), who mentioned that *guānxi* tuned into favouritism since is more often used at social cost instead of feeling obliged to increase social wealth – not only for oneself, but also for those in one's network (*cf.* Dunfee and Warren 2001).

This *guānxi* forming is not surprising, given the background of the institutional and historical conditions, which, in the long run, become – as mentioned by Gold *et al.* (2002) – inextricably linked to the society. In rural China in particular, the ongoing structural and demographic changes due to labour migration, as well as the weak agricultural economy and legal infrastructure make networking and mutual trust fundamental parts of economic transactions and the use of *guānxi* a coping strategy for institutionally uncertain environments (Gold *et al.* 2002). Simultaneously, *guānxi* is increasingly motivated by self-enhancing values. So, there is the risk that "institutional holes" – positively described by Bian (2002, p. 134) – will be utilised in future for individual benefit instead of universal community targets.

Hence, structures are needed that avoid personal gain and use the full capacity of personal relationships of public – in this case, of agri-environmental – utility.

People with high social network capital would be good knowledge multiplicators. They are most active and are able to take advantage of the best opportunities. However, they themselves must also profit from this function. In this regard, the results give evidence that farmers are morally motivated and have a collective relationship orientation.

Thus, even farmers who do not use the utilitarian character of *guānxi* for their personal gain have universally motivated pro-environmental attitudes, which is the best precondition for a planned behaviour change supported by training.

Finally, the results of the SEM provide evidence that differently aligned fundamental value positions and orientations regarding social relationships evoke differently directed agri-environmental attitudes, which in turn result in different behaviours or behavioural intentions. Thus, the comprehensive theoretical economic model of individual decision-making was verified while revealing that farmers do not consistently decide solely as rational economic utility maximisers.

In addition to financial reasons, there are socio-demographic factors, such as age, education and gender, that affect agronomic and economic decisions, as individuals' preconditions differ in socialisation, education and experience, in particular against the background of the remarkable political and economic developments in China of the last 60 years. Thus, the individual scope of action has an influence on the transitivity of fundamental value positions, the relevance of traditional *guānxi* traits and hence, on the specification of agri-environmental attitudes. These differ in non-constraining pro-environmental attitudes, non-understanding of the urgency to change agri-environmental behaviour and a primarily risk-averse stance placing economic security above environmental issues; furthermore, they influence the amount of mineral nitrogen fertilisers farmers apply as well as their willingness to pay for the provision of clean drinking water, depending on financial restrictions.

Having summarised and discussed the main results of the study, the following section adresses the strengths and limitations of the research.

5.2 Strenghts and limitations

As mentioned above, research on the agri-environmental decision-making of Chinese farmers is a topic of great relevance to the Chinese government, who is looking to improve the economic as well as the ecological situation of the rural population. As this can only be accomplished through the sustainable development of agriculture, the comprehensive socio-psychological approach presented here enhances the understanding of the main actors and thus, can contribute to better adapted policy recommendations.

In this regard, the research hearkens back to various economic as well as socio-psychological approaches to build a theoretical framework for the study. However, only very little literature was found providing empirical analysis of decision-making in the Chinese context. Moreover, the available studies focus on well-educated urban populations rather than rural subjects. Thus, one important achievement of this research was to provide – in addition to agronomic data – results concerning small-scale farmers' inherent decision-making, as this population makes up large parts of China's labour force and contributes in a remarkable manner not only to the country's food security, but also to its environmental problems.

Nevertheless, in a transitional system like China's, this topic is, at the local level, politically very sensitive. In particular, Tsai (2010) mentioned that quantitative population surveys are used as a measure of the performance of particular officials or local governments; furthermore, Cai (2000) added that such administrators seek to control the collection and flow of statistical data. In addition, foreigners are not allowed to administer surveys in China by themselves (Tsai 2010), so one of the principal achievements of this survey was the performance of this Sino-German-cooperative and officially sanctioned investigation into sensitive socio-psychological variables in rural China. Moreover, good progress was also made in collecting and analysing the agro-economic data.

Concerning the latter, the analysis of the basic data collected shows considerable agreement with the literature and with the findings and experiences of our project partners from other disciplines. Thus, although there were several concerns regarding the data set (*cf.* Chapter 3.4) as well as the difficulty of quantifying the factor use on small plot sizes and, moreover, on farms that do not practice detailed and penetrative accounting and bookkeeping, the study provided general evidence about the conclusions and tendencies stated.

Complying with the broader project framework and linking to the theoretical research approach, the study concentrated on a few crucial, decision-making factors, in particular sensitive socio-psychological variables. Due to the project framework, these findings are limited by the selection of the decision factors. For instance, some results, such as those of the structural equation model, show only moderate construct reliability since only a small number of items were included (*cf.* Section 4.6.1). In spite of that, it was possible to identify and verify tendencies, allowing for significant interpretations. However, further research based on these findings would increase the insights gained by including more precisely selected items reflecting decision-making determinants.

Hence, due to administrative burdens and the fact that our survey depended mainly on the efforts of our Chinese partners, who themselves had to rely in turn on local government contacts, errors could have slipped in during data collection. Limitations and tradeoffs lay in biases from interviewer and respondent effects that occurred due to the socio-culturally conditioned investigative situation and the performance of officials or local governments. These affected data quality and generalisability. Moreover, linguistic and cultural transfer also led to limitations that need to be considered, as did the fact that our cooperative partners had neither experience nor expertise in socio-psychological methods.

On the other hand, this interdisciplinary and application-orientated approach is one of this thesis' main strenghts. It was only possible due to the composition of the overall project and the interdisciplinary nature of our subproject. Thus, due to complicance with interdisciplinary objectives and the comprehensiveness of the overall approach, the individual cursory analyses could not follow the used methodologies in its entirety. On a higher level, the added value of this research is founded mainly on the conjunction of its main objectives, which target the sustainable development of Chinese agriculture based on a theoretical approach to individual decision-making.

Finally, with regard to data interpretation, little comparable literature was available in English. As a result, much of the discussion and interpretation stemmed from the author's own analysis, as well as from broadly related literature and information from personal communication, much of which was indeed biased by individual perception and interpretation, but which simultaneously carved an initial benchmark for subsequent researchers.

Overall, this research had to cope with a number of institutional and administrative difficulties and, faced limitations on a variety of levels; at the same time, it broke new ground in seeking to isolate the determinants of Chinese farmers' decision-making. Thus, based on the results, it is possible to identify preliminary policy implications that take into account the farmers and their inherent motivations to enhance sustainable agriculture.

5.3 Outlook – Policy implications

Concluding with an outlook, this research has outlined various perspectives regarding the agri-environmental decision-making of Chinese farmers. In terms of optimised fertilisation or – at a higher level – in terms of more sustainable agricultural practices, the focus was not only on economic, but also on socio-psychological and contextual determinants of individual decision-making, in particular.

Since this was the first interdisciplinary approach to study Chinese farmers' agri-environmental decision-making, relevant determinants have been touched in this initial attempt, and it is obvious that, besides the influencing factors selected here, more aspects should be taken into account in order to understand the ongoing processes involved in decision-making. Thus, further research is needed to consolidate this interdisciplinary, multi-factor approach. Moreover, in terms of applied research, the practical implementation of these results should be enhanced.

In this regard, in the following, policy implications are formulated on the basis of the conclusions discussed above in Chapter 5.1. The measures recommended draw a preliminary picture of an entire policy package instead of simply regarding the single problem of fertiliser overuse. However, in terms of a sustainable enhancement of agriculture in China, the proposed implications still need to be reviewed and extended by deeper analyses of the political and administrative framework and further research on other social and cognitive decision-making determinants.

As already mentioned by Ju *et al.* (2004) "command-and-control" policy measures, such as compulsory rules and the introduction of upper limits, as often implemented in developed counties, will not yet work in the Chinese situation. Although several governmental institutions have started to establish legal standards for more sustainable agricultural production,[56] the level of professionalism is still very low among the Chinese small-scale farmers, and adapted production techniques as well as related knowledge are rarely found (Ju *et al.* 2004). Nevertheless, according to proposals by our project partners, simple tools, such as soil sampling, could be introduced as an immediate means of testing amounts of mineral nitrogen in the soil and, thus, enable farmers to calculate plot-specific fertiliser demands. However, this presumes that farmers have knowledge and skills necessary regarding fertilisation practices.

To conclude, even these simple tools require precise policy steps at a higher level and, thus, concentrate on the development of a functional and broadly accepted extension system that is able to reach the individual farmer as the primary actor in the transition process indirectly, at the micro level.

Based on this, diverse recommendations for policy implications emerge in the fields of education, political incentives and institutional reforms. In terms of education, development of the extension system and a reliance on social networks as informative multiplicators are crucial. Monetary incentives and subsidies coupled with specific practices that will lead to a behaviour change in situations of financial scarcity are political measures for averting economic risk considerations.

Moreover, institutional reforms are indispensable in order to cope with negative effects involved in transitioning to sustainable agricultural practices.

---

[56] This includes, for example, thresholds for nitrogen concentrations in the Chinese Sanitary Standard for Drinking Water and environmental quality criteria for surface waters. Furthermore, the State Environmental Protection Administration (SEPA) regulates pollutants from livestock breeding (Ju *et al.* 2004).

Implication I: Enhance the extension service system

In order to implement agri-environmental technologies and to address farmers directly, the extension system has to be reestablished. Although, successful extension services existed in the past, Huang *et al.* (2001) have pointed out that the current system is ineffective since the payments for the public extension system were cut off at the beginning of 1988 and the stations are increasingly involved in commercial activities to cover their own costs. Given the fact that extension agents' salaries derive from commercial activities (including from fertiliser companies), they face conflicts of interest; hence, they tend to encourage farmers to overuse agro-chemicals. In addition, Hu *et al.* (2009) mentioned that the remote system lacks qualified personnel since the extension agents are mainly tied up with other administrative duties, such as family planning, budget management, *etc.*

Thus, as already recommended by Hu *et al.* (2009) one institutional policy is to separate commercial and administrative activities from public extension services. Moreover, better educated agents spend more time on agricultural extension services. This would seem to indicate that regularly trained agents would deliver more and better services. In addition, the results of this survey provide recommendations regarding enhancing the quality of extension services in order to promote effective adoption by the local farmers. Thus, there is evidence that advice from locally accepted representatives with strong *guānxi* relationships with the farmers would be acknowledged and trusted. Moreover, the agents employed should concentrate solely on farmers' best practices instead of being tied up with other administrative or commercial businesses. Thus, institutional changes are recommended at the administrative level.

Furthermore, in their farming, farmers rely heavily on traditional practices. In order to address farmers' socio-psychological motivations, agricultural extension agents should be encouraged to pick up and discuss farmers' indigenous knowledge and experiences regarding good agricultural practice. In addition, the damage inflicted by fertilisers on the environment and on human health should be included in local extension activities so that farmers increasingly internalise the negative externalities of fertiliser use. In the long run, this will lead to the rural society having a more sophisticated agri-environmental awareness. To this end, extension agents would need special training regarding to farmers' concerns and preferences.

Implication II: Disperse agri-environmental knowledge via *guānxi* networks

Given the results regarding farmers' reliance on their social networks, in addition to extension services, bottom-up approaches that seek to spread agricultural knowledge via informal networks should be implemented. For example, additional (financial) incentives might be offered to farmers and farmer cooperatives with self-enhancing, open and universal value orientations who express interest in agri-environmental issues and who agree to act as pilot farms. These commendable farmers should farm in close cooperation with the agricultural extension stations and follow their recommendations. Since it was found that *guānxi* relationships are still important in Chinese society, although the traits have already been adapted in a part to the ongoing value change, information exchange via personal ties in a collective sense is assumed to increase knowledge transfer informally. For instance, by organising private field days for surrounding farmers, these innovative farmers could explain their practices and thus act as multiplicators of specific agricultural information within the region. In this regard, these "early adopters" – following the term of Roger (1962) – have to be identified first. Then, their underlying motivations have to be determined in order to create adequate incentives and provide best-adapted extension programmes in agri-environmentally optimised practices.

Moreover, based on farmers' *guānxi* relationships, which essentially still rely on mutual exchange and trust (advantages public extension agents do not enjoy), privately coordinated local cooperatives, such as a machinery syndicates, would be more promising, for both economic and environmental goals. If knowledge is to be established, it will spread more easily through such network relationships, and the costs of technology use for precision farming could be shared. However, the establishment of such self-organised processes takes for granted a political framework at the institutional level that would permit forms of non-governmental self-organisations, which is not currently the case in China (for detailed information on NGOs, see Qing and Vermeer [1999]).

Implication III: (Monetary) incentives to compensate perceived economic risks

To adress farmers' risk perception concerning the economic security of their farm households, an obvious implication is well-placed (monetary) incentives.

The results on farmers' fundamental values revealed that – besides their traditional and still Confucian orientated universal values – farmers tend to be more achievement-orientated, self-enhancing and economically driven. Due to ongoing financial restrictions and insecurity, their preferences focus rationally on economically optimised agricultural practices. Thus, in order to comply with farmers' risk-averse agricultural coping strategies of nitrogen overuse, which result in environmental costs, well-placed incentives need to be developed.

First, monetary subsidies should be coupled with specific practices, for instance, the accomplishment of soil sampling aimed at plot-adapted nitrogen fertilisation or farmers' compliance with scientifically recommended practices. This presumes that sanctions are imposed if the nitrogen content of the soil samples is above a defined threshold value.

Second, indirect monetary incentives can include experienced positive economic effects from recommended technology changes. Concerning the latter, public extension training should include not only agronomic advice, but also advice economic matters, for instance, the emphasis on better SGMs as well as other benefits achieved if less chemical nitrogen fertiliser is applied. In combination with the removal of perverse incentives, such as high fertiliser subsidies, this would indeed be a convincing argument for farmers to optimise their fertiliser overuse and, at the same time, mitigate their risk-averse concerns. In addition to the reconsidering misleading subsidies, access to other production factors or production means should be improved.

Implication IV: Improve accessibility to agricultural production factors and land

Since decision-making faces geographical and political constraints, such as China's current system of land tenure and restricted access to water for irrigation, the agricultural infrastructure must be improved. Although the government has already put a great deal of effort into solving the main rural problems in a sustainable way

("The Three Rural Issues"), there is still a lot of work to do, in particular in terms of farmers' scope of action. Farmers decision-making and, thus, their agricultural productivity and agri-environmental behaviour, is strongly dependent on the administrative and legislative situation, in addition to natural conditions. In the long run, this causes negative external effects for the environment. Thus, even if farmers are willing to implement some optimised agricultural technologies, they still have to adjust their decisions to account for existing administrative regulations, such as, access to irrigation water, extension stations or to other agricultural inputs or markets.

Access to irrigation water

In Shandong Province, accessibility of irrigation water is not in farmers' hands, since they determine neither when the water channels next to their fields are flooded nor the amount of water made available to them. Thus, even if farmers have the necessary knowledge and would like to make decisions based on the best fertilisation practices, they are not able to time the water supply to meet their crops' demands. Thus, in order to increase nitrogen use efficiency, accessibility to necessary amounts of irrigation water must be guaranteed.

Moreover, the introduction of well water costs for agricultural water use is indispensable given that farmers' constraints, but also achievements and self-enhancing decisions are economically and rationally motivated. Especially on the North China Plain, where water is scarce and droughts occur from time to time, water usage is best regulated by water prices. This would have the effect that, in the long run, awareness of water as a scarce good increases environmental sensitivity. Economic considerations would factor into farmers' decision-making about water use; as a result, water would only be applied in times of real demand.

Establishment of secure property rights

A restrictive system of land ownership prevents any motivation on the part of farmers to invest in farming. Whereas a few try to expand their farm activities, the majority have no future plans for their farms and simply continue as in the past (*cf.* Figure 18).

Figure 18   Future perspectives of Chinese farmers

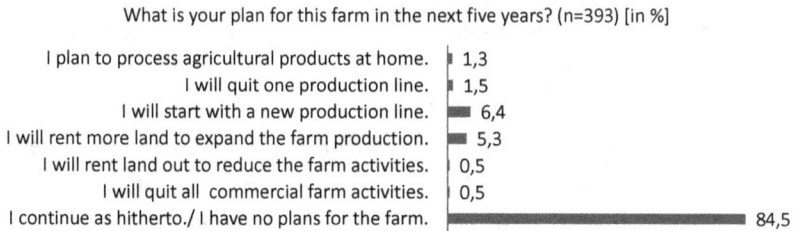

What is your plan for this farm in the next five years? (n=393) [in %]

I plan to process agricultural products at home.	1,3
I will quit one production line.	1,5
I will start with a new production line.	6,4
I will rent more land to expand the farm production.	5,3
I will rent land out to reduce the farm activities.	0,5
I will quit all commercial farm activities.	0,5
I continue as hitherto./ I have no plans for the farm.	84,5

As recently as 2008, the PRC announced a land reform allowing farmers to transfer or lease their land. Thus, the potential to boost agricultural activities on expanded plot sizes through technological investment and machinery use already exists. However, without other structural changes and developments, people will not trust the reforms of the current system. Magnier (2008) warns that farmers will sell their land use rights for a cheap price, with the result that they will remain impoverished after doing so without socio-economic safeguarding. Thus, a legal framework for totally private land ownership should be envisaged for the land transformation process. This would also entail further institutional and social reforms in rural areas, safeguarding the rural population's retirement and offering future perspectives, especially for the younger generation of farmers, so that some would agree to remain in the rural areas and continue farming on a larger scale.

Implication V: Mitigate vulnerability and empower the rural population

The policy implications discussed here will be only successful if they are not thought of as distinct from the problems of the rural population. In order to mitigate rural people's vulnerability, (1) farmers' decision-making should be empowered and guided by well-placed incentives to increase farmers' profitability, status and motivation to continue farming; thus, the focus should also be on the provision of advanced vocational training schools for farmers. (2) The Chinese social security system should be strengthened. Although a number of social security measures have been established in urban areas in the past years, the land contract system for rural families (*Hùkŏu* registration) – that is, farms – provides most farmers' living

(Xinhua 2003). If farmers become old or ill – that is, if they are no longer attractive for other labour markets – they need socio-economic safeguards to avoid impoverishment. Therefore, in order to conduct a land reform in terms of enhancing the growth and efficiency of more profitable farms, policies are necessary to ensure socio-economic well-being of the rural population who do not have additional money to purchase private insurance.

To conclude, the overall recommendation is to set up a package of interconnected measures encompassing agricultural policies in the fields of education, political incentives and institutional reforms. The enforcement of just one of the elements will lead to undesirable results. For example, focusing on education and the improvement of the extension system might, in a short run, lead to better agricultural practices, but, in the long run, it will not solve the problem of rural emigration and obsolescence of the agricultural population. To succeed sustainably, this effort has to be coupled with further (economic) incentives and structural changes. Thus, all elements have to operate simultaneously and in concert. While this is highly challenging, it is also very promising.

In the end, the study results not only identify farmers' agri-environmental decision-making determinants, but also offer policy implications that demonstrate the widespread dimensions of sustainable development in agriculture, addressing the demand for further research into a new agricultural paradigm in China.

6 REFERENCES

Addison, P., Fan, Y. H., Scully, G. and Woodbine, G. (2008) The impact of Chinese auditors' values on their ethical decision-making, AFAANZ/IAAER Conference. Sydney.

Ajzen, I. (1985) From intentions to actions: A theory of planned behavior. In: Kuhl, J. and Beckmann, J. (eds.) Action control: From cognition to behavior. Berlin, Heidelberg, New York: Springer-Verlag.

Ajzen, I. and Fishbein, M. (1980) Understanding attitudes and predicting social behaviour. Englewood Cliffs: Prentice-Hall.

Akerlof, G. A. and Kranton, R. E. (2000) Economics and identity. The Quaterly Journal of Economics 115 (3), pp. 715-753.

Albersmeier, F., Schulze, H. and Spiller, A. (2009) Evaluation and reliability of the organic certification system: Perceptions by farmers in Latin America. Sustainable Development 17, pp. 311-324.

Allport, G. W. (1961) Pattern and growth in personality. New York: Holt, Rinehart and Winston.

Alston J. P. (1989) Wa, guanxi, and inhwa: Managerial principles in Japan, China, and Korea. Business Horizons 32 (2), pp. 26-31.

Anosike N. and Coughenour, M. C. (1990) The socioeconomic basis of farm enterprise diversification decisions. Rural Sociology 55, pp. 1-24.

Ash, R. F. and Edmonds, R. L. (1998) China's land resources, environment and agricultural production. The China Quarterly 156, pp. 836-879.

Backhaus, K., Erichson, B., Plinke, W. and Weiber, R. (2000) Multivariate Analyse-methoden. Eine anwendungsorientierte Einführung. Berlin, Heidelberg, New York: Springer.

Banister, J. and Cook, G. (2011) China's employment and compensation costs in manufacturing through 2008. Monthly Labor Review (March) (Manufacturing in China).

Barning, R. (2008) Economic evaluation of nitrogen application in the North China Plain. Dissertation. Univeristy of Hohenheim (Institute of Farm Management). Online available at: http://opus.ub.uni-hohenheim.de/volltexte/2008/279/pdf/B arning_2008_Economic_Evaluation_of_Nitrogen_Application_in_the_North_Chin a_Plain.pdf [1.8.2011].

Becker, G. S. (1976) The economic approach to human behaviour. Chicago: University of Chicago Press.

Becker, G. S. (1965) A theory of allocation of time. Economic Journal 75, pp. 493-517.

Bell, D. (2000) Guanxi: A nesting of groups. Current Anthropology 41 (1), pp. 132-138.

Bian, Y. (1994) Guanxi and the allocation of urban job in China. China Quarterly 140, pp. 971-999.

Bian, Y. (2002) Institutional holes and job mobility process: Guanxi mechanisms in China's emerging labor markets. In: Gold T., Guthrie, D. and Wank, D. (eds.) Social connections in China: Institutions, culture, and the changing nature of guanxi. Cambridge: Cambridge University Press, pp. 117-36.

Borg, I. and Groenen, P. J. F. (2005) Modern multidimensional scaling: Theory and applications, 2nd edition. New York: Springer (Springer Series in Statistics).

Bossen, L. (2000) Women farmers, small plots, and changing markets in China. In: Spring, A. (ed.) Women farmers and commercial ventures. Increasing food security in developing countries. London: Lynne Rinner Publishers (Directions in Applied Anthropology), pp. 171-190.

Bourdieu, P. (1986) The forms of capital. In: Richardson, J. G. (ed.) The handbook of theory and research or the sociology of education. New York: Greenwood.

Bourdieu, P. (1972) Outline of a theory of practice. Cambridge: Cambridge University Press.

Brklacich, M., Bryant, C. and Smith, B. (1991) Review and appraisal of concept of sustainble food production systems. Environmental Management 15, pp. 1-14.

Buresh, R., Peng, S., Huang, J., Yang, J., Wang, G., Zhong, X. and Zou, Y. (2004) Rice systems in China with high nitrogen inputs. In: Moisier, A. R., Syers, J. K. and Freney, J. R. (eds.) Agriculture and the nitrogen cycle – Assessing the impacts of fertilizer use on food production and the environment. SCOPE Report 65. Island Press, pp. 143-154.

Burns, R. (1997) Introduction to research methods, 3rd edition. Melbourne: Longman.

Cai, Y. (2000) Between state and peasant: Local cadres and statistical reporting in rural China. The China Quarterly 163, pp. 783-805.

Chan, K. W. and Zhang, L. (1999) The Hukou system and rural-urban migration in China: processes and changes. The China Quarterly 160, pp. 818-855.

Chin, W. W. (1998) The partial least squares approach to structural equation modeling. In: Marcoulides, G. A. (ed.) Modern methods for business research. Hillsdale: Erlbaum.

ChinaTouristMaps.com (2010) Outline map of Shandong Province. Online available at: http://www.chinatouristmaps.com/provinces/shandong/simple-map.html [10.6.2010].

Chinese Network TV (CNTV) (2011) CCTV-7 military and agriculture. Online available at: http://bugu.cntv.cn/nettv/ibugu/28/CCTV7/20110928.shtml [29.09.2011].

CIA (1969) The Cultural Revolution and education in communist China. Intelligence report. Online available at: http://www.foia.cia.gov/CPE/POLO/polo-26.pdf [24.10.2011].

Coleman, J. C. (1988) Social capital in the creation of human capital. American Journal of Sociology 94, pp. 95-120.

Cui, Z. L., Chen, X. P., Zhang F. S. (2010) Current nitrogen management status and measures to improve the intensive wheat-maize system in China. AMBIO 39, pp. 376-384.

Davies, H., Leung, T. K. P., Luk, S. T. K. and Wong, Y. (1995) The benefits of 'guanxi' - the value of relationships in developing the Chinese market. Industrial Marketing Management 24, pp. 207-214.

Deci, E. L., Koestner, R. and Ryan, R. M. (1999) A meta-analytic review of experiments examining the effects of extrinsic rewards on intrinsic motivation. Psychological Bulletin 125, pp. 627-668.

Deci, E. L. and Ryan, R. M. (1985) Intrinsic Motivation and Selfdetermination in Human Behavior. New York: Plenum.

De Schutter, O. (2010) Mission to the People's Republic of China from 15 to 23 December 2010, 23 December 2010. Preliminary observations and conclusions (UN Mandate of the special rapporteur on the right to food). Online available at: http://www.srfood.org/images/stories/pdf/officialreports/de-schutter-china-stat ement.pdf [26.07.2011].

Deaton, A. and Muellbauer, J. (1980) Economics and consumer behaviour. Cambridge: Cambridge University Press.

Diekmann, A. (1998) Empirische Sozialforschung. Grundlagen, Methoden, Anwendungen, 4th edition. Hamburg: Rowohlt.

Duesenberry, J. (1960) Comment on "An economic analysis of fertility". In: National Bureau of Economic Research (ed.) Demographic and economic change in developed countries. Online available at: http://www.nber.org/chapters/c2387.p df [11.8.2011].

Dunning, J. H. and Changsu, K. (2007) The cultural roots of guānxi: An exploratory study. The World Economy 30, pp. 329-341.

Dunfee, T. W. and Warren, D. E. (2001) Is guanxi ethical? A normative analysis of doing business in China. Journal of Business Ethics 32 (3), pp. 191-204.

Durkheim, E. (1961) Die Regeln der soziologischen Methode. Deutsche Übersetzung. Neuwied: Luchterhand.

Ebertseder, T., Schmidhalter, U., Gutser, R., Hege, U. and Jungert, S. (2005) Evaluation of mapping and on-line nitrogen fertilizer application strategies in multi-year and multi-location static field trials for increasing nitrogen use efficiency of cereals. In: Stafford, J. V. (ed.) Precision Agriculture '05. Wageningen: Wageningen Academic Publishers, pp. 327-335.

Egri, C. P. and Ralston, D. A. (2004) Generation cohorts and personal values: A comparison of China and the U.S. organization science 15, pp. 210-220.

Errington, A. (1991) Getting out of farming? Part two: The farmers. University of Reading: Department of Agriculture (Farm Management Unit).

European Social Survey (ESS) (2010) European Social Survey. Online available at: htt p://www.europeansocialsurvey.org/ [10.6.2010].

Falk, A. and Fischbacher, U. (1999) A theory of reciprocity. Working paper 6. University of Zurich: Institute for Empirical Research in Economics.

Fan, C. C. (2008) China on the move: Migration, the state, and the householde. London: Routledge.

Fan, Y. (2002) Guanxi's consequences: personal gains at social cost. Journal of Business Ethics (38), pp. 371-80.

Feather, N. T. (1995) Subjective probability and fecision under uncertainty. Psychological Review 66, pp. 150-164.

Fehr, E. and Fischbacher, U. (2002) Why social preferences matter – the impact of non-selfish motives on competition, cooperation and incentives. The Economic Journal 112, pp. C1-C33.

Fornell, C. and Larcker, D. F. (1981) Evaluating structural equations models with unobservable variables and measurement error. Journal of Marketing Research 19 (1), pp. 39-50.

Frey, B. S. (2001) Inspiring economics: Human motivation on political economy. Cheltenham: Edward Elgar.

Frey, B. S. (1997) Markt und Motivation. Wie ökonomische Anreize die (Arbeits-) Moral verdrängen. München: Vahlen.

Frey, B. S. (1990) Ökonomie ist Sozialwissenschaft. München: Vahlen.

Frey, B. S. and Stroebe, W. (1980) Ist das Modell des Homo Oeconomicus „unpsychologisch"? Zeitschrift für die gesamte Staatswissenschaft 136, pp. 82-97.

Frey, D. and Irle, M. (1993) Theorien der Sozialpsychologie. Bern: Huber.

Fulton, D., Manfredo, M. J. and Lipscomb, J. (1996) Wildlife value orientations: A conceptual and measurement approach. Human Dimensions of Wildlife 1, pp. 24-47.

Fung, Y. L. (1976) A short history of Chinese philosophy, 2nd edition by Bodde, D. and Feng, C. L. New York: Free Press.

Gabriel, S. (2003) Introduction to heterodox economic theory. Online available at: www.mtholyoke.edu/courses/sgabriel/heterodox_defined.htm [11.10.2009].

Gale, F., Lohmar, B. and Tuan, F. (2005) China's new farm subsidies. USDA Electronic outlook report from the economic research service. Online available at: http://www.ers.usda.gov/publications/WRS0501/WRS0501.pdf [26.07.2011].

Gartrell, D. C. and Gartrell, J. W. (1985) Social status and agricultural innovation: A meta analysis. Rural Sociology 50, pp. 38-50.

Gasson, R. (1973) Goals and values of farmers. Journal of Agricultural Economics 24 (3), pp. 521-542.

Georgescu-Roegen, N. (1966) Analytical economics. Cambridge: Harvard University Press.

Gneezy, U. and Rustichini A. (2000) Pay enough or don't pay at all. Quaterly Journal of Economics 115 (3), pp. 791-810.

Godelier, M. (1999) The enigma of the gift. Chicago: University of Chicago Press.

Gold, T., Guthrie, D., and Wank, D. (2002) An introduction to the study of guanxi. In: Gold, T., Guthrie, D. and Wank, D. (eds.) Social Connections in China. Institutions, Culture, and Changing Nature of Guanxi. Cambridge: University Press, pp. 3-20.

Goodwin, R. (1999) Personal relationships across cultures. London: Routledge

Granovetter, M. (1985) Economic action and social structure: The problem of embeddedness. The American Journal of Sociology 91 (3), pp. 481-510.

Granovetter, M. (1973) The strength of weak ties. American Journal of Sociology 78 (6), pp. 1360-1380.

Götz, O. and Liehr-Gobbers, K. (2004) Analyse von Strukturgleichungsmodellen mit Hilfe der Partial-Least-Squares (PLS)-Methode. Die Betriebswirtschaft 64 (6), pp. 714-738.

Guthrie, D. (1998) The declining significance of guanxi in China's economic transition. The China Quarterly 154, pp. 254-282.

Guttman, L. (1968) A general nonmetric technique for finding the smallest coordinate space for a configuration of points. Pschometrika 33, pp. 469-506.

Hackley, C. A. and Dong, Q. (2001) American public relations networking encounters China's guanxi. Public Relations Quarterly 46 (2) pp. 16-19.

Hair, F. J., Anderson, E. R., Ronald, L. T. and Black, C. W. (1998) Multivariate data analysis. Englewood Cliffs, NJ: Prentice-Hall.

Harris, P. G. (2004) 'Getting rich is glorious': Environmental values in the People's Republic of China. Environmental Values 13, pp. 145-165.

Harris, P. G. (2006) Environmental perspectives and behaviour in China. Synopsis and Bibliography. Environment and Behaviour 38 (1), pp. 5-21.

Hedström, P. and Stern, C. (2008) Rational choice and sociology. The New Palgrave Dictionary of Economics 2, 1-17.

Herath, H. M. G., Hardaker, J. B. and Anderson, J. R. (1982) Choices of varieties by Sri-Lanka rice farmers: Comparing alternative decision models. American Journal of Agricultural Economics 64, pp. 87-93.

Hirel, B., Le Gouis, J., Ney, B. and Gallais, A. (2007) The challenge of improving nitrogen use efficiency in crop plants: towards a more central role for genetic variability and quantitive genetics within integrated approaches. Journal of Experimental Botany 58 (9), pp. 2369-2387 (Special issue paper).

Hoering, U. (2010) Landwirtschaft in China: Zwischen Selbstversorgung und Weltmarktintegration. Essen: Asienstiftung (EU-China: Civil Society Forum).

Hofstede, G. (2011) Cultural dimensions. China. Online available at: http://www.geert-hofstede.com/hofstede_china.shtml [12.8.2011].

Hofstede, G. (2001) Culture's consequences: Comparing values, behaviors, institutions, and organizations across nations, 2nd edition. London, New Delhi: Sage publications

Hofstede, G. (1991) Cultures and organizations. Software of the mind. London.

Homer, P. and Kahle, L. R. (1988) A structural equation analysis of the value-attitude-behavior hierarchy. Journal of Personality and Social Psychology 54, pp. 638-646.

Hu, R., Yang Z., Kelly, P. and Huang, J. (2009) Agricultural extension system reform and agent time allocation in China. China Economic Review 20 (2), pp. 303-315.

Hu, R. and Huang, J. (2001) Agricultural technology extension investment and its impact in China. Strategy and Management 3, pp. 25-31.

Huang, J., Qiao, F., Zhang, L. and Rozelle, S. (2001) Farm pesticides, rice production, and human health in China. Research Report 2001-RR3: International Development Research Centre (IDRC), pp. 49-52.

Huang, J., Hu, R., Song, J. and Rozelle, S. (1999) Agricultural technology from innovation to adoption: Behaviour analysis of decision maker, scientist, extension worker, and farmer. Impact of Science on Society 1, pp. 55-60.

Huimin Bureau of Statistics (2011) Huimin 2010. Economic and social development. statistical information. Online available at: http://www.huimin.gov.cn/art/2011/4/13/art_165_41855.html [18.8.2011].

Huimin Governmental Portal (2011) About Huimin. Online available at: http://www.huimin.gov.cn/ [18.8.2011].

Hwang, E. R. (1987) Face and favor: The Chinese power game. American Journal of Sociology 92 (4), pp. 35-41.

Inglehart, R. and Welzel, C. (2010) Changing mass priorities: The link between modernization and democracy. Perspectives on Politics 8 (2), pp. 551-567.

Inglehart, R. (1997) Modernization and postmodernization. Cultural, economic, and political change in 43 societies. New Jersey: Princeton University Press.

Ju, X. T., Liu, X. J., Zhang, F. S. and Roelcke, M. (2004): Nitrogen fertilization, soil nitrate accumulation, and policy recommendations in several agricultural regions of China. Ambio 33, pp. 300-305.

Ju, X. T., Kou, C. L., Zhang, F. S. and Christie, P. (2006) Nitrogen balance and groundwater nitrate contamination: Comparison among three intensive cropping systems on the North China Plain. Environmental Pollution 143 (1), pp. 117-123.

Ju, X. T., Kou, C.L., Christie, P., Dou, Z. X. and Zhang, F. S. (2007) Changes in the soil environment from excessive application of fertilizers and manures to two contrasting intensive cropping systems on the North China Plain. Environmental Pollution 145 (2), pp. 497-506.

Ju X. T., Xing, G. X., Chen, X. P, Zhang, S. L., Zhang, L. J., Liu, X. J., Cui, Z. L., Yin, B., Christie, P., Zhu, Z. L. and Zhang, F. S. (2008) Reducing environmental risk by improving N management in intensive Chinese agricultural systems. PNAS Early Edition. Online Available at: http://www.pnas.org/content/early/2009/02/13/08 13417106.full.pdf?with-ds=yes [28.07.2011].

Kahneman, D. and Tversky, A. (2000) Choices, values and frames. New York: Cambridge University Press.

Kahneman, D. and Tversky, A. (1979) Prospect theory: An analysis of decisions under risk. Econometrica 47, pp. 313-327.

Keeney, R. L. and Raiffa, H. (1976) Decisions with multiple objectives. Preferences and value trade-offs. New York: Wiley.

Kendy, E., Molden, D. J., Steenhuis, T. S., Liu, C. M. (2003) Policies drain the North China Plain: Agricultural policy and groundwater depletin in Luancheng County, 1949-2000. Research report 71. Colombo, Sri Lanka: International Water Management Institute.

Keynes, J. M. (1930) A treatise on money. London: Macmillan.

King, A. Y. (1991) Kuan-hsi and network building: A sociological interpretation. Daedalus 120 (2), pp. 63-84.

Kirchgässner, G. (2000) Homo oeconomicus: das ökonomische Modell individuellen Verhaltens und seine Anwendung in den Wirtschafts- und Sozialwissenschaften, 2nd edition. Tübingen: Mohr Siebeck.

Kluckhohn, C. (1951) Values and value orientations in the theory of action: An exploration in definition and classification. In: Parsons, T. and Shils, E. (eds.) Toward a general theory of action. Cambridge: Harvard University Press.

Knafo, A. and Sagiv, L. (2004) Values and work ennvironment: Mapping 32 occupations. European Journal of Psychology of Education 19, pp. 255-273.

Kohn, M. L. (1969) Class and Conformity. A study in values. Homewood: Dorsely.

Korsching, P. F. and Hoban, T. J. (1990) Relationships between information sources and farmers' conservation perceptions and behavior. Society and Natural Ressources 3 (1), pp. 1-10.

Kuratorium für Technik und Landwirtschaft (KTBL) (2005) Faustzahlen für die Landwirtschaft, 13th edition. Darmstadt: KTBL.

Kwong, J. (1994) Ideological crisis among China's youth: Values and official ideology. British Journal of Sociology 45 (2), pp. 247-64.

Lee, D. Y. and Dawes, P. L. (2005) Guanxi, trust, and long-term orientation in Chinese business markets. Journal of International Marketing 13 (2), pp. 28-56.

Likert, R. (1932) A technique for the measurement of attitudes. Archives of Psychology.

Lin, N. (2001) Guanxi: A conceptual analysis. In: So, A., Lin, N. and Poston, D. (eds.) The Chinese triangle of mainland China, Taiwan, and Hong Kong. Westport: Greenwood Press.

Lin, Y. J. (1992) Rural reforms and agricultural growth in China. The American Economic Review 82 (1), pp. 34-51.

Lund, P. and Price, R. (1998) The measurement of average farm size. Journal of Agricultural Economics 491, pp. 100-110.

Luo, Y. (2000) Guanxi and business. Singapore: World Scientific.

Luo, Y. (1997) Guanxi: Principles, philosophies, and implications. Human System Management 16 (1), pp. 43-51.

Magnier, M. (2008) China outlines land reform plans. Los Angeles Times. 20.10.2008. Online available at: http://articles.latimes.com/2008/oct/20/world/f g-land20 [17.8.2011].

Map-of-China.org (2011) China relief map. Online available at: http://www.map-of-china.org/relief-map.htm [16.8.2011].

Marggraf, R. (2008) Neoklassische (Mikro-) Ökonomik als Wissenschaft. Mimeo.

Markus, H. R. and Kitayama S. (1994) A collective fear of the collective: Implications for selves and theories of selves. In: Society for Personality and Social and Psychology 20 (5), pp. 568-579.

Mauss, M. (1924) The gift. The form and reason for exchange in archaic societies. London: Routledge.

Ministry of Agriculture (MOA) (2010) Market information of corn for October 2009. Online available at: http://english.agri.gov.cn/ga/ei/201001/t20100113_1588.ht m [16.09.2011].

Moll, R. H., Kamprath, E. J. and Jackson, W. A. (1982) Analysis and interpretation of factors which contribute to efficiency to nitrogen utilization. Agronomy Journal 74, pp. 562-564.

Morris, C. W. (1956) Varieties of human value. Chicago: University of Chicago Press.

Mußhoff, O. and Hirschauer, N. (2010) Modernes Agrarmanagment. Betriebswirt-schaftliche Analyse- und Planungsverfahren. München: Vahlen.

Napier, T. L. and Foster, D. L. (1982) The farm business perspective and soil conservation. In: Harlow, H. G., Heady, E. O. and Canter, M. L. (eds.) Soil conservation policies, institutions and incentives. Iowa: AMES, pp. 137-150.

National Bureau of Statistics (2011) Communiqué of the National Bureau of Statistics of People's Republic of China on major figures of the 2010 Population Census (No. 2). 29.4.2011. Online available at: http://stats.gov.cn/english/newsandcomi ngevents/t20110429_402722516.htm [18.8.2011].

National Bureau of Statistics of China (2010) China Statistical Yearbook 2010. Online available at: http://www.stats.gov.cn/tjsj/ndsj/2010/indexeh.htm [19.09.2011].

Noack, E., Weber, D. and Bergmann, H. (2011) Pluriactivity among Chinese farmers – A case study from Shandong Province. Conference paper, 85th Annual Conference of the Agricultural Economics Society (AES), Warwick. 18th-20th April 2011.

Olson, R. V. and Swallow, C. (1984) Fate of labeled nitrogen fertilizer applied to winter wheat for five years. Soil Science Society of American Journal 48, pp. 583-586.

People's Daily Online (2010) Soaring wheat prices in China make farmers reluctant to sell. 7.7.2010. Online available at: http://english.peopledaily.com.cn/90001/90778/90862/7056186.html [12.9.2011].

Polanyi, K. (1944) The great transformation. New York: Rinehart.

Potter, S. M. (1995) A nonlinear approach to US GNP. Journal of Applied Econometrics 10, pp. 109-125.

Qing, D. and Vermeer, E. B. (1999) Do good work, but do not offend the "Old Communists", in Draguhn, W. and Ash, R. (eds.) China's Economic Security. Surrey: Curzon Press, pp. 142-162.

Rabin, M. (1994) Cognitive dissonance and social change. Journal of Economic Behaviour and Organisation 23 (2), pp. 177-194.

Raun, W. R. and Johnson, G. V. (1999) Improving nitrogen use efficiency for cereal production. Agronomy Journal 91 (3), pp. 357-363.

Rawls, J. (1971) A theory of justice. Cambridge, MA: Harvard University Press.

Ringle, C. M., Wende, S. and Will, S. (2005) SmartPLS 2.0 (M3) Beta. Online available at: http://www.smartpls.de [10.08.2010].

Rockeach, M. (1973) The nature of human values. New York: Free Press.

Rogers, E. M. (1962) Diffusion of innovations. New York: Free Press.

Sahlins, M. D. (1972) The original affluent society. In: Sahlins, M. D. (ed.) Stone Age Economics. London: Routledge.

Sauer, U. (2010) Werte und tatsächliches Verhalten in der Kontingenten Bewertung. Eine empirische Studie im Landkreis Northeim. Göttingen: Ibidem.

Schnell, R., Hill, P. B. and Esser, E. (1999) Methoden er empirischen Sozialforschung, 6th edition. München, Wien: Oldenburg.

Schüller, M. (2004) Chinas Landwirtschaft – Neue Entwicklungstrends nach dem WTO-Beitritt. Hamburg: GIGA (China aktuell). Online available at: http://www.giga-hamburg.de/openaccess/chinaaktuell/2004_5/giga_cha_2004_5_schueller.pdf [27.7.2011].

Schwartz, S. H. (2006) Les valeurs de base de la personne: Théorie, measures et applications [Basic Human Values: Theory, Measurement, and Applications]. Revue française de sociologie 42, pp. 249-288.

Schwartz, S. H. (2006) Value orientations: Measurement, antecedents and consequences across nations. In: Jowell, R., Roberts, C., Fitzgerald, R. and Eva, G. (eds.)

Measuring attitudes cross-nationally – lessons from the European Social Survey. London: Sage.

Schwartz, S. H. (2005) Basic human values: Theory, methods, and applications. Jerusalem: The Hebrew University of Jerusalem.

Schwartz, S. H. (2001) Value hierarchies across Cultures: Taking a similarities perspective. Journal of Cross-Cultural Psychology 32, pp. 268-290.

Schwartz, S. H. (1999) A theory of cultural values and some implications for work. Applied Psychology: An International Review 48, pp. 23-47.

Schwartz, S. H. (1996) Value priorities and behavior: Applying of theory of integrated value systems. In: Seligman, C., Olson, J. M. and Zanna, M. P. (eds.) The psychology of values: The Ontario Symposium 8. Hillsdale, NJ: Erlbaum, pp. 1-24.

Schwartz, S. H. (1994) Are there universal aspects in the structure and contents of human values? Journal of Social Issues 50 (4), pp. 19-45.

Schwartz, S. H. (1992) Universals in the content and structure of values: Theory and empirical tests in 20 countries. In: Zanna, M. (ed.) Advances in experimental social psychology 25. New York: Academic Press, pp. 1-65.

Schwartz, S. H. (1977) Normative influences on altruism. In: Berkowitz, L. (ed.) Advances in experimentalsocial psychology 10. New York: Academic Press, pp. 221-279.

Schwartz, S. H. and Sagie, G. (2000) Value consensus and importance: A cross-national study. Journal of International Business Studies 14 (2), pp. 61-74.

Sellin, N. and Keeves, J. P. (1994) Path analysis with latent variables. In: Husen, T. and Postlethwaite, T. N. (eds.) International encyclopedia of education. London: Elsevier Publishers, pp. 4352-4359.

Shandong Bureau of Statistics (2010) Economic and social development. Statistical information. Online available at: http://translate.googleusercontent.com/translat e_c?hl=en&prev=/search%3Fq%3Dhttp://www.shandong.gov.cn/%26hl%3Den% 26newwindow%3D1%26client%3Dfirefox-a%26hs%3D8rH%26rls%3Dorg.mozilla: de:official%26prmd%3Divns&rurl=translate.google.com&sl=zh-CN&u=http://ww w.stats-sd.gov.cn/disp/tjgb.asp%3Faa%3D1101201100&usg=ALkJrhgITI2wROX73 JuQuJphmcReuISUbghgITI2wROX73JuQuJphmcReuISUbg [19.08.2011].

Shouguang Bureau of Statistics (2011) Shouguang 2010. Economic and social development. Statistical information. Online available at: http://hivc.blog.163.co m/blog/static/134349547201141115320386/ [18.3.2011].

Shouguang Government (2011) About Shouguang. Online available at: http://www.s houguang.gov.cn/ [18.3.2011].

Simon, H. (1959) Theories of decision making in economics and behavioural science. American Economic Review 49 (3), pp. 253-283.

Simon, H. (1957) Models of man. Social and rational. New York: Wiley.

Smart, A. (1993) Gifts, bribes, and guanxi: A reconsideration of Bourdieu's social capital. Cultural Anthropology 8 (3), pp. 388-408.

Smith, A. (1759) The theory of moral sentiments. University of Michigan.

Spiegel Online (2011) China. Explodierende Melonen entsetzen Landwirte. Online available at: http://www.spiegel.de/wissenschaft/natur/0,1518,763114,00.html [17.5.2011].

SPSS Inc. (2009) PASW Statistics 18.0. Chicago: SPSS Inc.

Stern, P. C. (2000) Toward a coherent theory of environmentally significant behavior. Journal of Social Issues 56 (3), pp. 407-424.

Stern, P. C. and Dietz, T. (1994) The value basis of environmental concern. Journal of Social Issues 50 (3), pp. 65–84.

Somwaru, A., Diao, X., Gale, F. and Tuan, F. (2001) China's employment and rural labor migration. American Agricultural Economics Association annual meeting. Chicago, 5.-8.8.2001. Online available at: http://ageconsearch.umn.edu/ bitstream/20459/1/sp01so05.pdf [18.8.2011].

Strack, M. (2010) Von Werten und Medien. Vortrag auf der 9. Tagung der Österreichischen Gesellschaft für Psychologie ÖGPs, 8.-10.4.2010, Salzburg.

Strack, M., Gennerich, C. and Hopf, N. (2008) Warum Werte? In: Witte, E. H. (ed.) Sozialpsychologie und Werte. Lengerich: Pabst, pp. 90-130.

The Economist (2010) The end of cheap Chinese labour? Washington, 18. July 2010. Online available at: http://www.economist.com/blogs/freeexchange/2010/07/ch ina [19.9.2011].

Tsai, L. L. (2010) Quantitative research and issues of political sensitivity in rural China. In: Carlson, A. et al. (eds.) Contemporary Chinese politics: new sources, methods, and field strategies. New York: Cambridge University Press, pp. 516-549.

UNDP (United Nation Development Programme) (2006) China Environmental Awareness Programme (CEAP) Project document: Government of People's Republic of China (United Nations Development Programme).

UNESCAP (United Nations Economic and Social Commision for Asia and Pacific) (2000) Shandong. Basic data. Online available at: http://www.unescap.org/ esid/psis/population/database/chinadata/shandong.htm [18.8.2011].

USDA (United States Department of Agriculture) (2009) Commodity intelligence report. China 2009/ 10 Winter wheat situation. Foreign Agricultural Service (FAS). Online available at: http://www.pecad.fas.usda.gov/highlights/2009/04/ChinaDr ought/ [11.09.2011].

Van den Bergh, J. C. J. M., Ferrer-i-Carbonell, A. and Munda, G. (2000) Alternative models of individual behaviour and implications for environmental policy. Ecological Economics 32, pp. 43-61.

Veblen, T. B. (1898) Why is economics not an evolutionary science. The Quarterly Journal of Economics 12 (4), pp. 373-397.

Vogel, S. (1996) Farmers' attitudes and behavior. A case study for Austria. Environment and Behavior 28, pp. 591-613.

Wen, J. (2006) Excerpts from Chinese Premier Wen Jiabao's speech on rural Issues. BBC Monitoring Asia Pacific. Online available at: http://www.redorbit.com/news/ international/364890/excerpts_from_chinese_premier_wen_jiabaos_speech_on _rural_issues/ [26.07.2011].

Weller, R. P. and Bol, P. (1998) From heaven-and-earth to nature: Chinese concepts of the environment and their influence on policy implementation. In: McElroy, M. B., Nielson, C. and Lydon, P. (eds.) Energising China: Reconciling environmental protection and economic growth. Cambridge: University Press, pp. 473-499.

Wertsch, J. (1998) Mind as action. NewYork: Oxford University Press.

Willock, J., Deary, I. J., McGregor, M. M., Sutherland, A., Jones, G. E., Morgan, O., Dent, B., Grieve, R., Gibson, G. J. and Austin, E. J. (1999) Farmers' attitudes, objectives, behaviors, and personality traits: The Edinburgh study of decision making on farms. Journal of Vocational Behavior 54, pp. 5-36.

WVS (World Values Survey Association) (2007) Study description: China. Online available at: http://www.wvsevsdb.com/wvs/WVSDocumentation.jsp [10.10.2009].

WVS (World Values Survey Association) (1990) Questionnaire. Online available at: http://www.worldvaluessurvey.org/wvs/articles/folder_published/survey_1990/ files/root_q_1990.pdf [10.10.2009].

Xinhua (2009) China to raise minium purchase price for wheat 2010. China daily. 13.10.2009. Online available at: http://www.chinadaily.com.cn/bizchina/2009-10/13/content_8787238.htm [11.2.2011].

Xinhua (2003) China yet to cover farmers in social security system. News agency. March 2003. Online available at: http://www.china.org.cn/english/government/5 7908.htm [1.12.2011].

Xu, J. L. and Wang, W. X. (2009) Current status of peasants' quality in China and cultivation of new peasants in the view of new countryside. Asian Agricultural Research 1 (2), pp. 12-16.

Zhang, B. and Dong, Z. (2002) Agriculture in Shandong marches into global market. Xinhua News Agency, 9.1.2002, translated by Feng, S. for China.org.cn. Online available at: http://www.china.org.cn/english/2002/Feb/26383.htm [17.08.2011].

Zhang, Y. M., Hu, C. S., Dong, W. X., Chen, D. L. and Zhang, J. B. (2004) The influencing factors of production and emission of N_2O from agricultural soil and estimation of total N_2O emisssions. Chinese Journal of Eco-Agriculture 12, pp. 119-123.

Zhen, L. and Zoebisch, M. (2006) Resource use and agricultural sustainability: Risks and consequences of intensive cropping in China. Kassel: Journal of Agriculture and Rural Development in the Tropics and Subtropics (Beiheft 86).

Zhen, L., Routray, J. K., Zoebisch, M. A., Chen, G., Xie, G. and Cheng, S. (2005) Three dimensions of sustainability of farming practices in the North China Plain. Agriculture, Ecosystem and Environment 105, pp. 507-522.

Zheng, Y. and Cui, R. (2008) Kluckhohn and Strodbeck's value model in Chinese and American culture. Sino-US English Teaching 4 (52), pp. 64-67.

Zheng, Y. and Fewsmith J. (2008) China's opening society. The non-state sector and governance. New York: Routledge (China Policy Series).

APPENDICES

Appendix 1 Theoretical model of relations among motivational types of values and bipolar value dimensions (Schwartz 1994)

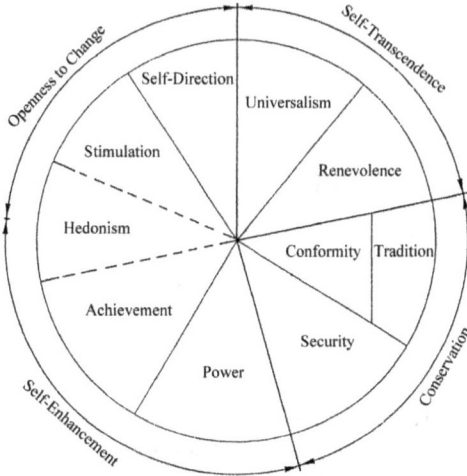

Self-Transcendence

Openness to Change

Self-Direction

Universalism

Stimulation

Renevolence

Hedonism

Conformity Tradition

Achievement

Security

Power

Conservation

Self-Enhancement

Note:
Tradition is outside of conformity, because the two value types share a single motivational goal. Conformity (self in favour) is subordinated to tradition, which is socially imposed (Schwartz 1992).

Appendix 2 Value structure averaged across 68 countries (Schwartz 2006)

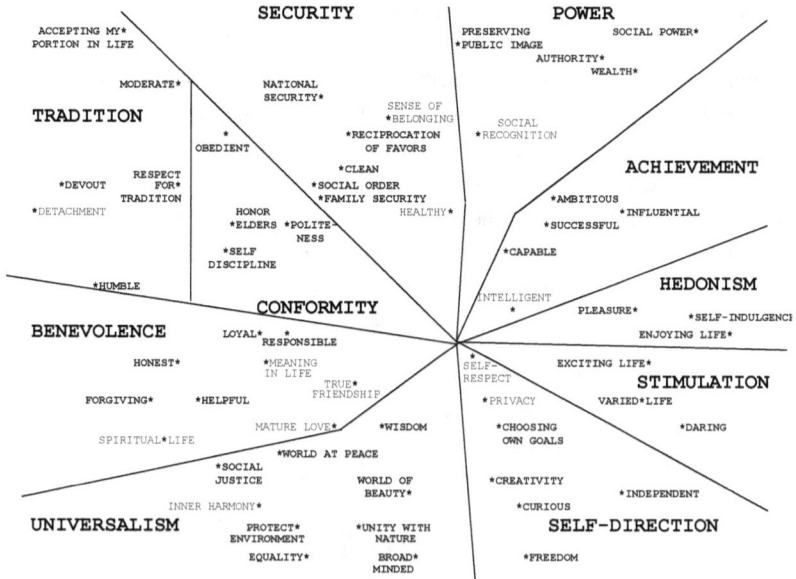

SECURITY   POWER

ACCEPTING MY*
PORTION IN LIFE

PRESERVING
*PUBLIC IMAGE

SOCIAL POWER*

AUTHORITY*

WEALTH*

MODERATE*   NATIONAL
SECURITY*

SENSE OF
*BELONGING

TRADITION   SOCIAL
*RECIPROCATION   *RECOGNITION
*   OF FAVORS
OBEDIENT

*CLEAN   ACHIEVEMENT
RESPECT   *SOCIAL ORDER
DEVOUT   FOR   *FAMILY SECURITY
TRADITION   HEALTHY*   *AMBITIOUS
*DETACHMENT   HONOR   *INFLUENTIAL
*ELDERS *POLITE   *SUCCESSFUL
NESS

*SELF   *CAPABLE
DISCIPLINE

*HUMBLE   HEDONISM
INTELLIGENT
CONFORMITY   *   PLEASURE*   *SELF-INDULGENCE
BENEVOLENCE   LOYAL* *   ENJOYING LIFE*
RESPONSIBLE

HONEST*   *MEANING   SELF-   EXCITING LIFE*
IN LIFE   RESPECT
TRUE*   STIMULATION
FORGIVING*   *HELPFUL   FRIENDSHIP   *PRIVACY   VARIED*LIFE

MATURE LOVE*   *WISDOM   *CHOOSING   *DARING
SPIRITUAL*LIFE   OWN GOALS
*WORLD AT PEACE
*SOCIAL
JUSTICE   WORLD OF   *CREATIVITY
BEAUTY*   *INDEPENDENT
INNER HARMONY*   *CURIOUS
UNIVERSALISM   PROTECT*   *UNITY WITH   SELF-DIRECTION
ENVIRONMENT   NATURE
EQUALITY*   BROAD*   *FREEDOM
MINDED

Appendix 3   PVQ 21 items allocated to each basic value (Schwartz 2005)

BENEVOLENCE
12. It is very important to him to help the people around him. He wants to care for their well-being.
18. It is important to him to be loyal to his friends. He wants to devote himself to people close to him.

UNIVERSALISM
3. He thinks it is important that every person in the world should be treated equally. He believes everyone should have equal opportunities in life.
8. It is important to him to listen to people who are different from him. Even when he disagrees with them, he still wants to understand them.
19. He believes that people should care for nature. Looking for the environment is important to him.

SELF-DIRECTION
1. Thinking up new ideas and being creative is important to him. He likes to do things in his own way.
11. It is important to him to make his own decisions about what he does. He likes to be free and not dependent from others.

STIMULATION
6. He likes surprises and is always looking for new things to do. He thinks it is important to do a lots of different things in life.
15. He looks for adventures and likes to take risks. He wants to have an exciting life.

HEDONISM
10. Having a good time is important to him. He likes to "spoil" himself.
21. He seeks every chance he can to have fun. It is important to him to do things that give him pleasure.

ACHIEVEMENT
4. It is very important to him to show his abilities. He wants people to admire what he does.
13. Being very successful is important to him. He hopes people will recognise his achievements.

POWER
2. It is important to him to be rich. He wants to have a lot of money and expensive things.
17. It is important to him to get respect from others. He wants people to do what he says.

SECURITY
5. It's important to him to live in secure surroundings. He avoids anything that might endanger his safety.
14. It is very important to him that his country be safe from threats from within and without. He is concerned that the social order will be protected.

CONFORMITY
7. He believes that people should do what they were told. He thinks people should follow rules at all times, even when no one is watching.
16. It is important to him always to behave properly. He wants to avoid doing anything people would say is wrong.

TRADITION
9. It is important to him to be humble and modest. He tries not to draw attention to himself.
20. Tradition is important to him. He tries to follow the customs handed down by his religion or family.

Appendix 4   *Guānxi* items (Dunning and Changsu 2007)

UTILITARIAN
1. Gaining favours/benefits 2. Exchange of favours
RECIPROCAL
3. Reciprocal obligations 4. Interdependence in a web of relationships
TRANSFERABLE
5. Navigating relationships in a social network 6. Third parties as a referral
PERSONAL
7. Personal relationship in daily life 8. Personal ties rather than organisational affiliation
LONG-TERM
9. Long-term personal relationships
INTANGIBLE
10. Personal commitment
COLLECTIVISM
11. Group interests over individual interests 12. Group harmony 13. Comfortable in a group

Appendix 5   Agricultural subsidies (Gale *et al.* 2005)

Subsidies	Description
Direct subsidies	Per area planted with grain; in general, farmers were paid about 10 *yuán* per *mǔ* planted with grain
Grain subsidy	Farmers are paid the difference between a "protection" price set by government authorities and a market price; therefore, commonly used is the previous year's market price.
Subsidy of agricultural inputs	Subsidies for impoved high-quality seeds and varieties are payed to seed supply companies, which are expected to pass on the subsidies to farmers. Up to 30 percent of the purchase price should be covered by the subsidies (improved corn seeds 10 *yuán*/ *mǔ*).
Machinery subsidies	Subsidies for purchase machinery

Appendix 6   **The WVS cultural map 2005-2008 (Inglehart and Welzel 2010)**

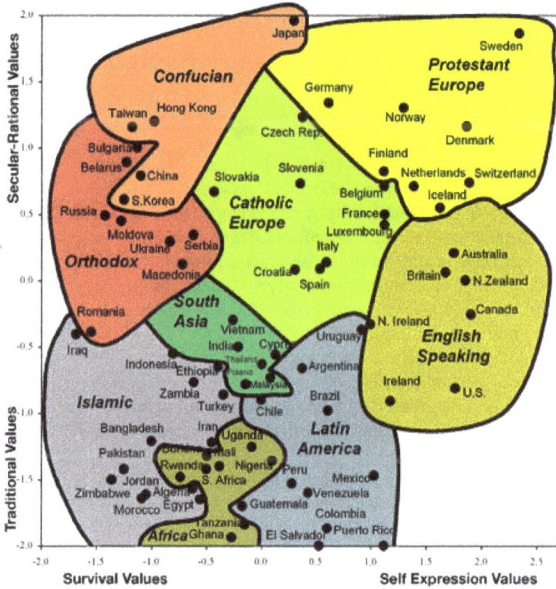

Secular-Rational Values

Japan
Sweden
Confucian
Germany
Protestant
Europe
Taiwan Hong Kong
Norway
Bulgaria
Czech Rep
Denmark
Belarus China
Slovakia Slovenia
Finland
Netherlands Switzerland
Russia S.Korea
Belgium Iceland
Catholic
Europe
France
Moldova
Luxembourg
Ukraine Serbia
Italy
Orthodox
Macedonia
Croatia
Australia
Britain N.Zealand
Spain
Romania
South
Asia
Canada
Vietnam
N. Ireland
Iraq
India Cyprus
Uruguay
English
Speaking
Indonesia Ethiopia
Thailand
Argentina
Ireland
Zambia
Malaysia
U.S.
Islamic
Turkey Chile
Brazil
Bangladesh
Iran
Uganda
Latin
America
Pakistan
Mali
Jordan
Rwanda
Nigeria Peru
Mexico
Zimbabwe
Algeria
S. Africa
Venezuela
Morocco
Egypt
Guatemala
Colombia
Tanzania
Africa
Ghana
El Salvador Puerto Rico

Traditional Values

Survival Values   Self Expression Values

Appendix 7   **Occupations by their value profiles (Knafo and Sagiv 2004)**

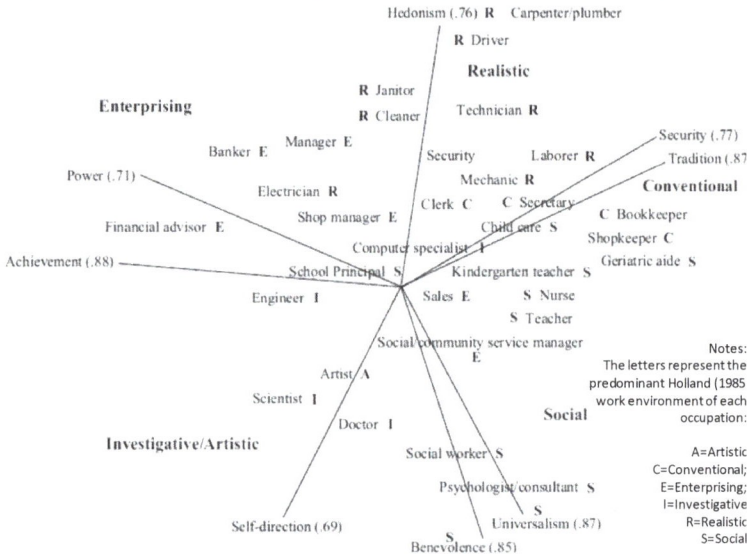

Hedonism (.76) R   Carpenter/plumber

R Driver

Realistic

R Janitor

Enterprising

R Cleaner   Technician R

Security (.77)

Banker E   Manager E

Security   Laborer R   Tradition (.87

Power (.71)

Electrician R   Mechanic R   Conventional

Financial advisor E   Shop manager E   Clerk C   C Secretary   C Bookkeeper

Child care S   Shopkeeper C

Computer specialist I

Achievement (.88)

School Principal S   Kindergarten teacher S   Geriatric aide S

Engineer I   Sales E   S Nurse

S Teacher

Social/community service manager
E

Artist A

Scientist I   Social

Doctor I

Investigative/Artistic

Social worker S

Psychologist/consultant S

S

Self-direction (.69)   Universalism (.87)

S
Benevolence (.85)

Notes:
The letters represent the
predominant Holland (1985
work environment of each
occupation:

A=Artistic
C=Conventional;
E=Enterprising;
I=Investigative
R=Realistic
S=Social

Appendix 8   Descriptive measurement items of the PLS model

Item code	Statements	Ø	δ	r
SD_1	Age group (1=young; 7=old)	5.27	1	0.998
SD_2	Gender (0=female;1=male)	0.70	0.458	0.996
SD_3	Education (1=low; 9=high)	6.22	3.287	0.995
HI	Income (metric scale)	18.104	14.761	1
TOV	Open-to change (negative sign) vs. Traditional values (positive sign)	0.32	0.73	1
USV	Self-enhanced (negative sign) vs. Universal values (positive sign)	-0.03	0.91	1
UMR_1	It is fair that people can gain benefits by depending on their network of contacts (utilitarian=1 vs. intrinsic motivated relationships=5)	3.55	1.381	0.913
UMR_2	Its natural that I give favours to and receive favours from my network of contact (utilitarian=1 vs. intrinsic motivated relationships=5)	2.99	1.255	0.839
CIR_1	I put group harmony above my own opinion. (collectivist=1 vs. individualist oriented relationships=5)	1.78	0.891	0.916
CIR_2	Related to work alone I like to work in a group (collectivist=1 vs. individualist oriented relationships=5)	1.95	1.165	0.704
ED_1	The groundwater burden resulting from the washing out of fertilizers is not so worse than many people imagine. (1=totally agree; 5=totally disagree)	2.88	0.932	0.592
ED_2	I don't think about environmenal aspects, I just do my work on the farm. (1=totally agree; 5=totally disagree)	3.06	1.325	0.907
ES_1	If I put more fertilizers, I will definitely have more yields. (1=totally agree; 5=totally disagree)	3.28	1.277	0.734
ES_2	Only people, who can't afford buying fertilizers, forbear from using fertilizers.(1=totally agree; 5=totally disagree)	2.94	1.303	0.885
ER	It is important to think upon environmental issues. (1=totally agree; 5=totally disagree)	1.80	0.932	1
WTP	WTP for clean drinking water (1=low 6=hig)	2.85	1.441	1
AN	Total amount of applied fertilizers (metric scale; calculated)	334.1	274.7	1

Scales in brackets; Ø = mean; δ = standard deviation; r = factor loading; Item code see Appendix 9

Appendix 9   Assessment of measurement model

Code	Item	Number of items	AVE	Composite reliability	Cronbach's Alpha
ED	Environmental disinterest/ Rejection of responsibility	2	0.59	0.73	0.34
AN	Amount of nitrogen fertiliser applied	1	1.00	1.00	1.00
CIR	'Collectivism' vs. individualism in relationships	2	0.67	0.80	0.53
ES	Fertilisers secure the agricultural outcome	2	0.66	0.80	0.50
EA	Environmental problem awareness	1	1.00	1.00	1.00
HI	Household income	1	1.00	1.00	1.00
SD	Socio-demographics	3	0.99	1.00	1.00
TOV	'Traditional axis' Traditional vs. open-to-change values	1	1.00	1.00	1.00
USV	'Universal axis' Universal vs. self-enhanced values	1	1.00	1.00	1.00
UMR	'Utilitarism' vs. intrinsically/ moral motivation in relationships	2	0.77	0.87	0.70
WTP	WTP for clean drinking water	1	1.00	1.00	1.00

Appendix 10   Effect size (f²) of the substantial constructs of the PLS model

Code		Socio-demogr.	Income	Tradit. values	Univers. values	Utilit.	Collect.
ED	Environmental disinterest/ Rejection of responsibility	.00	.00	.03	.03	.00	.02
AN	Applied nitrogen amount	.00	.00	.00	.00	.01	.00
CIR	Collectivist vs. individualistic oriented relationships	.00	.00	.00	.03	.00	.03
ES	Fertilizers secure the agricultural outcome	.00	.00	.01	.04	.07	.00
EA	Environmental problem awareness and responsibility	.00	.00	.01	.05	.02	.04
HI	Household income	.01	.01	.00	.00	.00	.00
TOV	Traditional vs. open-to-change value positions	.00	.01	.01	.00	.00	.00
USV	Universal vs. self-enhanced value positions	.01	.00	.00	.01	.00	.00
UMR	Utilitarian vs. intrisic/ moral motivated relationships	.00	.01	.00	.00	.01	.00
WTP	WTP for clean drinking water	.00	.04	.00	.00	.00	.00

Appendix 11   Quantitative farm household questionnaire (part I)

Household Code_____
Is this questionnaire about maize planting or wheat planting?   1=Maize; 2=Wheat

Farm Household Questionnaire

Province:_____
Prefecture: _____
County: _____
Township:_____
Village: _____
Team (xiaozu): _____

Name of interviewee: _____
Tel: _____
Mobile phone: _____

Interviewer:_____
Survey date: _____

Mobile phone of interviewer: _____
Person checking questionnaire:_____

A. Roster

A1. How many persons are there in your family? _____

Code			PID					
			1	2	3	4	5	6
A2	Relation to the head	[Code 1]						
A3	Sex	1=male 0=female						
A4	Born year	Year						
A5	Length of education	Years (0 if uneducated)						
A6	Position in village committee	1=none 2=village Party secretary/ head 3=village Party branch committee members/village committee members 4= team head 5=others (specify)						
A7	Time spent on farm from Sep., 2008 to Aug., 2009:	1=all working time 2=part of working time 3=non-farming 4=others____						
A8	Proportion of time spent on farm?	%						
A9	Which industry, if A7>=2?	[Code 2]						
A10	What is the working place?	1=this township 2=other township in this county 3=other county in this province 4=other province 5=others						
A11	Which month do non-farm	9						
A12	work from Sep., 2008 to	10						
A13	Aug., 2009?	11						
A14	(mark "X" if do non-farm	12						
A15	work)	1						
A16		2						
A17		3						
A18		4						
A19		5						
A20		6						
A21		7						
A22		8						
A23	Whether participate in the maize training during this maize planting season?	1=yes 0=no						
A24	Whether participate in the wheat training during last wheat planting seaon?	1=yes 0=no						

Code 1: 1=the head himself; 2=spouse; 3=son/daughter; 4=grandchild; 5=parents; 6=brother/sister; 7=son-in-law/daughter-in-law; 8=brother-in-law/sister-in-law; 9=parent-in-law; 10=other relatives; 11=non family paid

Code 2: 1=enterprise; 2=public institutions; 3=government offices; 4=craftsman; 5=engineering-constructions; 6=transportation; 7=restaurant; 8=wholesale/retail trade; 9=mining; 10=others (specify)

B. Transportation

Code		
B1	How far is the township government from your home (li)?	
B2	How far is the nearest shop selling fertilizer (li)?	
B3	How far is the nearest bituminous concrete road or cement concrete road (li)?	

C. Land owning (from Sep., 2008 to Aug., 2009)

Code			
C1	Cultivated land your family managed	Total area	mu
C2		Area of irrigable land	mu
C3		Area of greenhouse	mu
C4	Cultivated land you rent in	Total area	mu
C5		Area of irrigable land	mu
C6	Cultivated land swaped in	Total area	mu
C7		Area of irrigable land	mu
C8	Cultivated land you rent out	Total area	mu
C9		Area of irrigable land	mu

D. Planting structure

D1 How big did you plant summer maize this year? _____mu
D2 How big did you plant winter wheat last year?_____mu

What else have you grown since Sep. 2008? (please fill in the following blank)

Code			Crop 1	Crop 2	Crop 3	Crop 4
D3	Other food crop	[Crop code]				
D4		Area in mu				
D3	Cash crop	[Crop code]				
D4		Area in mu				
D3	Outdoor fruit or vegetables	[Crop code]				
D4		Area in mu				
D3	Fruit or vegetables grown in	[Crop code]				
D4	greenhouse	Area in mu				
D3	other crops	[Crop code]				
D4		Area in mu				

E. Poultry and livestock

Code			Animal 1	Animal 2	Animal 3	Animal 4	Animal 5
E1	[Animal code]						
E2	**Standing stock (end of 2008)**						
E3	**Fattened stock in 2008**						
E4	**Standing stock at present**						
E5	**Fattened stock this year**						
E6	**How to**	used on field (%)					
E7	**deal**	Discard (%)					
E8	**with**	Used for methane %					
E9	**animal**	Sell (%)					
E10	**feces?**	Other (%)					

F. How to deal with your feces?

Code			
F1		used on field (%)	
F2	**How to deal with your family's feces?**	Discard (%)	
F4		Used for methane (%)	
F5		Sell (%)	
F6		others (%)	

G. Plot and field management

Note: This table only record information about the largest plot of maize or wheat and field management during this maize (or wheat) production season.

Code			Unit	
Plot information				
G1	**Name of this plot**		Words	
G2	**Area of this plot**		Mu	
G3	**How far is it from your home**		Li	
G4	**How far from nearest township-level cement paving road?**		Li	
G5	**Fertility:** 1=good; 2=medium; 3=poor		[Code]	
G6	**Soil type:** 1=loamy soil; 2=clay soil; 3=sandy soil; 4=两合土; 5=tidal marsh; 6=others(specify)		[Code]	
G7	**Type of ownership:** 1=Contracted from collective; 2=rent in; 3=swap in; 4=Contract in jidongdi; 5=others (specify)		[Code]	
G8	**Nearest historical crop**		[Crop code]	
G9	**Whether return straws of nearest historical crop to the field?**		1=yes 0=no -> G11	
G10	**How to return:**	1=mechanical crushing; 2=cover after processing; 3=return directly; 4=others (specify)	[Code]	
G11	**Whether undersow with other crops? (Maize/wheat)**		1=yes 0=no -> G13	
G12		**With which crop**	[Crop code]	

G13	Whether intercrop with other crops? (Maize/wheat)		1=yes 0=no -> G15	
G14		With which crop	[Crop code]	
Ploughing land				
G15	Whether plough land before sowing?		1=yes 0=no -> G20	
G16	How much spent on ploughing land?		Yuan	
G17	How long your family spent?		Day	
G18	How long the employees spent?		Day	
G19	How much spent on employees?		Yuan	
Sowing				
G20	Name of the seeds		Words	
G21	Whether get subsidies while buying seeds?		1=yes 0=no	
G22	Whether coating seeds?		1=yes 1=no	
G23	Price of the seeds		Yuan per jin	
G24	Date of sowing		month-day	
G25	Amount of seeds sown in this plot		Jin	
G26	How much spent on sowing		Yuan	
G27	How long your family spent?		Day	
G28	How long the employees spent?		Day	
G29	How much spent on employees?		Yuan	
Irrigation				
G30	Times for irrigation		Time	
G31	First	How long your family spent	Day	
G32	irrigation	How much your family spent	Yuan	
G33		How long the employees spent	Day	
G34		How much spent on employees	Yuan	
G35	Second	How long your family spent	Day	
G36	irrigation	How much your family spent	Yuan	
G37		How long the employees spent	Day	
G38		How much spent on employees	Yuan	
G39	Third	How long your family spent	Day	
G40	irrigation	How much your family spent	Yuan	
G41		How long the employees spent	Day	
G42		How much spent on employees	Yuan	
Spraying Pesticide				
G43	Times for insect disease prevention		Time	
G44	Times for using herbicides		Time	
G45	Times for using growth regulators		Time	
G46	How long your family spent?		Day	
G47	How long the employees spent?		Day	
G48	How much spent on employees		Yuan	

Intertillage			
G49	Times for intertillage		Time
G50	Whether use machine or animal labor?		1=yes 0=no -> G53
G51	If yes,	how much spent on machine?	Yuan
G52		how much spent on animal labor?	Yuan
G53	How long your family spent?		Day
G54	How long the employees spent?		Day
G55	How much spent on employees		Yuan
Other management			
G56	Is there other management?		1 = yes 0 = no -> G61
G57	What management?		Words
G58	How long your family spent?		Day
G59	How long the employees spent?		Day
G60	How much spent on employees		Yuan
Nature disaster			
G61	Have you had nature disaster in maize (or wheat) production?		1 = yes 0 = no -> G63
G62	If yes, what disaster: 1=flood; 2=drought; 3=snow; 4=storm; 5=hail; 6=frost; 7=soil erosion; 8=others (specify)		[Code]
Harvest			
G63	Date of harvest		month-day
G64	Way of harvest: 1=use your own machine; 2=use rent machine; 3=use your own livestock or human labor; 4=use employee; 5=other(specify)		[Code]
G65	How long your family spent on harvest?		Day
G66	How long the employees spent on harvest?		Day
G67	How much spent on employees		Yuan
G68	Way of threshing: 1=use your own machine; 2=use rent machine; 3=use your own livestock or human labor; 4=use employee; 5=other(specify)		[Code]
G69	How long your family spent on threshing?		Day
G70	How long the employees spent on threshing?		Day
G71	How much spent on employees		Yuan
G72	Total product		Jin
G73	Yield per unit		Jin per mu
How to deal with the straw			
G74	Left on field		%
G75	Feed livstocks		%
G76	Burn in the field		%
G77	Burn for cooking		%
G78	Discard		%
G79	Sell		%
G80	Other		%

H1. Fertilizing management 1 + 2

How many times do you fertilize during this maize (or wheat) production season? _

Code				1	2	3	4	5
H2	Sequence			1	2	3	4	5
H3	Date for fertilizing		month-day					
H4	Season for fertilizing		[code 1]					
H5	Family Labor input		Day					
H6	Employees' labor input		Day					
H7	Expenditure on employees		Yuan					
H8		Specific type	[code 2]					
H9		If compound fertilizer,	N in %					
H10		labeled NPK ratio is	P in %					
H11	Fertilizer 1		K in %					
H12		Source	[code 4]					
H13		Amount	Jin					
H14		Expenditure	Yuan					
H15		Specific type	[code 2]					
H16		If compound fertilizer,	N in %					
H17		labeled NPK ratio is	P in %					
H18	Fertilizer 2		K in %					
H19		Source	[code 4]					
H20		Amount	Jin					
H21		Expenditure	Yuan					

Code				1	2	3	4	5
H2	Sequence			1	2	3	4	5
H22		Specific type	[code 2]					
H23		If compound fertilizer,	N in %					
H24		labeled NPK ratio is	P in %					
H25	Fertilizer 3		K in %					
H26		Source	[code 4]					
H27		Amount	Jin					
H28		Expenditure	Yuan					
H29		Description	[code 3]					
H30		Dry or wet?	1=dry; 2=wet					
H31		Whether use after ageing?	1=yes; 0=no					
H32	Manure 1	Source	[code 4]					
H33		Amount	Jin					
H34		Expenditure	Yuan					
H35		Description	[code 3]					
H36		Dry or wet?	1=dry; 2=wet					
H37		Whether use after ageing?	1=yes; 0=no					
H38	Manure 2	Source	[code 4]					
H39		Amount	Jin					
H40		Expenditure	Yuan					

Code 1 (fertilizing season of wheat):
1= 播种前; 2=越冬前; 3=越冬期; 4=返青期; 5=拔节期; 6=孕穗期; 7=灌浆期; 8=其他 (请注明)
Code 1 (fertilizing season of maize):
1=播种前; 2=小喇叭口期; 3=大喇叭口期; 4=孕穗期; 5=灌浆期; 6=其他 (请注明)
Code 2 (fertilizer type):
1=尿素; 2=碳酸氢铵; 3=硫酸铵; 4=过磷酸钙; 5=钙镁磷肥; 6=氯化钾; 7=硫酸钾; 8=磷酸二铵; 9=
配方肥 (特指测土配方施肥); 10=其他复合肥; 11=叶面肥; 12=其他 (请注明)
Code 3 (manure):
1=chicken; 2=cow; 3=pig; 4=human; 5=straw; 6=commercial manure; 7=manure with organic
materials; 8=commercial manure; 9=others (specify)
Code 4 (source):
1=yourselves' remaining fertilizer; 2=agricultural input agency; 3=Extension institution;
4=cooperative; 5=factory; 6=other households; 7=others (specify)

J. Extension service of maize production

J1. Have you seen extension technicians providing
extension service since April?
_____(1=yes; 0=no)

J2. If yes, how many times？_____
J3. Which technician?   _____ (name)

Code				improved seeds	techniques of fertilizing	techniques of crop protection	other farming techniques	techniques of breeding animals	techniques of animal epidemic prevention	selling agricultural input	others (specify)___
J4				1	2	3	4	5	6	7	8
J5		Whether received following services?	1=yes 0=no -> J12								
J6		Whether received training in the way of meeting	1=yes 0=no								
J7		Whether received door-to-door service	1=yes 0=no -> J9								
J8	If have seen technicians	He voluntarily or you requied that?	1=voluntarily 2=unvoluntarily								
J9		Whether received services in the way of phoning	1=yes 0=no -> J11								
J10		He voluntarily or you requied that?	1=voluntarily 2=unvoluntarily								
J11		Whether received materials	1=yes 0=no								

J12		Whether received following services from other people	1=yes 0=no -> next page								
J13		Whether received training	1=yes 0=no -> J15								
J14		Who is the director?	[code]								
J15		Whether received door-to-door service	1=yes 0=no -> J18								
J16		Who provided the service	[code]								
J17		He voluntarily or you requied that?	1=voluntarily 2=unvoluntarily								
J18		Whether received materials	1=yes 0=no -> J20								
J19		He voluntarily or you requied that?	1=voluntarily 2=unvoluntarily								
J20		Whether received materials	1=yes 0=no -> next page								
J21		Who give you?	[code]								

(rows J14–J19 labelled vertically: If have not seen technicians)

Code: 1=village cadre; 2=people from factory; 3=team head; 4=farmers' cooperatives members; 5=others (specify)

K. Extension service of wheat production

K1. Have you seen extension technicians providing extension service from Sep. 2008 to Jun. 2009? _____

(1 = yes; 0 = no)

K2. If yes, how many times? _____

Code			improved seeds	techniques of fertilizing	techniques of crop protection	other farming techniques	techniques of breeding animals	techniques of animal epidemic prevention	selling agricultural input	Others (specify)_____
K3			1	2	3	4	5	6	7	8
K4		Whether received following services?	1=yes 0=no -> K11							
K5		Whether received training in the way of meeting	1=yes 0=no							
K6		Whether received door-to-door service	1=yes 0=no -> K8							
K7		He voluntarily or you requied that?	1=voluntarily 2=unvoluntarily							
K8		Whether received services in the way of phoning	1=yes 0=no -> K10							
K9		He voluntarily or you requied that?	1=voluntarily 2=unvoluntarily							
K10		Whether received materials	1=yes 0=no							

(rows K5–K10 labelled vertically: If have seen technicians)

K11		Whether received following services from other people	1=yes 0=no -> next page							
K12		Whether received training?	1=yes 0=no=>K14							
K13	If have not seen technicians	Who is the director?	[code]							
K14		Whether received door-to-door service	1=yes 0=no -> K17							
K15		Who provided the service?	[code]							
K16		He voluntarily or you requied that?	1=voluntarily 2=unvoluntarily							
K17		Whether received materials	1=yes 0=no -> K19							
K18		He voluntarily or you requied that?	1=voluntarily 2=unvoluntarily							
K19		Whether received materials?	1=yes 0=no next page							
K20		Who give you?	[code]							

Code: 1=village cadre; 2=people from factory; 3=team head; 4=farmers' cooperatives members; 5=others (specify)

M. House assets

M1. How many houses do you have?

Code					
M2	[House code]		1	2	3
M3	House type	1=buildings with two or more storeys 2=bungalow			
M4	How many floors	Floor			
M5	How many rooms	Room			
M6	Construction materials	1=earth 2=wood 3=brick 4=concrete 5=others (specify)			
M7	Whether share the house with other household	1=yes 0=no			
M8	How many rooms your household have	Room			
M9	When built	Year			
M10	Expenditure of building this house	Yuan			
M11	Present value of this house	Yuan			

N. Consumer durables

Note: only record consumer goods whose value are more than 500 yuan

Code			colour TV	camera	washing machine	fridge	car	motorcycle	air-condition	computer	mobilephone	gas stove	others
N1			1	2	3	4	5	6	7	8	9	10	11
N2	Whether have	1=have 2=none											
N3		If have, amount?											
N4	When buy it	Year											
N5	The price	Yuan											
N6	Present value	Yuan											

Note: if the amount is more than 1, N5 and N6 record the total value!

P. Open question

Code			
	What do you care most when you buy fertilizers? (Sort)		
P1	1=quality	most important	
P2	2=Price	second important	
	3=Whether goods can be returned		
	4=Others (_____)		
	How do you decide the amount of fertilizer while fertilizing? (Sort)		
P3	1=the price of fertilizer	most important	
P4	2=past experiences	second important	
	3=the state of crop growth and the weather		
	4=quality of fertilizer		
	5=do as fertilizer seller told		
	6=extension service		
	7=Others (_____)		
	Have you bought following agricultural inputs in the past 3 years?		
P5	low-quality fertilizer	1=yes; 0=no	
P6	low-quality seeds	1=yes; 0=no	
P7	low-quality pesticide	1=yes; 0=no	
P8	**Do you know the meaning of symbol N, P2O5 or K2O?**	1=yes; 0=no	
P9	**Do you know the meaning of "15-15-15" marked on the fertilizer bags**	1=yes; 0=no	
P10	**Do you think that putting more fertilizer would get more yields**	1=yes; 0=no	
P11	**How should you fertilize if you want to get higher yields?** 1=putting all fertilizer at a time; 2=fertilizing by several times?		
P12	**Is it better to put more fertilizer on earlier stage during crop production?**	1=yes; 0=no	

Crop code：D3, G8, G12, G14				
1.summer maize	**Outdoor fruit or vegetables**		**Fruit or vegetables grown in greenhouse**	
2.winter wheat	301.西红柿	327.芥菜	401.西红柿	427.芥菜
Other food crops	302.黄瓜	328.甘蓝	402.黄瓜	428.甘蓝
101.rice	303.大葱	329.苹果	403.大葱	429.苹果
102.kaoliang	304.小葱	330.梨	404.小葱	430.梨
103.谷子	305.大蒜	331.桃	405.大蒜	431.桃
104.糜子	306.生姜	332.家杏	406.生姜	432.家杏
105.荞麦	307.青菜	333.李子	407.青菜	433.李子
106.红薯	308.白菜	334.葡萄	408.白菜	434.葡萄
199.其他(注明)	309.韭菜	335.红枣	409.韭菜	435.红枣
Cash crops	310.莴笋	336.核桃	410.莴笋	436.核桃
201.花生	311.茄子	337.板栗	411.茄子	437.板栗
202.油菜籽	312.丝瓜	338.山楂	412.丝瓜	438.山楂
203.芝麻	313.苦瓜	339.柿子	413.苦瓜	439.柿子
204.向日葵	314.芹菜	340.山杏	414.芹菜	440.山杏
205.棉花	315.包菜	341.菜花	415.包菜	441.菜花
206.红黄麻	316.油麦菜	342.香菜	416.油麦菜	442.香菜
207.萱麻	317.西葫芦	343.茴香	417.西葫芦	443.茴香
208.胡麻	318.青椒	344.胡萝卜	418.青椒	444.胡萝卜
209.桑叶	319.辣椒	345.萝卜	419.辣椒	445.萝卜
210.烟叶	320.西瓜	346.西兰花	420.西瓜	446.西兰花
211.甘蔗	321.香瓜	347.生菜	421.香瓜	447.生菜
212.甜菜	322.草莓	348.药材	422.草莓	448.药材
213.大豆	323.樱桃	349.花椒	423.樱桃	449.花椒
214.绿豆	324.土豆	350.草坪	424.土豆	450.草坪
215.红豆	325.豆角	351.苗圃	425.豆角	451.苗圃
299.其他（注明）	326.冬瓜	399.其他（注明）	426.冬瓜	499.其他（注明）
			other crops	
			501.other（specify）	

Animal code：E1
1.pig
2.cow
3.sheep
4.ass
5.mule
6.horse
7.fowl（鸡、鸭、鹅等）
8.rabbit
9.other（specify） ____

Appendix 12   Quantitative farmers' survey (part II)

Intensive Farmers' Survey

Interviewer:_____
Survey date: _____

Mobile phone of interviewer: _____
Person checking questionnaire:_____

Code	Questions	Unit	
hcode	Household code		
nm_inter	Name of Interviewee		
ph_inter	Tel:		
mp_inter	Mobile Phone		
G1	Name of this plot	Words	
G2	Area of this plot	Mu	
G63	Date of harvest	month-day	
G64	Way of harvest: 1 = use your own machine; 2 = use rent machine; 3 = use your own livestock or human labor; 4 = use employee or; 5 = other(specify)	Code	
G89	Mechanic expenditure	Yuan	
G65	How long your family spent on harvest?	Hour	
G66	How long the employees spent on harvest?	Hour	
G67	How much spent on employees	Yuan	
G68	Way of threshing: 1 = use your own machine; 2 = use rent machine; 3 = use your own livestock or human labor; 4 = use employee or; 5 = other(specify)	Code	
G90	Mechanic expenditure of threshing	Yuan	
G69	How long your family spent on threshing?	Hour	
G70	How long the employees spent on threshing?	Hour	
G71	How much spent on employees	Yuan	
G72	Total product	Jin	
G73	Yield per unit	Jin per mu	
	Remarks		

The following questions should be finished by farmer himself.

Interview duration (minute):   _____

1. Household income

Q1: To which of the following income groups does your farm-household belongs to?
(added net-income from every household member as well as remittances from other family members included)

Code:			Code:		
1	Under 1,000 Yuan		6	30,000 – 40,000 Yuan	
2	1,000 – 5,000 Yuan		7	40,000 – 50,000 Yuan	
3	5,000 – 10,000 Yuan		8	50,000 – 100,000 Yuan	
4	10,000 – 20,000 Yuan		9	>100.000 Yuan	
5	20,000 – 30,000 Yuan		10	Refused/ Don't know.	

2. Specific income

Q2.1 In the past year (2008.9-2009.8), what was the household income composition in percentage?

Q2.1.1	Crop income	
Q2.1.2	Livestock / Fishery income	
Q2.1.3	Off-Farm-Income (non-farming income)	
Q2.1.4	Income from subsidies	
Q2.1.5	Other household income (non specified)	

Q2.2 How much remittances (money transfer) did you get in the past year (8-2008 to 8-2009) from your relatives that don't live at home?

Q2.2.1	Relatives	
Q2.2.2	Friends	
Q2.2.3	Immediate family but not your household	
Q2.2.4	Other people	

3. Future Plans for the Farm / Farmer's motivation

Q3.1 What are your future plans for this farm in the next 5 years?
(If you have no future plans, you don't need to answer the following question 3.2)

Code:		
1	Means further processing of their agricultural products at home. (Which one?	
2	I quit one production line. (Which one? Please specify!)	
3	I start with a new production line. (Which one? Please specify!)	
4	The farmer rents more land/ buys more animals to expand the farm.	
5	The farmer rents land out/ sells some animals to reduce his farm activities.	
6	Quit all his commercial farm activities (eg. wheat or maize production)	
7	I continue as hitherto./ I have no future plans for the farm.	

Q3.2 (Only for those who have future plans for the farm!)
What are your reasons for the considered change in your farm activity? (headwords!)

_____

_____

_____

_____

4. Average yields

What are the yields of the main crops in a good and in a bad year?
Please state in Jin/ Mu!

	Bad year yield	Good year yield
Wheat	Q4.1.1	Q4.1.2
Maize	Q4.2.1	Q4.2.2
Cotton	Q4.3.1	Q4.3.2
Soy beans	Q4.4.1	Q4.4.2

5. Disasters and yield depressions

Q5.1 Which disasters/ yield depressions have you had in the last 10 years in wheat and maize production?

	Frequency					If have, the trend is:
		1	2	3	4	1=unchanging;
	Disasters	Never	Irregular	Yearly	More than one time per year	2=better and better; 3=more and more severe
Q5.1.1	Drought					
Q5.1.2	Heavy rain					
Q5.1.3	Hail/ Snow					
Q5.1.4	Storm					
Q5.1.5	Frost					
Q5.1.6	Other					

If no disasters occurred in the last 10 years please go to question 6!

Q5.2 What is your average reduction of yield by disaster?

Disasters	Reduction in % of harvest if disaster is happening	
	Wheat	Maize
Drought	Q5.2.1.w	Q5.2.1.m
Heavy rain*	Q5.2.2.w	Q5.2.2.m
Hail/ Snow	Q5.2.3.w	Q5.2.3.m
Storm	Q5.2.4.w	Q5.2.4.m
Frost	Q5.2.5.w	Q5.2.5.m
Other please specify	Q5.2.6.w	Q5.2.6.m

Code: 1=0-10%; 2=10-20%; 3=20-30%; 4=30-40%; 5=40-50%; 6=50-60%; 7=60-70%; 8=70-80%; 9=80-90%; 10=90-100%

Q5.3/ 4/5 Did you get a compensation for the reduction of yields (latest disaster)?

	Disasters		Drought	Heavy rain	Hail/ Snow	Storm	Frost	Other
Q5.3 Crop	Wheat		Q5.3.1.w	Q5.3.2.w	Q5.3.3.w	Q5.3.4.w	Q5.3.5.w	Q5.3.6.w
		Code1						
	Maize		Q5.3.1.m	Q5.3.2.m	Q5.3.3.m	Q5.3.4.m	Q5.3.5.m	Q5.3.6.m
		Code1						
Q5.4 Source of Compen-sation	Wheat		Q5.4.1.w	Q5.4.2.w	Q5.4.3.w	Q5.4.4.w	Q5.4.5.w	Q5.4.6.w
		Code2						
	Maize		Q5.4.1.m	Q5.4.2.m	Q5.4.3.m	Q5.4.4.m	Q5.4.5.m	Q5.4.6.m
		Code2						
Q5.5 Amount of Comp-ensation	Wheat		Q5.5.1.w	Q5.5.2.w	Q5.5.3.w	Q5.5.4.w	Q5.5.5.w	Q5.5.6.w
		RMB						
	Maize		Q5.5.1.m	Q5.5.2.m	Q5.5.3.m	Q5.5.4.m	Q5.5.5.m	Q5.5.6.m
		RMB						

Code 1: 1=Yes; 2=No; **Code 2:** 1=Government, 2=Insurance, 3=other (Please specify!)

6. Who are your principal customers for your crops?

			Q6.1	Q6.2	Q6.3	Q6.4	Q6.5	Q6.6
			Other households	Bazaar	Hawker	Whole-salers	Govern-ment	Other
.1.w	Local or unlocal?	1=this township 2=other places						
.2.w	Number							
.3.w	Type of Agreement [Code 4]							
.4.w	Since years							
.5.w	Price determination [Code5]							
.1.m	Local or unlocal?	1=this township 2=other places						
.2.m	Number							
.3.m	Type of Agreement [Code 4]							
.4.m	Since years							
.5.m	Price determination [Code5]							
.1.o	Local or unlocal?	1=this township 2=other places						
.2.o	Number							
.3.o	Type of Agreement [Code 4]							
.4.o	Since years							
.4.o	Price determination [Code5]							

Code 4: 1=Written contract; 2=Oral Agreement; 3=other; 4=None

Code 5: 1=Set by me, 2=Negotiated on daily basis, 3=Negotiated on long term basis, 4=Set by customer, 5=Common marked price (unofficial), 6=Fixed market price (according to Government), 7=other

7. Decision-making on the annual production

How do you decide on your annual production progam? (State the three most important!)

Code:		
1	Which was the best in the last year / According to the best yield of the last year	Q7.1
2	Which was the best in average in the last years / According to the best yield average of the last years	Q7.2
3	The Crop I expect to get the best Price for/ According to that crop with the best expected price for the coming year	Q7.3
4	That crop I get the highest subsidies	
5	I look for best crop rotation	
6	I check and test new strategies	
7	I do what my neighbour do	
8	I follow the advice of the extension service	
9	Other	

8. Willingness to pay for weather insurance

Imagine, you can get a full compensation (by insurance) for your weather caused (disasters) crop losses in wheat or maize. What is your Willingness to pay for this?

Code:			Q8.1	WTP for wheat	
1	5	RMB/ Mu	Q8.2	WTP for maize	
2	10	RMB/ Mu			
3	20	RMB/ Mu			
4	25	RMB/ Mu			
5	50	RMB/ Mu			
6	75	RMB/ Mu			
7	100	RMB/ Mu			
8	150	RMB/ Mu			
9	200	RMB/ Mu			

The following part contains questions that are related to your decision-making and the way that costumes and moral influence your behaviour. There is no right or wrong, so don't worry about answers you give.

9. Knowledge-based decision-making

Q9.1 What was your most important support in the farm's decision-making on nitrogen- and manure management? (Please write the most important Code for the answer on top, then the second, followed by the third)

Code:		Q9.1.1	
1	Established habits and traditions	Q9.1.2	
2	Advices from relatives and friends	Q9.1.3	
3	Agricultural extension services		
4	TV/ braodcast		
5	Agricultural articles / newspapers		
6	Private provider for agricultural inputs / "gòng xiáo shè"		
7	Others (please specify!)		

Q9.2 How well informed are you about the following problem areas. ! When "never heard of it" skip question 8.3 and go directly to question 9!

		Code:	1	2	3	4
			Well informed	Informed	Not informed	Never heard of
			+++	++ -	+ - -	- - -
Q9.2.1	Groundwater pollution caused by fertilizer-overuse?					
Q9.2.2	Pesticide residues in vegetables?					

Q9.3 Where did you get information about groundwater and pollution caused by nitrogen and pesticide over-use? (Please write the most important Code for the answer on top, then the second, followed by the third)

Code:		Q9.3.1	
1	Family members	Q9.3.2	
2	Community members / Friends	Q9.3.3	
3	Agricultural trainings and extension services		
4	TV		
5	Radio		
6	Newspaper		
7	Trader		
8	Others (please specify!))		

10. Environmental attitudes

Q10.1 I am now going to read out some statements about the environment. For each one read out, can you tell me whether you strongly agree, agree, neigther agree nor disagree, disagree or wheather you strongly disagree) (WVS 2007)

Code:		1	2	3	4	5
		Strongly agree	Agree	Neither agree nor disagree	Disagree	Strongly disagree
		++++	+++ -	++ - -	+ - - -	- - - -
Q10.1.1	I agree to pay money to the government if I use more fertilizer than allowed.					
Q10.1.2	The government should reduce environmental pollution, but it should not cost me any money.					
Q10.1.3	Talk about the environment makes people worried.					

Q10.2 Environmental Attitudes as a Farmer

Code:		1	2	3	4	5
		Strongly agree	Agree	Neither agree nor disagree	Disagree	Strongly disagree
		++++	+++ -	++ - -	+ - - -	- - - -
Q10.2.1	If I stop N-use in order to reduce the harm of the environment that would be too risky for the household's income.					
Q10.2.2	The groundwater burden resulting from the washing out of fertilizer is worse than many people imagine.					
Q10.2.3	Farmers are the best protectors of the natural environment, because they know at the best, what is good for the natural resources; therefore don't work against the natural environment					
Q10.2.4	Sometimes as protectors of the environment farmers have made mistakes, for example in fertilizer and pesticide use					
Q10.2.5	Mineral fertilizers pesticides promote high quality. Beside they have no harmful effects.					
Q10.2.6	The use of chemicals in agriculture makes sense as long it brings greater returns than costs.					

Q10.3 Risk-related enviromental attitudes

Code:	1	2	3	4	5
		Strongly agree	Agree	Agree nor disagree	Disagree	Strongly disagree
		++++	+++ -	++ - -	+ - - -	- - - -
Q10.3.1	For the sake of the environment, stopping N-use is too risky for the household's annual income.					
Q10.3.2	People should have the choice if they will reduce their N-application on farm.					
Q10.3.3	It is important to think about environmental issues.					
Q10.3.4	If I put more N, I will definitely have more yields.					
Q10.3.5	Only people, who can't afford buying fertilizers, forbear from using fertilizers.					
Q10.3.6	Environmental problems are not related to my behaviour in fertilizer usage.					
Q10.3.7	I don't think about environmental aspects, I just do my farm work.					

11. Willingness to pay

There are environmental problems. Some of them are related to groundwater pollution through fertilizers, pesticides and improper waste disposal. These can be found in drinking/ well water as well as in food that might cause health problems. In order to avoid such pollution, water prizes must increase due to higher cleaning costs and waste collection services must be established that also costs additional money. If you then have the choice between two kind of water, on the one hand your untreated somehow polluted well/ drinking water which is for free and on the other hand clean drinking/ well water, but you have to pay for the service. How much would your household be willing to pay per month for the provision of clean drinking/ well water and how much for waste collection services?

Code:	1	2	3	4	5	6
		0 ¥	1 ¥	5 ¥	10 ¥	15 ¥	20 ¥
Q11.1	Clean drinking/ well water						
Q11.2	Waste collection services						

12. Guanxi

The questions are related to your guanxi. Which comes closest to reflecting your opinion?

	Code:	1	2	3	4	5
		Definitely agree	Tend to agree	Neither Agree nor disagree	Tend to disagree	Definitely disagree
		++++	+++ -	++ - -	+ - - -	- - - -
12.1	It is fair that people can gain benefits by depending on their network of contacts.					
12.2	It is natural that I give favours to and receive favours from my network of contacts.					
12.3	When someone helps me, I will want to repay it by all means, rational and irrational ones					
12.4	In my network of contacts, people depend on one another.					
12.5	I can make use of my contacts' contacts as long as I have a good relationship with my contacts.					
12.6	My limited contacts do not matter, for my contacts are able to introduce me to their network of contacts.					
12.7	A personal relationship with others is part and parcel of daily life.					
12.8	A personal connection that a person brings to a group disappears when the person leaves the group.					
12.9	People should help one another at all times; you never know when you might need their help.					
12.10	A personal connection is developed and reinforced through personal care and commitment.					
12.11	It is fair that group interests prevail over individual interests.					
12.12	I put group harmony above my own opinion.					
12.13	Related to work alone I like to work in a group.					

13. Personal Values

In the following, some persons will be described. How similar or dissimilar is this person to you?

Code:	1	2	3	4	5	6
	This person is <u>definitely</u> <u>not</u> <u>similar</u> to me.	This person is not similar to me.	This person is only a little bit similar to me.	This person is a little bit similar to me.	This person is similar to me.	This person is <u>very</u> <u>similar</u> to me.
	-----	---- +	--- ++	-- +++	- ++++	++++ +
13.1	Thinking up new ideas and being creative is important to him. He likes to do things in his own original way.					
13.2	It is important to him to be rich. He wants to have a lot of money and expensive things.					
13.3	He thinks it is important that every person in the world be treated equally. He believes everyone should have equal opportunities in life.					
13.4	It's important to him to show his abilities. He wants people to admire what he does.					
13.5	It is important to him to live in secure surroundings. He avoids anything that might endanger his safety.					
13.6	He likes surprises and is always looking for new things to do. He thinks it is important to do lots of different things in life.					
13.7	He believes that people should do what they're told. He thinks people should follow rules at all times, even when no-one is watching.					
13.8	It is important to him to listen to people who are different from him. Even when he disagrees with them, he still wants to understand them.					
13.9	It's important to him to be humble + modest. He tries not to draw attention to himself.					

13.10	Having a good time is important to him. He likes to "spoil" himself.							
13.11	It is important to him to make his own decisions about what he does. He likes to be free and not depend on others.							
13.12	It's very important to him to help the people around him. He wants to care for their well-being.							
13.13	Being very successful is important to him. He hopes people will recognize his achievements.							
13.14	It is important to him that his country be safe from threats from within and without. He is concerned that social order be protected.							
13.15	He looks for adventures and likes to take risks. He wants to have an exciting life.							
13.16	It is important to him always to behave properly. He wants to avoid doing anything people would say is wrong.							
13.17	It is important to him to get respect from others. He wants people to do what he says.							
13.18	It is important to him to be loyal to his friends. He wants to devote himself to people close to him.							
13.19	He strongly believes that people should care for nature. Looking after the environment is important to him.							
13.20	Tradition is important to him. He tries to follow the customs handed down by his religion or his family.							
13.21	He seeks every chance he can to have fun. It is important to him to do things that give him pleasure.							

Thank you very much for your participation!

***ibidem*-**Verlag

Melchiorstr. 15

D-70439 Stuttgart

info@ibidem-verlag.de

www.ibidem-verlag.de
www.ibidem.eu
www.edition-noema.de
www.autorenbetreuung.de